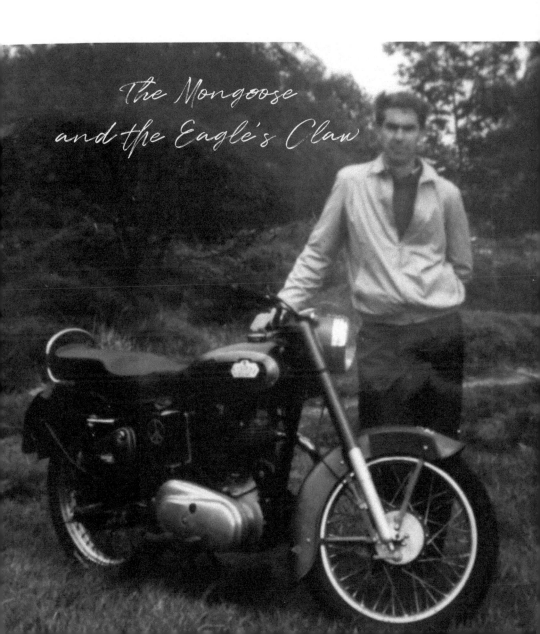

The Mongoose
and the Eagle's Claw

The Mongoose and the Eagle's Claw

A JOURNEY BY BOOT AND MOTORCYCLE

Michael R Whittle

The Book Guild Ltd

First published in Great Britain in 2021 by
The Book Guild Ltd
9 Priory Business Park
Wistow Road, Kibworth
Leicestershire, LE8 0RX
Freephone: 0800 999 2982
www.bookguild.co.uk
Email: info@bookguild.co.uk
Twitter: @bookguild

Typeset in 12pt Minion Pro

Printed and bound by CPI Group (UK) Ltd, Croydon, CR0 4YY

ISBN 978 1913551 582

British Library Cataloguing in Publication Data.
A catalogue record for this book is available from the British Library.

From the Pilbara of West Australia to the Nepal Himalayas. A ride along the Grand Trunk Road of India, Kashmir, Pakistan, Baluchistan, Iran and Anatolia, to the fateful hills and shores of Gallipoli.

Acknowledgements

To my mother Violet for the visits to libraries and museums to appreciate books, far-away places and many things of interest, and for all the years keeping a roof over our heads, never discouraging my interests.

To my father James (Jem) who taught me to ride a bike and fix a puncture, and on losing his sight declined to accept a guide dog when so many younger people needed one more then he.

To Barbara for all the help, love and hospitality, over all the years, always in my thoughts.

To Uncle Frank for the camera and teaching me that walking is one of life's pleasures. To Aunt Bea for the summer holidays in Anglesey, and the present of the world atlas, still a treasured possession.

In memory of Trev, and our travels in Africa and Australia, too young and green to fully appreciate where we were going and what we were seeing, – no regrets.

I have always been lucky with the friends I have made, my thanks to all of you.

To the many strangers, who guided me along the roads and tracks of many countries, – thank you.

I am grateful to all the staff at The Book Guild and Troubador Publishing for their encouragement support and advice during an entirely new experience. It couldn't have happened without them.

Any financial profit that may come to me from book sales will be shared between – 'The Guide Dogs for the Blind Association' – who need no introduction, and – 'Mines Advisory Group' (MAG).

MAG works in 80 countries to locate and destroy mines and munitions left behind in villages and fields after the combatants have long gone, that kill and maim the rural poor and a disproportionate number of children. I have worked alongside and witnessed the work of MAG in Cambodia and Vietnam, and seen the children maimed by mines, not to mention the many more fatalities.

MAG trains local women to locate and destroy mines and bombs in local villages. It is an expensive process to train and equip these women with the skills needed to do this very dangerous work, to make their fields and food gardens safe: so they can be cultivated once again, providing a livelihood that was lost when their land was sown with mines, often decades earlier. See the MAG website for more information. http://www.maginternational.org/

If you are reading a borrowed copy of this book please consider a small donation to either or both these great charities, whose work is so important – thanks.

M W.

Introduction

The book I treasure most is my grandfather's school prize for arithmetic in the midsummer examination of 1887, a copy of Capt. James Cook's *Three Voyages Round the World*, which thankfully I still have. As a schoolboy I read the usual adventure novels my English teacher Mr Jenkins recommended when he realised this kind of escapism from the grey skies of Lancashire interested me. Robert Louis Stevenson's *Treasure Island* and William Golding's *Lord of the Flies* imprinted a vision of the South Seas that would later take me to the Pacific Islands to work and travel. Arthur Grimble's *A Pattern of Islands* kept my interest alive. Walter Lord's *Lonely Vigil: Coastwatchers of the Solomons*, the story of fugitive islanders who sometimes paid with their lives to send radio messages to the US Navy of Japanese shipping movements during the war in the Pacific, still evokes memories of the time I worked on Gizo Island.

I read Heinrich Harrer's *Seven Years in Tibet* and Nepal went onto my must-visit list – you couldn't travel in Tibet then, but the Solu Khumbu region of Nepal was every bit as Tibetan in its traditional customs and free of Chinese influence. I discovered Bill Tilman and Eric Shipton in a West Australian country town library; their accounts of Himalayan exploration whetted my appetite. In my late twenties I made a first trek to Everest base camp and the Himalaya became a much-loved destination for trekking to ethnically diverse villages only accessible on foot, and is still my favourite travel region.

I spent five years working in the islands of the Pacific – Papua

New Guinea, the Solomon Islands, Tonga and Nauru – and travelled to others; none of these countries had television. Trekking in the bush and hiking the mountain trails, radio and reading were my entertainment. I read Jack Hides's *Through Wildest Papua*, and J. K. McCarthy's *Patrol into Yesterday* and I still have them in my library. *My Father Is a Cannibal* by Sten Bergman had me wanting more.

India has also been a favourite destination, if I were limited to travelling in just one region, the Indian sub-continent would top the list; it has every geographical and climatic variation, as well as hundreds of ethnic and linguistic variants, besides timeless history, art, architecture and ancient feats of engineering long before the Romans spread their expertise across Europe. Eric Newby's *Slowly down the Ganges* caused me to visit the Ganges Delta. And I worked there on the construction of a rural hospital and high school, the first in Bangladesh providing free secondary education for girls from disadvantaged villages (Kumudini Welfare Trust).

I have ridden motorcycles since my teens. The first was a third share in a 1956 Royal Enfield Bullet 350cc 'one pot' (single cylinder), bought for £5 from a partner at the building firm I was apprenticed to a week after my fifteenth birthday. I earned £3 a week and gave £2 to my mother for my keep. The Enfield was a bargain I couldn't let pass but could little afford. I beat the price down from £8; with a feigned 'Oh, all right', Roy accepted the crisp new £5 note that was part of my bargaining plan, climbed back into his plumber's van and drove off with a scowl. Two mates both chipped in a third and we bashed it around the country lanes and the fields of a friend's farm till we were reported to the police by a 'concerned citizen' and cautioned for underage driving, having no licences, insurance or road tax. It went into a farm shed and disappeared who knows where – 'If only I had kept it' is the mantra of every old biker.

I read Ted Simon's *Jupiter's Travels* while working in Papua New Guinea and knew that someday I had to make a motorcycle journey, and, though my journey and account of it is not even moderately as inspiring as Ted's journey, it had plenty enough danger for my taste.

Though I have named a few favourite travel books, I don't wish to imply my story is in the same league. What follows is no more than an account of a year in my life when a lot happened, some of which I wanted to happen and some I didn't.

I have tried to recall as much as possible a journey made forty years ago. Some of it is imprinted in clear detail in my memory, some recollected from old passports and surviving artefacts; much has been lost, including photos and documents in the many moves I have made since. I apologise to the enthusiast travel book reader who will have read better accounts of a journey. It is not written in the elegant style of Patrick Leigh Fermor's *Between the Woods and the Water* – never sure where his day's journey would lead, just as my daily destinations were never certain - but I hope it is in the same spirit.

With an unhealthy obsession with travel and limited motorcycling touring experience, I suppose it was only a matter of time before I would make a journey on a motorbike. This is my account of it.

But first I must start with a condensed account of the famous West Australian prospector Lang Hancock, the discoverer of the Pilbara's vast iron ore deposits, who contributed more to West Australia's wealth and development than any other person, enabling me to earn the means of the journey. Unless born into wealth or a lucky win in a lottery, whoever wishes to travel must find the means of paying for it. In my case, I worked as a carpenter in the Pilbara district of Western Australia, the largest iron ore mining region in the world, where the journey materialised during hot sleepless nights in a small caravan.

Lang Hancock's discovery

In November 1952 the prospector and pastoralist Lang Hancock and his wife, Hope, were flying from their Mulga Downs pastoral station south-west of Marble Bar – the hottest town in Australia – to Perth in their single-engine Auster aircraft, when they encountered storm clouds. 'I was flying down south with my wife Hope, and we left a bit later than usual and by the time we got over the Hamersley Ranges, the clouds had formed and the ceiling got lower and lower. I got into the Turner River, knowing full well if I followed it through, I would come out into the Ashburton. On flying through a gorge in the Turner River, I noticed that the walls looked to me to be solid iron and was particularly alerted by the rusty looking colour of it, it showed to me to be oxidised iron.'

Hancock assumed the ore he saw must be of low grade as no one had reported its existence, though surveys had been done in the region. When he later flew back over the area more thoroughly, he saw that it continued for many miles and therefore that it must have commercial value. He collected rock samples and sent them to Perth for analysis. They turned out to have significantly higher iron content than the standard blast furnace feedstock. West Australia's future wealth was assured.

Hancock's find was technically worthless as there was an embargo on exporting iron ore from Australia. The embargo was in place because it was claimed that Australia's iron ore reserves were only 358 million tons. Hancock had been involved in prospecting and small mining ventures since 1938, and knew that at some future date the iron ore would be worth millions, but only if mines could be developed and the ore exported.

Before the Second World War, as Japan began emerging as a military threat, the Australian government banned the export of iron ore, fearing getting it back in the form of bullets and bombs. This later eventuated when Prime Minister Robert Menzies, in an attempt to mollify the Japanese, began selling them scrap iron, much of which was turned into war material. Menzies was given the nickname 'Pig Iron Bob' for that decision.

By the 1950s Japan was deemed a 'friendly' nation and, as its need for iron grew, it was seen as a potential market for the ore that was lying in the Pilbara unmined. The problem was the lack of infrastructure in this remote region. Towns, power plants, railways, ports, roads and mine development would need to be constructed; this would take millions of dollars the state didn't have.

Hancock spent more time flying around the Pilbara, mapping iron ore deposits. He found over 500 large ore deposits, while the state government and BHP aerial exploration hadn't found any while prospecting over the same country.

The reason for the government's oversight of the huge resource was embarrassingly simple. Aerial ore body detection was done with instruments that were supposed to spike in the presence of iron ore. The instruments had shown no major spikes so it was believed there was no iron. The problem seems to have been that, because the areas explored had very high concentrations of iron and the instruments were calibrated to respond to the usual lower concentrations, they failed to respond properly. Hancock had simply used his eyes and prospecting experience to discover high-grade ore. Hancock is quoted saying the following about his discovery and the problems of getting others to recognise what he had found:

Well people interested in iron ore, knew that there was no iron ore in Australia and here was I, a boy from the bush, no experience, no education, no letters after his name, trying to tell them that I'd found by far the world's largest iron ore deposits, a whole field actually and you know, 30 or 40 firms throughout the world said 'run away, it's a lot of rubbish'. Unbeknown to me, they rang up what was then known as the Bureau of Mineral Resources in Canberra and Doctor Argot, the head of it, said 'Hancock's talking through his hat, we've done a magnetometer survey of all that area and there's nothing there'. So then they came back to me and I said well look if there's something there you pay me a royalty — if there's nothing there it doesn't cost you anything.

Hancock was faced with the problem of getting overseas mining companies interested in starting up without revealing exactly where the huge deposits were. His approaches to big miners met with little success, and he was even frozen out of the first mining venture. Gradually overseas investors started to take notice and the first Pilbara mine at Goldsworthy was opened. It was nothing compared to what would follow.

Finally, in 1961, the giant British mining conglomerate Rio Tinto sent its best geologist, Bruno Campana, to check Hancock's finds. Bruno was impressed, but the head office of the Australian arm of Rio Tinto dithered. Hancock went over their heads to the CEO, Val Duncan, in London. This made Hancock very unpopular with the Australian staff of Rio Tinto, who refused to give him any credit for his discoveries, despite having his maps on their office walls and having to pay Hancock and his partner's royalties. At last, in June 1963, an agreement was finalised and Hancock lived to see the development he had so long worked for in the remote Pilbara.

Through all of this Hancock had made powerful enemies in Rio Tinto Australia and in WA state government. He was an outback cattle station bushy, a practical and a rather blunt man who didn't suffer fools gladly. His lack of diplomacy and servility when dealing with politicians rubbed West Australian state premier Charles Court the wrong way. Hancock made no secrets of his dislike of bureaucratic management, committees and self-serving politicians that held up progress. He appreciated men who made things happen and learned early that, if you wanted to get something done, you went straight to the top.

In 1966, at the opening of the Hamersley Iron project, Hancock's name on the guest list was conspicuous by its absence. He was not even mentioned in any of the speeches that day. The local bureaucracy had shut him out, and went on to spend many years denying him credit for his discoveries.

The dream was eventually realised by Hancock's daughter Gina and, in her mother's honour, the 'Hope Downs' mine was developed for $1.34bn. Hancock Prospecting started exploration procedures at Hope Downs mine in 1992. Production started in November 2007; it takes a lot of time and money to start up a big mine. Since then further Hope Downs deposits have been opened and more are under development. Of Australia's top fifty iron ore mines operating today, no fewer than seven were discoveries by Lang Hancock.

The result was the industrial development of the 'Pilbara', the world's biggest iron ore region, resulting in massive infrastructure development. Migrants arrived from almost every country of the world to work in the mines and build the infrastructure, myself among them in 1973.

Where the journey began:
red dust - 1979

I had a recurring dream as the rattling air conditioner above my head fought its nightly contest against the stifling heat in the small caravan that had been baking in the sun for twelve hours. I lay on sweat-dampened sheets with a cold can of beer at the end of each long day of hard physical work under the unrelenting Pilbara sun, thinking of what to do with my hard earned savings. Buy a boat and go shark fishing? Maybe a hedonistic trip to North America? Or a deposit on the latest V8 Holden muscle car.

These were just some of my workmates' preferences, but my dream was different, and even less responsible. I would first go to the Himalayas. It would be cooler there, and how good would that be after the ceaseless Pilbara heat? I would trek to Everest base camp – and after that? I wasn't sure. I'd see what it led to; let it be an adventure that led wherever it did.

I had recently read Alan Moorehead's famous book *Gallipoli*, his vivid account of that WW1 naval and military disaster. I thought perhaps I would travel on from Nepal through northern India and then across Asia to the Gallipoli battlefields, a place I wanted to visit after reading Moorehead's book, and decided I would try to get there one way or another.

By Christmas 1979 I had been working a year in the mining towns and remote bush camps of the Pilbara in north-west Australia. A year sweating under a remorseless sun in the rust red dust that infiltrated everything – we breathed it, ate it and wore it; the joke went that a long-term North-Wester's bed sheets could be identified on a washing line by the red rings left from farting in bed.

I had done some reading in the South Hedland library, the only place in town to escape the hot nights in air conditioned cool without getting a hangover. It was usually empty. I enjoyed the hushed peace after the long hot noisy days of compressors and construction machinery. I searched the shelves for anything on Nepal and the Himalayas. There wasn't much available but it was there that I made my first acquaintance with William 'Bill' Tilman and his climbing partner Eric Shipton; their writings on mountain travel and Himalayan exploration inspired me then and since.

It was in the small South Hedland library where I first learned the Everest base camp trek route started from the roadhead village of Lamosangu, 90km due east of Kathmandu but 200km of boneshaking switchbacks by bus to the road's end. From there it continued along 300km of ancient foot trails through ethnically diverse remote villages, down steep rhododendron and pine-filled valleys and over high snow-covered passes to the foot of the Khumbu icefall, the site of Everest base camp, where international climbing expeditions begin their attempts on the summit of Everest, or Sagarmatha – Mother of the World – as the Nepali people know it.

In those intoxicating north-west Pilbara days you could work for a year 'up north', as we called it, and earn enough to travel the world for a year. The tax department even helped, giving fast two-day tax refunds on production of an airline ticket out of the country. Try that now and a six-year audit is all you'd get; it was a simpler time.

The plentiful construction work in the north-west Pilbara attracted a variety of young and not-so-young tradesmen and chancers from Australia's southern cities and all around the world, some of them leaving a fresh skeleton in a hometown cupboard. There was a saying in the mining camps of the north-west that the Pilbara attracted three types of characters – the infamous three Ms – 'mercenaries, missionaries and misfits'. The mercenaries were the majority; their driving force was earning money. I was one of them. Missionaries were fewer but could be found collecting money in the pubs on Fridays for worthy causes such as the flying doctor service, a collection for a new church roof and the Salvation Army slush fund – in support of reforming the many alcoholics. The Pilbara and especially Port Hedland had much need of the Sally Ann.

The most interesting characters were the misfits. These included men on the run from prison, others avoiding tax debts or alimony payments, conmen and bankrupts of all shades, and the more sinister and not-uncommon international war criminal, and a variety of villains of interest to Interpol if the bar rumours were only partly true. Among these worthies, bashings over gambling debts were no rarer than a hangover. An occasional murder or gunfight would result in the local constabulary having their weekend leave cancelled, to the dismay of the officers posted there as punishment for indiscretions in more law-abiding southern towns.

Bar brawls were no rarer than a sweat rash. I was on hand to witness one, on a Saturday night in the beer garden of the Victoria hotel at Roebourne, involving fifty or more drinkers in town from the construction camp at Cape Lambert, a dis-United Nations of nationalities from Albania to Zimbabwe. For five minutes a table or chair was airborne till the overworked bouncers finally evicted them into the street, where they carried on till they couldn't. The touring rock band to its professional credit kept on playing 'Jumping Jack Flash' throughout. A few innocents were injured but no women were caught up in it; the only women in the Vic worked behind the bar, and the bar was behind a steel mesh barrier, where the drinks were pushed through a small hatch, after payment had first been pushed through it.

Next morning the Roebourne sergeant and a couple of side-armed constables drove out to the construction camp at Cape Lambert, where 600 sweating men were building an iron ore shipping terminal, and began rounding up all those with black eyes and bruises. These were paid off by Bechtel Pacific, the engineering contractor, then escorted out of town by the police and told to get going. Where the police were during the brawl no one could say; the station was less than 100m from the Vic's beer garden.

Ted

One of the more affable misfits and workmate was a Melbourne larrikin called Ted, though there was no certainty that was his real name. Like me, Ted was employed as a roofing carpenter; in his mid-forties, Ted was a tad long in the tooth for roofing work in the daily 40°C temperatures. Short-statured with a growing beer paunch, some missing teeth and a sun-ravaged appearance, he was still in strong physical condition. Rough as he looked, Ted never failed to shave on Sundays or keep his jet-black hair neatly slicked with hair oil in a 60s Elvis-style quiff and his wedge-shaped sideburns neatly trimmed. I was envious of Ted's sideburns.

On Friday afternoons we all finished work an hour early to gather around two forty-four-gallon drums filled with ice and Emu Export beer, known as 'super', due to its high-octane content. For the last two hours of daylight and often longer we drank icy cans of Emu under the sparse shade of a few sun-withered bottlebrush trees, burning sausages on a gas ring and listening to each other's lies.

One particularly hot Friday afternoon Ted was his usual extrovert self, as we approached the trees he pronounced he was 'As dry as a wooden God'; he had drunk more than his usual share by the time we emptied the drums. In the dark I helped him stagger to his caravan next to my own. By then Ted had lost whatever inhibitions he ever had about revealing his past; as we sat in the caravan annex having a few more cans from the Esky box he unloaded his story on me.

He was on the run from prison for grievous bodily harm to a

building contractor who owed him a lot of money. He thought he was still married but didn't know if his wife had by now already divorced him. Ted was only five foot six so had set about the bigger man with a crowbar, and was lucky not to have been serving a sentence for attempted murder. But Ted wasn't satisfied with his revenge; it had cost him his marriage, his house and a prison sentence, saying he was saving money to have the contractor killed by a budget hitman he'd met in prison. As most of his wages went on beer, smokes and gambling, the contractor seemed safe enough.

Ted had gained the trust of the jail's governor and on day release to visit his sick father had gone on the run. With help from some drinking mates he borrowed money to head to the Pilbara. He had since heard his father had died, and as his parents had been managing a pub his mother could no longer manage it alone. Ted desperately wanted to go home and run the pub but knew he would be picked up by the police if he did. Torn between his perfect job and a return to prison if he went home, he had turned to heavy drinking.

I knocked on Ted's caravan at 6 am and heard the clump of work boots hitting the floor as he got off the bed; he opened the door, still in the stubby shorts, ripped shirt and dusty work boots he was wearing when he'd collapsed on his bed six hours earlier. I lit the gas ring and made coffee while he went behind the van for a piss and a swill from the hosepipe. It was clear he hadn't eaten last night: no plate was in the sink, just empty beer cans. He was still well under the influence so we took my car, stopping at the bakery for sausage rolls, before another day sweating under the already-hot sun.

Among the mercenaries and misfits, gambling was a way of life. Whenever there was a bush town race meeting all work stopped for the day. And wearing our finest mocker and best rubber flip-flops we went to 'the races'. On one memorable occasion of the Roebourne race meeting the contractor building the Cape Lambert iron exporting facility threatened to fire anyone who didn't show for work that day. However, this minor hitch was overcome when a kitchen hand found a maggot in the camp kitchen and 600 of us went on strike for the day.

Such was the hold gambling had on Pilbara life. I miss some of those good old days when the workers had the upper hand.

The last time I saw Ted was the Sunday before I left town. He was standing in the red dust ring of a two-up game at the end of a potholed dirt track near the South Hedland rubbish dump, losing his wages to a syndicate of 'knife fighters', as we referred to the East Europeans and others who had slipped through the Iron Curtain and found their way to the Australian Wild West.

These gentlemen ran the illegal bush casinos where local police turned a blind eye, keeping well clear, where a week's wages could be lost in minutes on the throw of two coins. When a punter had lost his roll bets were taken on credit against next week's wage; failure to pay debts had serious consequences. Even the Italian mafia didn't interfere in these gambling schools. It wasn't unusual to see a party of 'knife fighters' visiting work sites on Friday afternoon to collect a debt as soon as a punter got paid.

Any who wouldn't pay could expect a serious beating or a curly knife between the ribs one dark night. Occasionally someone vanished and we never knew if he'd 'shot thru' or been shot dead. It was rumoured the rubbish dump had a few bodies in it – it smelled likely enough when the wind was from the east coming in off the Gibson Desert.

To break the monotony and escape the relentless heat and dust, every few months we went down to the 'big smoke' – Perth – for a week, propping up the bar at Sassella's tavern or less respectable watering holes where skimpies (bikini barmaids) were employed. A day's pay placed on the counter and the girls told to 'give us a hoy when that's finished' – which was quicker than expected if you didn't keep an eye on it.

They were boom times and we thought they'd always be. But this time around I wasn't returning to the red dust of the Pilbara; I was ready for a sea change. Had I known what lay ahead, I would have bought that 150mph muscle car or gone shark fishing instead; it would have been far less risky.

I dreamed a few dreams in that calm cool library in South Hedland. It's still there today and still used on a hot night to while away an hour or two, offering a more civilised alternative to the Last Chance Tavern at the other end of the street. I wonder how many other dreamers started a journey in that library or one like it.

The Nepal Himalayas

I was unable to find a like-minded mate to join me trekking in the Himalayas. It was considered eccentric and a bit weird by my mates to go mountain trekking. 'What are the pubs like in Nepal'? I was asked. 'There are none,' I replied. 'But what will you do every night?' they asked. Early to bed, I'd say; after a day of hiking 30k up steep hills, down valleys and over snow-swept passes and back down their far sides, all you want to do is eat and go to bed, I'd tell them. They couldn't see the point of it. So, not for the first time, I was travelling on my Jack Jones. But, as that great witness of nineteenth-century customs among the peoples of the Himalayan hills – Rudyard Kipling – tersely observed,

> Down to Gehenna, or up to the Throne, He travels the fastest who travels alone.

I was off to the Throne of the Himalayas – to see Mount Everest and some of its pals, but at this stage I had no reason to suspect Gehenna would soon follow.

With inoculation card, two passports and my tax refund in my money belt, the cooler world of the Himalayas waited. I kitted out with boots, sleeping bag and cheap hiking clothes at the army and navy stores on Wellington Street, Perth, and took the Friday-night Thai Airways flight to Bangkok. After a short stay to get a Nepal visa, I flew on to Kathmandu.

Arriving in Nepal from the backblocks of Western Australia, Kathmandu was a culture shock. It was still a lingering hippy sanctuary, though well past its heyday of the late 60s, when it had been the vital destination for the dedicated hippies of the flower power movement, led by the Fab Four. And it still is for those who want to turn back time and give hippy retro life a try where no one will recognise you and some people actually still do.

Mercenaries, missionaries, misfits and hippies

The Pilbara had its share of the three Ms but Kathmandu had them and hippies. The city was as I remembered it from a visit six years earlier: narrow, congested streets bustling with pedal trishaws, pony carts, and cantankerous cows lifting their tails when you least expected. Three-wheeled tractors pumping out clouds of two-stroke fumes, hauled trailers of rural produce through the narrow lanes to the daily markets. Street dogs and beggars rummaged through piles of garbage; soldiers marched through the narrow lanes with rifles at the slope; traffic police manned road junctions armed with whistles and bamboo lathi sticks, keeping order where it wasn't needed.

A persistent tiger balm seller followed me for a mile; I gave in and bought some for anticipated stiff leg muscles. Processions of white-robed nuns and orange-robed priests ringing brass bells stepped warily around the scavenging dogs and cow patties. Undercover police posing as hashish dealers operated in dim doorways, extracting bribe fines from gullible hippies who fell for the ruse.

I was surprised to still see a few hippies with grey ponytails chilling in the street cafes and pudding shops. On my first visit to Kathmandu in the monsoon season of 1974, I had also hung out in the pudding shops, strictly for the puddings. There were some good pudding shops in Kathmandu then.

The cult of the overland hippy reached its highpoint in Kathmandu about 1970. Hippies were not persecuted in Kathmandu as they were in conservative Asian cities such as Singapore and Kuala Lumpur, where travellers were not welcome unless they had haircuts like a WW2 sergeant major and where possession of ganja ensured a prison sentence and a flogging. Kathmandu with its dirt cheap ganja, hash puddings and cheap digs was nirvana to the 1970s' wandering hippies.

The Nepalese had no real idea what the citizens of Europe or America looked or dressed like; there was no TV and few Nepalese had travelled further than India. The average Nepalese thought all Europeans and North Americans to be like the hippies who had come among them, with their strange appearance and stranger needs, ganja, hashish puddings, long hair and strange dress.

The 1970s were also the height of the short-lived era of the 'Asian overland trip', the drug-fuelled psychedelic magic bus ride that officially started in Turkey and ran through Iran, Afghanistan, Pakistan and India, ending in Kathmandu. The adventure began at the 'Pudding Shop' at Sultan Ahmet in Istanbul and ended at the pudding shops of Freak Street in Kathmandu. I'm not sure why puddings were such an important foundation of hippy culture, but it was so. Kathmandu had pudding shops on every corner of Freak Street and Thamel bazaar.

The Asian overland trip was an experience where anything might happen and something always did, ranging from religious enlightenment to an indefinite sentence in a crowded cell with a communal bucket for a toilet. Some hippies were seeking religious illumination; others were just 'hanging loose, man'. 'Man' was used to end every sentence whatever gender was being addressed. It would be used multiple times in a sentence, such as 'Hey, man, what's going down, man?' 'Just had a pudding with Melanie, man, she's got a fresh stash man, knows a guru at a temple, man; she'll be in the spotted yak pudding shop if you want some good hash, man.'

Kathmandu was the best place on the planet to live the hippy life. It was easy to get a visa; your hair could be longer than a yak's. There were no religious or political zealots, the dope was cheaper than bread and the puddings were world class. Even the name was right:

'Kathmandu'. Hanging loose in Kathmandu was nirvana, man; even the Beatles were there.

I have heard the Asian overland trip, described by those who never did it, as the '70s' equivalent of the Victorian-era grand European tour – a ridiculous comparison, unless the grand European tour was all about, drugs, rock and roll, ganja-laced chocolate puddings, and dank communal dormitories where if you spent too much time you developed rickets.

Besides the hippies there were other types in Kathmandu, such as wealthy mountaineering wannabees with custom-tailored designer clothes and hand-made Italian boots – worth a year's wages to a Nepali expedition porter. These pseudo expedition climbers thought themselves a few levels above the idling hippies and stayed in a better class of hostelry, the Kathmandu Guest House being a favourite, where the Beatles had once crashed, and me too on my first visit, though in the low-end dormitory wing.

American evangelical missionaries were also active, waging war against three thousand years of Hinduism by distributing English-language Bibles nobody could read. During times of famine due to a bad monsoon or a blighted crop, the missionaries cashed in, converting low-caste, hungry families in return for a sack of rice. The recipients of this charity are still known as rice Christians by the Hindu higher castes.

The cream of Kathmandu's expatriate life was the Diplomatic Corps, who kept to themselves, insulated behind high lichen-covered brick walls, where uniformed gardeners manicured the lawns with hand sickles, tidied up the leaves and shooed away scavenging dogs and destitute hippies. Chowkidars in knife edge-creased embassy uniforms and gold-braided caps guarded the gates of these enclaves of worldly privilege, armed with bamboo lathis to keep the hippies in order when they came a knocking for a replacement passport, having sold their old one to a rickshaw wallah for hashish money or to bribe their way out of jail.

Outside the high defensive walls of the tranquil embassy gardens was a world of dust, debris and beggars, including a few Westerners dressed as Hindu sadhus. Diplomatically, Kathmandu was not an appointment to boast of; those posted there were usually first-time diplomats or ones who had displeased the service mandarins and received a hardship allowance for their difficulties.

Inside the embassy walls the consuls and attachés lived in cloistered splendour – by Kathmandu's standards – attending a merry round of incestuous soirees, at each other's embassies and dining on imported delicacies such as foie gras and smoked salmon that arrived in the diplomatic bag. How those bags must have hummed when delayed by the many airline strikes of the 1970s. It was a world apart from the vegetarian noodles and hashish puddings the hippies survived on.

In the 1970s Kathmandu's now-ubiquitous international NGO community had not established itself. The Nepalese had not then come to associate expatriate Westerners with an array of free services such as nutrition education programmes taught by obese Western aid workers, or World Health Organization immunisation programmes for diseases they had never heard of, believing all ailments to be payback for some misdeed in a previous life.

Any destitute hippy suffering from one of the many diseases found in the city, and most of them were, had a good chance of dying in a Freak Street dormitory unless fortunate enough to be repatriated home by a junior diplomat unlucky enough not to be on compassionate leave. Hepatitis was more common than dandruff among the feringhee hippy community.

A passable hippy wardrobe could be had for a few rupees in any Kathmandu bazaar. Wearing your 108-bead yak-bone necklace – I've still got mine – you were all set to hang loose on the temple steps in Durbar Square, but not too early: real hippies don't get up till afternoon. The number 108 has great significance in Hinduism and Buddhism. In Hindu astrology, there are twelve zodiacs and nine planets, giving a total of 108 combinations. There are also twenty-seven lunar houses, divided into four quarters, giving a combination of 108 padas. I bet you didn't know that.

There can't have been another city in the world like it during the five years each side of 1970. An academy of misfits, missionaries and hippies, where Janis Joplin and Led Zeppelin thumped from tape decks in every backstreet pudding shop, and John Lennon glasses were on sale at every tiger balm vendor's pitch. How the Nepalese must have wondered what it was all about.

Two days' hanging loose was all I could spare, man – I hadn't come to Nepal just to be a weekend hippy. I hired a rickshaw pedalled by an elderly gent who looked like he had been pedalling since George VI's coronation to take me to a government office, where, under a creaking ceiling fan that kept the mosquitos in order till the power failed, I filled out carbon triplicate forms detailing my life history, and a good part of my parents'. Eventually, a trekking card and Sagarmatha National Park permit were issued after my rickshaw driver hinted a modest baksheesh would expedite things saving me from coming back next day.

This done, under the straining might of the thinnest legs in Kathmandu we pedalled off to Thamel bazaar to stock up on trek ammunition – chocolate, mango jam and yak cheese, followed up by a stop at the Rum Doodle bar for a cold beer.

The bar was named after W.E. Bowman's book *The Ascent of Rum Doodle*, the world's highest mountain at 40,000½ ft, an out-of-print satire of the mountaineering genre books that always follow every climb in the Himalayas. The expedition cook, named Pong, is a central character whose culinary skill caused many problems for the expedition.

Also savouring a cold one in the Rum Doodle was an Australian trekker just arrived from India. We swapped information and inevitably got into a beer session. In the interval my driver, a pious Muslim, grabbed a nap in his rickshaw before returning me to my lodging, which I wouldn't have found without him. I was roused at 6 am the next morning from a state of grogginess by a loud knocking; as promised, he had arrived early to pedal me to Ratna Park bus station for the 7 am departure to Lamosangu.

The trek to Everest

There's a race of men that don't fit in,
A race that can't stay still;
So they break the hearts of kith and kin,
And they roam the world at will.
They range the field and they rove the flood,
And they climb the mountain's crest;
Theirs is the curse of the gypsy blood,
And they don't know how to rest.
Robert Service 'The Men That Don't Fit In'

The Indian-built Ashok Leyland bus looked to be at the limits of its endurance, its broken springs and creaking chassis held together with dobs of rusting weld and twisted wire. Its crumpled body work displayed a history of head-ons, side swipes and rollovers. Garish hand-painted murals of Hindu deities and mountain scenes adorned its dented panels. My favourite was a bloody-mouthed tiger carrying off a sari-clad damsel, while pukka sahibs with wing commander moustaches dressed in khaki jungle kit and solar topees aimed their rifles at it from the back of an elephant. It wasn't clear whether the lady's bleeding wounds were caused by the tiger or the sahibs. It was more than a road-worn ramshackle bus at the end of its days – it was a mobile pop art exhibition.

In the overcrowded interior, each wooden bench held a family or two, the aisle was chock full with jute sacks of bazaar goods. Further back, a goat was bleating; cock-a-doodling came from somewhere among it all. Bags of cement and steel rebars were being manhandled onto the roof. At my rickshaw wallah's sage advice, I paid extra for the seat by the door in case of an emergency. Latecomers were climbing the rear ladder onto the roof with their weekly shop of rice, fruit, vegetables, chickens and kid goats; in the cramped, sweat-scented interior I envied their airy perches.

The unbreakable Leyland Comet engine spluttered to life after a vigorous bout of crank handle turning by the driver's mate, who by my judgement should have been in school. We began groaning and huffing through the litter of plastic bottles and rotting vegetation out of the dusty station through a fog of diesel fumes and dried animal manure dust. As we entered the highway the driver hit the air horn, blasting a passage through the congestion. Then we hit the first of many potholes, causing me to bang my head on the seat post. A Hindi film song was screeching from oversized speakers hung from the sagging roof. It might have been a worn-down bus but it had character and very strong lungs.

The long stroke comet engine beat rhythmically in low gear as we squeezed between similar buses competing for road space in the chaotic morning traffic. The Leyland's creaking chassis, wooden carriage work, splintered seats and glassless windows didn't inspire confidence in its ability to complete the journey, and I was grateful I had a seat by the door for a fast exit. Statistics show a chance of a road accident is thirty times greater in Nepal than in Europe, but I didn't know that then; I was young and bulletproof. It was to come in handy later.

The five-foot-tall gap-toothed driver was dressed in an oil-stained lunghi; a threadbare cotton singlet clung with sweat to his protruding ribs; a frayed Nepali topi and a worn-down pair of tyre rubber slippers completed his uniform. He looked in need of a T-bone steak, but the gruesome image of the Hindu goddess Kali swinging from the broken mirror told me he wouldn't have let me on the bus if he'd known I'd eaten one a week earlier. He was barely able to haul the steering wheel around as we crawled through the jammed streets, road dust and exhaust fumes choking us to the city's fringe.

Clearing the city sprawl, we began climbing out of the Kathmandu valley; the dust haze and humidity were replaced by the clean cool air of the hills gusting through the broken windows. I breathed it gratefully. We began a laborious low-geared progression of rising switchbacks cut into the hillsides, narrow precipitous ledges that served as the road to the middle hills. Our destination was Lamosangu village, the limit of the motor road in 1979 and the last village of any size I would see till I reached Namche Bazaar, the main settlement of the famed Sherpas I had first read of in the hushed cool of South Hedland library.

From Lamosangu, narrow foot trails led down deep valleys across rickety wooden footbridges before climbing back up their far sides. Days ran into weeks as I crossed the many ridges and spurs running down from the higher ranges of the Himalayan chain. The ridges and valleys continuing all the way to Namche Bazaar, and then on to Thangboche monastery, and finally Everest base camp, where the trail ended at the foot of the Khumbu Icefall. I was no longer dreaming beneath a struggling air conditioner in a hot caravan; the journey had begun I was in the cool clear air of the Nepal hills.

One memory from that bus ride still gives me cold feet whenever I think of it. A road block was in place before the bridge over the fast-flowing Sun Khosi (*khosi* means river). Our bus was stopped by a party of men waving banners; a passenger explained it was a ban against bus companies refusing to pay increased bridge tolls. The bridge owners were not allowing some bus companies to cross, ours being one of the damned.

Some passengers with only small loads to carry walked down to the bridge, but they were turned back; these passengers were the rural poor, for whom a ticket on a third-class bus had to be saved for. I watched them as they began climbing down the bank to wade across the fast-flowing river. As I considered my own options, the old man and his grandson who had shared my seat began scrambling down the bank. I watched them take off their shoes and roll up their trousers to wade the river; grabbing my rucksack off the roof, I went to join them. I could walk on to Lamosangu once across the Sun Khosi.

I got down the bank just as the hill man and his young grandson were taking their first cautious steps into the rushing water. Taking off my trekking boots, I threw them over to the far side to keep my hands free; they landed safely on the shingle bank. I was committed now. The old man stopped and asked me to throw their plastic slippers across. With my rucksack straps loosened in case I had to get free of the pack in a hurry, I began wading across.

Stepping into the river, I flinched at the numbingly cold water, the old man and boy were working across diagonally, while I waded more directly. I was nearly halfway over, where the current was at its fastest and strongest, when I noticed the old man struggling to keep his balance in the strong flow while keeping hold of his grandson who was beginning to panic, the water now up to the boy's waist.

Moving as quickly as I could over the stony river bed, my soft feet slipping on the water-polished stones, I reached them just as the boy lost his balance and stumbled. Wedging him between us, we stood still to take stock and then locked arms. A bank of shingle broke the surface lower down in midstream, causing the flow to divert; if we could get to it we could rest a bit and recover. With me acting as downstream anchor and the boy held between us, we inched through the turbulence and some nervous minutes later reached the slack water of the shingle island.

After a few minutes' rest observing the best route to take, we entered the river again, pushing diagonally upstream to where the water looked shallower. Some edgy minutes later there was relief all round as we reached knee deep shallows and then the far bank. It had been touch and go in midstream, where the river was fastest. Few Nepalese hill dwellers can swim; the young boy and his grandfather had been badly scared and so had I.

Boots retrieved, we climbed the bank; a short walk took us to a roadside chai stall overlooking the scene, where we sat in the sun warming up, our wet clothes spread steaming on the warm rocks. The old hill man offered to pay for the tea, but I could see from their clothes they were very poor, and insisted it was my shout. We argued a while before the chai wallah who had watched us crossing refused payment: our chai was on the house.

We finished our tea and in damp clothes walked on till we reached a steep path leading up a rice paddy-terraced hillside towards my new friend's village, where, by gestures, I was invited to spend the night, but I wanted to reach Lamosangu, so, shaking hands, we parted ways.

Walking briskly to keep warm in the gathering chill of late afternoon, I watched the sky turning crimson as the sun fell behind distant snow peaks and then turn to deep blue. I reached Lamosangu as darkness fell, and found a corner to sleep in on the compacted earth floor of a teashop, among a party of porters and their dhoka baskets of goods destined for the villages ahead. I lay among the snoring blanket-shrouded bodies, contemplating my first day on the trail to Everest and my first experience of the hospitality and culture of village Nepal, feeling pleased I had at last come.

At the village of Junbesi I took a rest day, staying at the monastery guest house, where I watched local carpenters and monks working on the construction of a trekker's dormitory in anticipation of increased future numbers of trekkers, and the money they would bring to the monastery in return for food and lodging.

It took me ten days, trekking up to ten hours a day, to cross the many ridges and valleys of the middle hills and high passes to Namche Bazaar in the Solu Khumbu, the high-altitude homeland of the famed Sherpas. A day's rest seemed in order; I took a dormitory bed in one of the two lodges on the main street of Namche, to explore the area and acclimatise for the higher altitudes ahead. Another week's trekking would take me to my goal of Everest base camp.

Sitting round the stove drinking chai in the International Footrest Lodge I first met Martin Zabaleta, the leader of the 'Expedicion Vasca Everest 1980' (the 1980 Basque Everest Expedition). Martin was accompanying a party of porters carrying supplies to establish the base camp for the rest of the Basque expedition climbers who were waiting at Lukla airstrip for their equipment to arrive. My luck was in: he invited me to spend a night as his guest at Everest base camp.

Months later I would learn Martin and Temba Sherpa summited Everest on 4 May 1980. A great feat for them; they had summited the world's highest mountain before any other Spanish expedition – a moment of pride for the Basque cause.

Also staying at the Footrest was Dan, who I had shared a few beers with at the Rum Doodle bar back in Kathmandu, who had been working in London and was overlanding home to Australia. After his Pokhara trip he had flown into Lukla, as he didn't have the time to hike all the way from Lamosangu. We were to team up and trek together for mutual safety. Trekking alone in the Himalayas carries a risk: a leg break or a fall from a steep trail with no one to know you have not arrived at your evening destination is all it takes to die of exposure. It happens every year.

Teaming up lessens risks and makes for evening company in the quiet teashops and lodges along the trail. We would set out together after breakfast each morning, but walked apart most of the day. Dan walked faster. I stopped to take a photo, or just sit on a rock absorbing the magnificent scenery. I asked Martin if Dan could also stay at their base camp and this was agreed. Next morning we set out on the trail to Khumbu.

It was a fine blue sky day as most are in winter months. The trail wound through rhododendron forest, along the valley above the Dudh Kosi River. Mount Everest, Lhotse, Nuptse, and Ama Dablam all standing majestically in the distance, we stopped at small wayside chai stalls wherever we found them; they always seemed to appear whenever we developed a thirst. There was a very steep climb up to Tengboche monastery, where we arrived for lunch before reluctantly moving on, as it seemed too early to stop for the night. I could always stay longer on the way back down.

We arrived in the late afternoon at Pangboche, the small village clustered around the oldest monastery in the Khumbu region and famous for the relics of a Yeti skull and hand, kept in a wood box. Perhaps I'm a cynical philistine but neither of us was interested enough to pay the fee to view them, preferring to spend the money on a pre-dinner Kukri rum and put our feet up round our lodge fire instead. We made a plan to climb the small peak of Kala Pathar before going on to base camp as we dined on the Nepali staple diet of dhal bhat – lentils, rice and whatever vegetables are locally available. This vegetable diet is always cooked fresh and very organic – fertilised naturally with goat and yak manure. As the Nepalese porters say, 'Dhal bhat power last 24 hour'.

We toasted our adventure with another khukri rum before laying our sleeping bags on the rough boarded floor. With the cold drafts coming through the chinks in the dry stone walls and the bleating of goats from the enclosure outside, sleeping was fitful. Today there are more comfortable lodges, with hot solar showers, and printed menus on the tablecloths, but it wasn't always so.

Early next morning, after a breakfast of chapattis and the last dregs of the mango jam I had carried all the way from Kathmandu, we left for Kala Pathar – Nepali for 'black rock' – a small peak on the south ridge of Pumori. At 5,570 metres, many Everest trekkers had a go at summiting Kala Pathar, not everyone makes it. We reached the summit but the effort was surprisingly hard, and I was reduced to stopping every ten paces to get my breath, I became acutely aware of the fitness and stamina needed to attempt to climb to the summit of Everest.

We arrived at Everest base camp late in the afternoon. A dozen yellow tents belonging to a Polish expedition were scattered among car-sized boulders and blocks of ice that had worked their way down the icefall from the heights of Everest and its neighbour Pumori over centuries of avalanches and glacial advance. The rock and ice beneath our feet had once been high on Everest; now it was a slowly moving glacial moraine, as we stood there we moved along with it at less than a snail's pace.

Martin had made arrangements for the three of us to sleep in one of the Polish expedition tents equipped with foam mattresses. It was a luxurious indulgence compared to my thin cell-foam mat on the cold earth floors of teashops and goatherd shelters. Six of the Polish climbers and their Sherpa porters were high on the mountain, carrying up supplies to advance base camp for their summit attempt, hence the empty tents. Fortunately I had brought a pack of dehydrated beef curry from Namche Bazaar to contribute to the base camp kitchen without feeling guilty eating the Polish expedition supplies. My bottle of khukri rum was even better received.

As night fell the stars emerged and we gathered for dinner in the mess tent sitting on cell-foam mats on blocks of sculpted ice around a rough table cobbled together from packing cases in the hissing light of a dented kerosene Tilley lamp. After dinner we drank khukri rum in our coffee while listening to the radio schedule with the climbing party on the mountain. The nightly contact provided those high at advanced base with next day's weather forecast, followed by a music tape played over the two-way radio. The climbers' spirits were high as they settled in for the night in their small tents on the South Col at camp IV at 26,000ft (7,925m).

Then it was time for bed; by 8 pm base camp was silent and deserted as the climbers and porters headed for the warmth of their tents and sleeping bags. It went very cold very quickly as night fell and the stars came out. Before I turned in I walked alone up the glacial moraine to the foot of the icefall, marvelling at the star-crowded sky in the silent night, the giant peaks all around illuminated by starlight. Beautiful as the night sky was, it was too cold to stay out long.

I crawled into the tent and lay half clothed in my sleeping bag, with the warm luxury of the foam mattress under me, thinking of all the hot days sweating in the Pilbara and the nightly respites dreaming of this in the South Hedland library. I wasn't dreaming anymore: this was the real thing, dozing in an expedition tent on the Khumbu glacier at the foot of Everest. The tent canvas was flapping lazily in a light breeze, a world away from rattling air conditioners in hot caravans.

A rising moon faintly illuminated the tent interior. Dan and

Martin were both snoring, but it didn't spoil the moment nothing could have. The library dream had become reality; I slept the sleep of tired contentment, the best sleep there is.

Next morning, after a breakfast of biscuits and coffee, we walked up to the head of the moraine at the foot of the Khumbu icefall and I pocketed a few pebbles that may once have been near the top of the mountain.

This was as high on the slopes of Everest as I would be going. The huge tumbled slabs of ice and rock brought down by centuries of avalanching meant climbing permits were required to go higher, and you can't get one of those with a small baksheesh to a rickshaw driver. We returned to camp, packed our things, thanked our Polish hosts and wished them good luck. Reluctantly we started trekking back to Namche Bazaar.

Two of the Polish climbers, Leszek Cichy and Krzysztof Wielicki, were successful in making the first ever winter ascent of Mount Everest on 17 February. On their way down the mountain they found the body of Hannelore Schmatz, a German woman who died after summiting Everest in autumn 1979. The Polish were late in the race to the highest mountains in the Himalayas; for political reasons they couldn't travel abroad. So, when it was finally possible for them to, all that was left was attempting the mountain in winter – a feat many thought to be impossible.

In 1979 Namche Bazaar boasted only three lodges, several small stone and slate houses and teashops, a bakery, and two small general stores, the butcher's shop was a blood-spattered slab of rock by the trackside selling cuts of goat and yak. We returned to the International Footrest with its one dormitory of Tibetan-carpeted sleeping benches around the walls and the cosy wood-fired stove in the middle of the room – it was an easy decision; it had the best menu.

Namche Bazaar is the main town in the eastern Sherpa region, though it was only a small village in 1980. It makes a welcome stop for the thousands of trekkers who today pass through on the trek to Thangboche monastery and Everest base camp. In 1979 there were very few winter trekkers; even so, apple pie could be ordered at breakfast in time for dinner – where the apples came from was a mystery. We celebrated our Everest trek with a dinner of baked beans, chips and fried eggs, followed by apple pie and khukri rum coffee. Porridge and yak cheese omelette was on offer for breakfast.

Today there are more than fifty hotels and lodges arranged around the horseshoe of scree slopes that shelters Namche Bazaar, and more on the ridge above it, ranging from four stars to minus a few, and nearly as many cafes, bakeries and Italian pizzerias. The Sherpa population is a part-transient population of around 1,800, living in stone and slate houses. There is even a karaoke bar, patronised mostly by gap year students from Japan and Korea – I wonder what Tilman and Shipton would make of that; probably they wouldn't have had need of a screen prompt.

The Solu Khumbu is Nepal's wealthiest district due to the money generated by trekking groups and climbing expeditions. The Sherpa's have become astute business operators, travelling the world in the monsoon off season. Many lodge owners have visited America, Europe and Australia, and some have visited the summit of Everest. Although well informed and travelled, many still prefer traditional Tibetan dress. The careful observer may glimpse a real Rolex as a wrist protrudes from a yak wool sleeve; some of the women wear expensive antique Tibetan pink coral necklaces alongside their Cartier earrings – real ones.

Fortified by two days' dining on baked beans, chips, apple pies, Thukpa Sherpa stew and chocolate cake, washed down with butter tea and khukri rum, we set out after a breakfast of yak cheese omelettes for Lukla, the only airstrip in the Khumbu, originally built by the Sir Edmund Hillary Foundation fund, which has also built many schools and health centres for the Sherpa people. A short walk beyond Lukla a sign pointed to the trail south to the Arun Valley. We were now off the main Everest trekking route there would now be very few lodges or tea shops until the town of Dhahran seven days away.

Our route – done in reverse – was first taken by the famed British climber and explorer H.W. 'Bill' Tilman, whose Himalayan travels had inspired me when I first read of them in the South Hedland library. Tilman was a prolific mountain traveller and writer of exploration books that have provided many quotes and advice for those following his footsteps. His laconic style makes entertaining reading for anyone trekking in the Himalayan hills, or wishing they could. His statement on all that's needed to have an adventure – 'Put on a pair of boots and walk out the door' – has been a motivation for me and many others.

Tilman was the first foreigner to take the direct route from the tropical Terai of Nepal to the mountains of Solu Khumbu, to reconnoitre a new route to Everest in 1950, early groundwork that was later used for the successful 1953 British Everest expedition. Tilman was a great believer in small and light expeditions, as noted in another of his quotes: 'Any expedition that can't be planned on the back of a cigarette packet is too big.'

Another of Tilman's sayings is: 'No conscientious traveller ever turns homeward by the route on which he came if a reasonable alternative offers itself.' I could hardly ignore such advice when the reasonable alternative now offered us had been pioneered by Tilman himself.

I had explained all of this to Dan over khukri rums at the Footrest lodge, he also became keen to follow Tilman's route down to the Terai, rather than fly back to Kathmandu. I had first read of this route in the South Hedland library, and was keen to follow it to Dhahran, the roadhead town where a bus to Kathmandu could be found. The trek would take us through traditional villages of the Rai and Limbu communities as we crossed the watershed of the Arun river.

It was some of the hardest and best trekking I have done; the small trails were often steeper than those in Solu Khumbu, and villages fewer and further between. Food supplies were limited to rice, chapattis, corn cobs and an occasional egg. We spent the nights sleeping on the open verandas of village houses or in rough animal shelters and fire wood sheds. One memorable night I slept on a wooden hay platform above a livestock pen, where the rising heat from the village cows and the ploughing buffaloes tethered below kept me warm through the night. Though the smell was hardly fragrant, and I swear they snored.

The clear sunny days slipped by as we climbed hills and descended them, along the Arun Valley and across its side valleys and then back up their far sides. I had read of one particularly deep valley made famous in Tilman's writings as he looked across from the village of Gudel to the far village of Bung. Resting there at the end of a long day's march, he wrote:

> For dreadfulness naught can excel
> The prospect of Bung from Gudel;
> And words die away on the tongue
> When we look back at Gudel from Bung.

The name Bung, Tilman said, 'Appeals to a music-hall mind'.

Tilman's exploration partner, the equally no-nonsense Eric Shipton – onetime British ambassador at Kunming in China – was not to be outdone and wrote, 'There is no greater vision of hell than the view from Bung to Gudel'. Not quite true: the views are stunning.

Bung is a village of the Rai people who are hill farmers; their fields spread over steep hillsides where rice, maize, potatoes and green vegetables are grown in their season. Ancient Buddhist chortens and mani walls are found on the high trails. The whitewashed Rai houses are traditionally roofed with shingles, but long lasting corrugated steel roofs are now replacing them. The maize crop is protected from vermin and pigs by suspending it to dry on racks of poles high above ground. The Rai claim to be the original people of these hills, well before the Hindu tribes migrated there from the south and Tibetan Buddhists from the north; they still practise forms of ancient animism.

It is a two-hour hike between Bung and Gudel villages. A 1,000m descent to the Hongu Khola before a 1,000m ascent to achieve a forward distance of 1km, and best avoided in the heat of the day. Today if you are lucky you can find a cold beer in the small teashops in either village. Tilman and Shipton were less fortunate; they had developed a taste for locally made spirits, especially the rice liquor called raksi, and the fermented millet beer chang, drunk warm through a bamboo straw from a bamboo mug.

When they arrived at Bung, Tilman and Shipton had worked up a thirst and hoped to find some local spirits 'to warm heart and soul and sooth aching feet'. But none was to be had: 'Its abundant well of good raksi, on which we were relying, had dried up.' Tilman's style is never too serious, but always perceptive and entertaining. In one typical book passage he writes that he and his companions failed to summit Annapurna IV (24,688 ft) 'because of an inability to reach the top'. Tilman irony.

In the days trekking Tilman's route we met only one foreign trekker coming up from the Terai as Tilman had, an Englishman who was tracing Tilman's journey. I would not have liked to trek the route up from the Terai; it was steep enough going down it. We talked Tilman anecdotes for an hour and swapped information on what food and shelter lay ahead then went our separate ways and saw no other foreign trekker till we reached Dhahran.

At Dhahran we met the tropical heat of the Terai. It seemed unbearable after the cold high mountains, though it was still 10°C cooler in Dhahran than it had been when I left Port Hedland two months earlier. We celebrated our trek with a hotel room and a café dinner washed down with good Nepal beer. I was scruffy and thin, in need of a bath, shave and haircut, and my clothes were a bit ragged after 600 miles on rough trails, through remote valleys and little-visited villages. But I have never felt as pleased with a long trek before or since.

There can't be many outdoor experiences better than a long trek in Nepal, and I am grateful I trekked to Everest base camp before it became the international tent city it is today during the climbing season. From Dhahran an overnight bus ran to Kathmandu, in twenty-four hours we covered what had taken me six weeks on foot. I took a room at the Tibet guest house and spent an hour in a big hot bath, then went sightseeing.

I walked the backstreets of Kathmandu, visiting ancient temples and traditionally built wooden Newari palaces, admiring the intricate Newari carpentry of the old houses in the back alleys of old Kathmandu and the stately buildings of Durbar Square. I stood for a while in a narrow lane watching the passers-by praying at the small shrine to the Hindu goddess of teeth – namastying to the toothache shrine and leaving a coin ensures you don't get toothache, and is cheaper than a dentist. I complied willingly.

The Enfield Bullet 3.5 horsepower

Next morning on an early walk through Kathmandu's winding backstreets I watched an Indian Enfield Bullet motorcycle squeezing through the crowded medieval alleys of the old city, the topee-hatted rider coolly weaving through the commuting throngs. His two children, casually riding pillion on their way to school rugged up in shawls against the late winter chill, gave me a grinning wave. I knew at that moment I had to have an Enfield for a vaguely planned tour of North India.

Unable to find one for sale in Kathmandu I took the night bus to Delhi, where with the confidence of ignorance I bought a gunmetal-grey 350cc Indian Enfield Bullet from Essar Motors on a chaotic street of wheeler dealers near Kashmir gate in Old Delhi. It was to be an impulse buy with consequences.

Before I saddled up for a tour of North India, I visited the Indian Automobile Association office off Connaught Circle in New Delhi to buy a North India road map. I loved the subtle atmosphere of the timeworn rosewood cabinets of motoring memorabilia and the fading sepia photographs of maharajas at the wheel of their vintage cars. The sagging shelves of maps and motoring books gave an impression of importance. Perhaps, I thought, an AA membership would be good insurance if I broke down in an Uttar Pradesh backwater; I could call the AA to get me out of trouble. Perhaps it was the timeless office where blue wash paint flaked off the mould specked walls, and elderly babus tapped unhurriedly on black enamelled typewriters as old as themselves.

The Hindu gentleman with the squadron leader moustache in his immaculately ironed white dhoti who sold me a map upon hearing what my plans were insisted I take out a membership. 'It is going well, tik hai, if you are member being, but if member not being, very risk trouble achha.' He had a lifetime of experience that I didn't. I weakened and joined; it was one of my better decisions.

In the tradition of Indian hospitality a chai wallah was summoned and tea served in a chipped cup while my membership card was typed. And forty years later I still have the badge, an artefact that may well have saved me from incarceration in an Iranian jail surviving on a diet of rice and goat fat. It was an unlikely outcome but it seemed real enough later.

The mongoose

I left my pitch on the Old Delhi campsite early on a misty February morning for a practice run to the Taj Mahal, nervously riding through the busy morning traffic along Sir Edwin Lutyens's magnificent Raj Path Avenue to the India Gate. The memorial stands in honour of more than 80,000 soldiers of the British Indian Army who died serving between 1914 and 1921 in the First World War in France, Flanders, Mesopotamia, Persia, East Africa and Gallipoli. The memorial is also the modern site of India's Tomb of the Unknown Soldier, and the eternal flame in their honour.

The memorial was inaugurated by Lord Irwin on 12 February 1931, saying in his address, 'Those who after us shall look upon this monument may learn in pondering its purpose something of that sacrifice and service which the names upon its walls record.' It says much about the British administration, that records were kept in such detail, a full record of the names of all the fallen, both Indian and British, regiments, rank and service records.

Once clear of Delhi's rush hour traffic it was an enjoyable ride through small villages and sunlit fields of early spring crops of mustard and young wheat. The fields being tended by both young and old in the manner of their ancestors, with buffaloes harnessed to wooden ploughs in a method unchanged for millennia. I stopped occasionally at a roadside daba for chai and a smoke, but not for too long; I had not yet got used to how easily I attracted a crowd at this stage.

As I was writing my details in the guest ledger at a cheap Agra hotel the resident mongoose asleep on the check-in desk suddenly woke and looked at me, and I stroked it; startled, it gave me a nip. The hotel manager immediately inspected my hand, saying, 'Skin not broken, acha, not likely rabies.' This was news. I looked closer: a small red graze was visible. Was the thing rabid, I wondered, and hurried off to the bazaar to buy disinfectant. I didn't sleep too well that night; it would become one of many anxious sleepless nights.

Next morning, still smelling of Dettol, I left the hotel to have breakfast at the railway station cafeteria, the standby of budget travellers in India. Entering the toilets to wash my hands, I found a man lying in front of the urinals; commuters were walking in stepping over him and having a piss. He was immobile and pale. I checked for a pulse; there was nothing, and he was cold. Realising he was dead, I hurried to the station master's office to report it. A mass of petitioners were haranguing the great man pleading for refunds on expired tickets or trains missed. I waited irritably, then, losing patience with the gabbling supplicants, I barged to his desk and reported my find. He looked up and said, 'I am knowing this since two hour, police being tardy today.'

The toilets were still in use; men were stepping over the body, having a piss, then stepping back over him to catch their trains, as though this was a normal part of the morning rush hour, and maybe it was. No one had cordoned off the area or kept a guard over the body. It could only happen in India, it probably still does.

My appetite gone, I returned to the hotel, keeping clear of the dozing mongoose. It was a friendly beast but not to be trusted. The manager saw me circling it to get my key and gave a cringing smile. 'Mongoose good, sir; no having snake in hotel with mongoose on duty.' I never found out how many snakes it had dispatched, and wondered how many other guests had been mauled.

I parked the Enfield under the Taj Mahal's Moghul-red sandstone entrance arch in the shade, and tipped a twelve-year-old lad selling peanuts to keep an eye on it. He immediately placed his younger sister on the saddle. I bought my entrance ticket and walked through the arch into the grounds. I hadn't gone twenty paces before I had to return and disconnect the battery to stop her flattening it; playing an Indian jingle on the horn.

Walking around the formal Mughal gardens, I watched a gardener harnessing a team of cows to a mechanical grass mower. I sat on a marble bench as the cows were driven around the lawns; whenever they slacked off the gardener prodded his stick where it hurts and off they took at the double mower blades spinning smoothly, grass cuttings left in neat lines. A boy raked the grass into piles to be used as fodder for the cows. Later they would be milked to make ghee and cheese, providing an income to the gardener's family. As they pulled the mower, they dumped on the turf, fertilising the ground so the grass would grow faster and need mowing again. It wouldn't satisfy the Royal Society as an example of Isaac Newton's second law of motion, but it will do me until I see better, and to date I haven't.

Next morning I crept out past the mongoose and in the clear early chill rode south to Fatepur Sikri, the ancient capital of Emperor Akbar. A magnificent abandoned Mughal city baking in the dry, sunny countryside. Quarried from the local red sandstone, the buildings are a superb example of the stonemasons' skills. The marble floors and finely carved tracery screens surrounding the Zenana provided privacy and cool ventilation to the concubine's quarters.

Sitting on a cool marble bench, I contemplated I was sitting on the same time-polished marble that had once cooled the posteriors of Emperor Akbar's wives and concubines; I tried to visualise the past rituals and events of Akbar's court life, imagining myself among the splendours of the Mughal court. My thoughts were soon interrupted by a procession of peanut and cola vendors. Such are the historic glories and modern trials of India.

I decided to return to Delhi via Bharatpur to visit the bird sanctuary, with its more than 360 species of avifauna and variety of other animals. Originally a hunting ground and duck shooting reserve of the Maharaja of Bharatpur. In 1938 the British viceroy, Lord Linlithgow, and his shooting party bagged over 4,270 birds. I guess no one in Bharatpur went to bed hungry that night. With no camping sites available I treated myself to a room in the forest lodge bungalow, and dined in its restaurant.

Up till now I had eaten vegetarian. I broke the rule and ordered chicken curry: a bad decision. Later that night I started feeling sick and spent most of it sat on the toilet, or bending over it; no sooner back to bed, I was up again. I had no medicines for food poisoning with me. After a long sleepless night, I felt I was over the worst but, still feeling weak, I decided to stay another day to rest and see more of the sanctuary.

Wanting only a light breakfast, I ordered toast, scrambled eggs and black chai. At the table beside me were a German couple, both professional wildlife and bird photographers, who had just arrived and planned on staying for a week. They had come hoping to photograph the Siberian cranes, which migrated there during the Siberian winter. We chatted for an hour and still our breakfasts hadn't come; the Germans had ordered before me and were still waiting.

They called the waiter over, who explained there was only one cook today, but as we were the only guests and toast and eggs did not require the services of a Michelin chef and an hour's wait the Germans started demanding better service. Eventually the breakfasts came: cold toast, cold, rubbery eggs and lukewarm tea. I didn't envy them a week's stay, but you can't hurry India, or, as Rudyard Kipling better put it:

> And the end of the fight is a tombstone white with the name of the late deceased. And the epitaph drear: 'A Fool lies here who tried to hustle the East.'

After breakfast the Germans set off, walking through the forest with their cameras and tripods while I sat reading in the sun for an hour. Then, feeling slightly better having secured some medicine from the manager's office, I set off walking along the forest road following the photographers. I found them at the lake setting up their tripods.

His preparations done, the man waded into the lake up to his waist to shorten the distance between his camera and a flock of ducks resting on the water at a distance. And, having set his tripod in the water, just as he was about to take his first shots a family in an ambassador taxi drove up the small track and the driver gave a great blast on the horn to scare up the birds so their kids could see them fly. Off they took in a loud gaggle to the skies, not to be seen again that day. In a rage he threw his tripod after the disappearing taxi, where it sank near the bank. He retrieved it and climbed up the bank, gesticulating after the taxi as it disappeared in a cloud of dust; as his wife tried to calm him. I thought it best to quietly disappear: the situation seemed beyond commiserations.

At dinner that night I went back to my vegetable standby of channa dhal and chapattis; the photographers had ordered dinner before I could warn them what to expect. It looked likely things might get even worse for them the following day. I sympathised on the morning's events, explaining tactfully that you couldn't change India, you had to adapt to it, and that Indian taxi drivers didn't understand the importance of avian photography. Dinner was no more appetising than breakfast; my companions looked troubled. It looked likely to be a challenging week for them.

The trial ride had gone without incident unless you consider being bitten by a mongoose, finding a corpse in a toilet and contracting food poisoning in the space of three days to be anything much: nothing any old India hand would think worth mentioning. So, not discouraged for the unknown roads ahead, I felt confident to make my next excursion along the historic Grand Trunk Road to Kashmir and all being well continue west to Pakistan.

Back in Delhi I began the tedious process of collecting the permissions needed to export the Enfield out of India. Had I known what this involved I would never have considered it; there is always a price to pay for impulsive actions. It was a saga that took all week. Trips to the reserve bank of India to verify I had bought the bike with foreign currency and receive a foreign currency exchange declaration. Then two trips to the Pakistan embassy, queuing among Muslim families applying for visas to visit relatives in Pakistan. I shared their chapattis and listened to their personal histories as we waited in shade-less lines in the hot sun.

Eventually word got through of a feringhee outside attracting a crowd with a story about a transit permit for a motorcycle. Finally I got to see the second secretary – or maybe he was the seventh. I explained my problem: I needed a transit permit to ride my shiny new Enfield across Pakistan to Iran. He looked amazed at such a notion – in today's jargon, 'gobsmacked' would describe it best. He began warning me against such a folly and only by pleading and grovelling did he give in. An elderly babu with a henna-dyed beard was summoned from a darkened corner, and began typing my letter of transit on a red-embossed letterhead.

My final task was a day long effort at the New Delhi Department of Customs and Excise to show my foreign currency exchange form and get a vehicle export permit; after a full day of form filling, waiting and tea drinking I was finally done – formally, physically and mentally. A week of queuing and cajoling at banks, government offices and embassies was finally over but had taken its toll.

It could all probably have been done in two days if I'd hired a Mr Fixit and paid the requisite baksheesh, but at this early stage I still thought myself a bona fide traveller with a task to complete that had to be done authentically, overcoming difficulties and bureaucracy as part of the mission: more fool me.

One evening during the week after the government offices had closed, and my sufferings were over for the day, I walked through the streets of Old Delhi and came upon the remains of the old munitions magazine, where, during the 1857 Indian mutiny (the First War of Independence to Indian citizens), the British army's munitions and armaments were stored. An old brass plaque, unpolished by its look since Indian independence, was embedded in the crumbling wall, commemorating the action when the men defending the magazine blew it up along with themselves, to prevent the 'besieging forces' (the politically correct term for mutineers) from seizing the weapons and munitions.

Theo

On the fateful morning of 11 May 1857, Theophilus Metcalfe – they don't moniker them like that anymore – the British magistrate sent for Lieutenant George Willoughby, the officer in charge of the Great Magazine, as it was known, to warn him he must prevent at any cost the munitions falling into the hands of the mutineers. Theo, as he was known to his friends – his servants used a different name – was born at Delhi on 28 November 1828, the eldest son of Sir Thomas Theophilus Metcalfe, 4th Baronet.

Young Theo was educated at Addiscombe College and East India College; a childhood illness cost him the sight in his right eye, ruling out a military career. In 1848 he entered the Bengal Civil Service. Theo succeeded to the baronetcy in 1853 after the elder Theophilus died in mysterious circumstances, thought to be poisoning on the instructions of Zinat Mahal, the Mughal emperor Bahadur Shah Zafar's favourite wife. Perhaps that's why she was his favourite.

In 1857 young Theo was appointed joint-magistrate and deputy-collector at Meerut, the centre of the Indian mutiny rising. On the morning of 11 May 1857 Theo galloped into Delhi with the news that the Meerut mutineers were then crossing the river to march on the city. Theo was instrumental in aiding the escape of the wives and children of the city's European civilians. Later he led the cavalry contingent that defeated the rebels at the Battle of Najafgarh.

Theo's poisoned father Sir Thomas Theophilus was the son of the Rev. Thomas Metcalfe, who served as an officer in the army of the East

India Company, obtaining the lucrative post of military storekeeper in 1782 'by most perseveringly courting the heads of the government', as one contemporary put it. Young Theo's grandfather was described by a colleague as a 'time-serving, pompous, and sycophantic officer'. However, he returned from India with a handsome fortune, bought a Berkshire estate and entered Parliament. He had four sons, all Theophiluses, and two daughters, both named Theophila.

The family seat at Delhi Theophilus House was the grandest residence on Theophilus Road, but it was looted and burned during the mutineers' assault on Delhi in May 1857. Thomas Theophilus had bought the land for Theophilus House from local Gujjar people, who lost no time in ransacking it during the uprising. A library of 25,000 books, said to be the best in India, and young Theo's treasured collection of Napoleonic relics were destroyed, along with many valuable oil paintings and his collection of Georgian furniture.

Young Theo was known by his servants as 'One-eyed Matka'; they found Metcalfe difficult to pronounce and Theophilus impossible. Young Theo had some eccentric habits; the one I like best was his donning of a white kid glove to publicly pinch the ear of any retainer who had displeased him. Odd, perhaps, but quite civilised when you consider some maharajas were not averse to having a servant trampled to death by elephant when displeased.

Young Theo had a reputation as a brave resolute man, who seemed to bear a charmed life, closely escaping death on several occasions. He knew every inch of ground in and around Delhi. He piloted the cavalry charge that fell on the mutineers' rear at the Battle of Mejgufghur. Colonel George Campbell, commanding the 52nd Light Infantry, reported the invaluable assistance he received from Theo, 'who was at my side throughout, and fearlessly guided me through many intricate streets and turnings to the Jumna Musjid, traversing two-thirds of the city, and enabling me to avoid many dangers and difficulties'. After the city fell to the British, Theo, on whose head the mutineers had set a high price, was said to be foremost in seeking revenge hunting the rebels throughout the city.

After British rule was re-established, young Theophilus was appointed assistant to the agent at Delhi and deputy-collector at Futtepore in 1858. He was sent home on sick furlough in 1859; his health prevented him returning to India. He was made a C.B. in 1864 and retired on an invalid pension in 1866. He died and was buried in Paris in 1883 aged 54, still mourning his lost collection of Napoleonic artefacts.

Anyway, back to the action. Willoughby did not have enough men under his command to hold the great magazine from a sustained attack. With a total force of eight officers and other ranks, he arranged his few cannons at the gates, and set charges to blow up the arsenal if his force were overrun, in the knowledge he and his men would be killed if they had to fire the charges. Early that afternoon the first rebel sepoys (from the Persian word *sepahi* – a soldier) arrived at the gates and began laying siege to the arsenal's outer walls with scaling ladders. As the fighting wore on into the afternoon, the rebels breached the outer walls and the situation became hopeless.

The cannons were loaded with double grape; Willoughby gave the order to fire as the mob broke through the inner gate, causing the rebels ('freedom fighters' in Indian history) to suffer heavy losses and fall back. But, as more scaled the walls, there was no time to reload or reposition the guns. Willoughby then gave the fateful order to light the trail of gunpowder leading to the magazine. At 4 pm it exploded; the huge blast was heard throughout the city. Willoughby and two others survived, making their escape badly wounded. Willoughby was killed the following day making his way to British lines.

In 1888 the memorial plaque I had come upon was erected at the site of the old magazine reading:

On the 11th of May 1857 nine resolute Englishmen, Lieutenant Geo. Dobson Willoughby, Bengal Artillery in command, Lieutenant William Rayner, Lieutenant Geo. Forrest, Conductor Geo. William Shaw, Conductor John Buckley, Conductor John Scully, Sub Conductor William Crow, Sergeant Benjamin Edward, Sergeant

Peter Stewart, defended the magazine of Delhi for more than four hours against large numbers of rebels and mutineers until the walls being scaled and all hope of succour gone these brave men fired the magazine – five of the gallant band perished in the explosion which at the same time destroyed many of the enemy. This tablet marking the former entrance gate of the magazine is placed here by the Government of India.

(Not of course the Indian government of India, but the British one of the time.)

The street of the old magazine was now a lively bazaar selling all manner of things a housewife needed and plenty more they didn't. I bought a plastic tarpaulin to serve as a groundsheet or tent, and some jute rope; they would prove to be needed and serve me well in the weeks ahead.

I was almost ready to hit the road, but Delhi hadn't finished with me yet, and a strange incident took place on my last night at the campsite when a party of Italians arrived in a camper van. While I was having my supper of channa dhal in the camp café the Italians began arguing with the waiters over the price of their meal. And, before you could say Theophilus, it escalated into a fist fight; outmanned by the kitchen staff, the Italians retreated to their campervan.

As I sat with the waiters discussing the odd behaviours of feringhee campers, suddenly the Italians returned with knives and confronted the waiters, who wisely retreated into the kitchen. I swallowed the last of my tea, deciding things were getting a bit hot, and was about to head for my bed, when out came the waiters, cooks and bottle washers, armed with bamboo lathis, cleavers and the biggest soup ladle I've ever seen.

A skirmish ensued in which the Italians got a beating with lathis and were forced to retreat again. I backed out, afraid I would be misidentified as reinforcements began arriving from the servants' quarters. It ended with the Italians driving off the campsite under a hail of stones and dented body panels. And so to my camp bed, weary but unscathed, and grateful I was well known to the kitchen staff after a week's stay and nightly discussions on all manner of worldly things.

I had serviced the Enfield, and changed the oil and filter. It was necessary to set the tappets and push rod clearance every 2,000km, a task I became proficient at, as well as regularly tensioning the drive chain, which, while new, kept stretching. I paid the café waiter's young son to give the bike a final wash and polish. With my camp kit tools and spare cables packed in the panniers, rucksack strapped on the rear carrier and the canary yellow 'Upper India Automobile Association' badge mounted proudly on the handlebars, I was as ready as I could be.

With my documents zipped into my money belt and tucked inside my shirt, I left early on a cool misty March morning after a last breakfast from the camp kitchen, first handing out small tips to the waiters in appreciation of their great judgement in not mixing me up with those hot-headed Italian feringhees. The grand excursion along the Grand Trunk Road was to begin with a ride to Kashmir.

The Grand Trunk Road

The GT Road from Delhi to Kashmir in the spring of 1980 was a single lane in both directions; in many places road works and hazards such as landslides and broken down trucks reduced it to one lane, overloaded trucks climbing the steep hills caused long tailbacks, and wherever roadworks were in place it was necessary to wait in a queue till a flagman waved us on. I overtook smaller traffic but often got stuck behind a crawling, smoke-spewing, overloaded, clanking Bedford ten-tonner with a rhyming message painted on the tailboard such as 'Drive to Survive', 'Arrive Alive' or 'Dip Light at Night', and the ubiquitous 'Horn Please'. I horned loudly as I raced past.

I will never forget the Jawahar tunnel at Banihal, a 3km-long dripping cavern where a man dressed in an old army greatcoat and balaclava waving a flag directed the traffic, not quite like a race starter at a grand prix but similar in an Indian way. Traffic was allowed through one way at a time; I waited half an hour while the oncoming traffic cleared the tunnel till it was our turn. I had wormed my way to near the front and as the flag dropped and the roar of Bedford and Ashok Leyland diesel engines reached their screaming peak we were off and racing for the dark cave-like entrance. I overtook the slower trucks and got to the front. I didn't want to get trapped behind the queuing mob; if one of the old wrecks broke down inside it would be chaos and possibly curtains.

The tunnel was full of lingering exhaust fumes. I had foreseen this and wrapped a scarf over my nose and mouth. Inside the sunless cavern it was icy cold and 200m in became darker than night. Water was dripping from fissures in the bare rock roof, forming pools in the uneven road surface that had frozen to ice. It was the most frightening ride of my life. The convoy of following trucks and buses were picking up speed, coming up fast behind me, and they weren't going to stop in time if I was lying on the road after losing control on a patch of black ice. I went as fast as I dared, weaving through patches of black ice and small rocks fallen from above. I could hardly pick them out in the blackness; there were no tunnel lights only my dim yellow headlight and those from the gaining convoy behind speeding up forcing me to go faster than it was safe to.

At last light at the far end appeared and I emerged into the welcome daylight. It had taken ten minutes but it seemed like an hour; I was never more pleased to be greeted by a leaden-grey snow-filled sky as I exited the tunnel. I pulled over at the first chai stall and sat drinking tea while the convoy of tinsel-clad horning trucks shot past. I didn't care they were in front of me now; I just wanted to calm down and warm up by the chai wallah's fire. There was no other route to Srinagar; I would have to return the same way.

It was spring in Delhi but it was still winter in Kashmir; the mornings and nights were cold but pleasant once the day warmed up. I took a room in a Srinagar lakeside hotel. I would have liked to stay on a houseboat but that meant leaving the bike unattended on shore. My hotel was owned by an ex-Indian Army officer who made me very welcome, I was the only guest. In late afternoon he would bring tea to a table on the front lawn and his wife joined us with homemade cake, the three of us rugged up against the early evening chill. We chatted about my trip and the route ahead, while eating apples and cake looking out over the green lake. It was cold but the sun setting over the snowy Himalayas seemed special. 'If there is heaven on earth, it is here, it is here, it is here', as the well-quoted statement of Emperor Jahangir says.

My host had fought in the first Indo-Pakistan war following

partition, and was instrumental in the defence of the Indian Kashmir position; he told me how undisciplined Pakistani units had stopped their advance to loot the towns and villages on their way instead of pressing forward quickly, giving the Indian army just enough time to bring up reinforcements and strengthen their defences, which successfully held. But he held no grudges. He had bought the hotel with his army pension savings, and perhaps he also did a bit of part-time soldiering or played the great game as a sideline.

I didn't have the benefit of time or enough funds to stay long in Kashmir, so I left on the third morning for the ride to Amritsar. I would have liked to spend a month in Kashmir riding the mountain roads but it was not possible. I wished my hosts goodbye; they waved me off, wishing me a safe journey. I said I would be back in a year or two for a longer stay. But life has a way of intervening: forty years on, I still haven't returned. The situation in Kashmir is still not resolved. India and Pakistan still don't allow trekkers to walk in their stunning mountains; perhaps it will not be possible in my lifetime, but my fingers are crossed.

The tunnel was waiting where I had left it; there was less traffic going down early and I was first in the queue. As the last of the up traffic emerged I started the bike and got ready. After a minute or so and, seeing no more headlights in the tunnel, I took off without waiting for the man with the flag to emerge from his hut. The trucks behind me were horning impatiently, and I was worried they would be too close behind me, and I would have to go faster than was safe once again all the way through. As I approached the entrance the chowkidar came out of his hut and waved me to stop. Too late: the trucks behind were moving and I wasn't going to be sucking fumes at the back of all those. Away we went in a cacophony of blaring horns and clouds of black smoke, daunting and so very Indian.

This time I was away well clear of the mob, the tunnel roof was dripping more than before, the sun melting the snow on the hills. As I emerged into welcome sunlight, the down side flagman was waiting for me with a red flag. I pulled up; he started telling me off for jumping the gun: his mate had phoned through to tell him. The trucks were nearly out of the tunnel. I could hear them roaring, and I gunned it; he could stop them if he could. I was off and racing; it was good to be alive, out of the hellish tunnel and under the sunny blue sky.

A prophecy

Other than seeing the Golden Temple and having my palm read I remember little else of my stay in Amritsar. I found a bed in a pilgrim's hotel on the dust-choked Grand Trunk Road. A disabled young Sikh wearing a bright blue turban had a pitch on the pavement outside my hotel; from where he sold combs, pens, schoolbooks, snacks, cigarettes and other small needs from a bicycle-wheeled wooden cart.

What I do remember clearly was his prophecy, if that's the right description. It was the first and only time I have had my palm read or tried any form of knowing the future. His withered leg was the result of polio, which was common in India then. I felt sympathy for his situation, scraping a living as a small vendor in the noise and dust outside a cheap hotel, though he may well have thought it a fine one. I bought a stock of cigarettes and a school atlas on the morning I left, and to give him a little extra cash I succumbed and let him read my future.

India is full of impostors offering to read fortunes by one method or another, and I was no believer in it. But I had stayed two days in the dusty, dark dormitory of the cheap hotel and bought peanuts and cigarettes from him; he had tried numerous times to persuade me to have my palm read. Fortune telling was his second job; he probably had some others.

It started as hopelessly as I expected: he wrote on a piece of paper, folded it and gave it to me. Then he asked me to name my favourite flower – Indian men have no awkwardness asking girly questions like this, unlike Australian culture, where such a question might result in a thick ear. I said violet: my mother's and grandmother's name. I unfolded the paper: he had written rose. It was obvious most of his victims thought of roses. Indians believe Inglesies are all rose lovers, no doubt a hangover from when the gardeners of the Raj grew roses for homesick memsahibs. It wasn't a good start, especially as he had never heard of violets. I wrote it down for him, for his next reading to a foreigner, when he would be faced with the dilemma of a one-in-two guess. He would be better off sticking with rose, I thought.

He started the reading with the safe opening gambit 'You will be rich soon' – wrong again, though it's all relative. Trying to soften me up for a tip, I cynically thought. He could see my clothes were mostly green and announced my favourite colour was green. I didn't have a favourite colour; my choice of clothes was a result of the army surplus gear bought back in Perth. Then he announced I was going on a long journey and there would be some danger ahead. He already knew I was leaving for Pakistan, Iran, Turkey and Europe from the conversations we'd had. The 'some danger ahead' was as obvious as night following day.

On it went until he saw I was looking more and more sceptical and decided to conclude the reading before he did further damage to his chances of a good tip by more bad guesses. To finish off he took a pen and paper and, shielding it from me, he wrote something on it, then folded and sealed it with gum. He made a bit of a fuss, saying there would be dangerous days ahead, but that I would be safe as long as I kept the note sealed and unopened till I reached my destination.

I was tempted to open it but he emphasised that if I opened it before the journey was over bad luck would follow. I put it down as hocus-pocus, and when I asked for a hint he would only say it was based on my star sign, and emphasised I would be safe as long as I kept it with me and it remained sealed until I was home.

What was written, I wondered. Was it along the lines of 'Feringhee miser a thousand punctures upon you' or something less tactful? I tucked the paper inside my money belt with my passports and bike documents, and paid his fee, adding what I thought a fair tip, though it brought no smile. Then I kicked the Enfield into life, checked my panniers were fastened down and my one-gallon fuel can secure, and a minute later I set off down the GT Road towards Pakistan. The scary part was about to begin.

The saga at Wagah

The single-lane rural road from Amritsar to the Pakistan frontier post at Wagah was almost deserted. It was bitumen surfaced in two parallel strips roughly equal to the width of a bus wheelbase, with loose gravel in-between and a generous sprinkling of potholes. It was necessary to keep the bike's front wheel aligned carefully on the centre of the strip, with the fewest potholes, requiring frequent passing from one side to the other.

There was little other traffic and none overtook me: small country buses with a few rural passengers and some small-acre farmers working in the fields was all I saw. The road was raised a little above the cultivated land, and flanked by ditches. Crops of wheat and mustard were irrigated by ditches and small canals. Malnourished cows, their ribs showing through their stretched skin, and ploughing buffaloes grazed on what little grass grew on the roads verges. A few scattered small kutcha (wattle and daub) homes of the tenant farmers dotted the fields, their owners out tending their few acres.

It was the bucolic Indian scene of a thousand years, yet only thirty-three years earlier these peaceful green fields had been a scene of slaughter as thousands of refugees, unable to protect themselves, were forced to flee across this land, reliant for their safe passage on a British colonial army and police force unprepared for what unfolded.

The last viceroy of India appointed to oversee the withdrawal of the British administration and bring India to independence was Lord Louis Mountbatten, uncle of Prince Charles. He was a reluctant viceroy, who had been strong-armed into accepting the post by a British government fearful that the Indian independence movement was becoming uncontrollable. Mountbatten wanted to get the job done quickly and be out of it. He was the wrong choice for such a monumental task. It was a job that needed someone with great patience, strong diplomatic political and negotiating skills and a solid knowledge of Indian history and religions, as well as a firm grip of its security forces.

Few such men existed and Mountbatten wasn't one of them; he was the quick fix political appointment of a worried government in London still reeling from WW2, and afraid India was about to blow up in its face; the time to bring India to independence was now. But what should have been planned and implemented over a couple of years was condensed into months. The human cost of this was as horrendous as it was politically irresponsible.

Mountbatten's plan allowed two and a half months to complete the task of handing political and military control of India and the newly formed nations of East and West Pakistan to their newly elected governments. It was a task that needed at least a year or two to implement. The human cost in lives lost and property destroyed was immense; after 200 years in India, Britain was to depart within weeks, leaving millions to their fate.

The refugees created by the division of India into East and West Pakistan were left to the mercy of their enemies to be slaughtered in thousands as law and order collapsed. Much of it had happened in the quiet, peaceful fields I was riding through; the road I was on was once crowded with fleeing refugees. It was a sobering ride, more so because it was so quiet, peaceful and empty under the pale-blue morning sky, the snipe and ducks rising from the roadside ditches startled by the Enfield's noise as I passed.

The division of old India into the two new dominions was a result of what became known as the Mountbatten Plan. It was announced at a press conference on 3 June 1947; the date of independence was set for 15 August 1947. The biggest event in modern Indian history, its complete independence after 200 years of British rule caused over 12.5 million people to become displaced with estimates of up to a million killed, five million left homeless and thousands of women and girls abducted and enslaved.

Millions of mostly poor villagers and rural farmers found themselves on the wrong side of a hastily planned dividing line between the two states. Suddenly becoming religious minorities in a country ruled by new untrusted politicians of a different religion, Muslims fled from the Indian side to the newly created Pakistan, while Hindus and Sikhs abandoned ancestral villages of countless generations to become refugees in the new independent India.

I was already aware of this history as I rode along the same road so many refugees had fled along carrying their possessions in bundles on their backs, and where many had died exhausted by hunger. A peaceful road now, where white egrets, snipe and wild ducks were taking flight at the unfamiliar sound of the Enfield, where thin men dressed in traditional dhotis led their bony cows yoked to wooden ploughs, a scene unchanged for centuries since before the British had arrived.

The border posts at Wagah came into being after the partition of India and the creation of Pakistan in 1947. It has become world famous in recent years, but it was just a dusty little outpost in March 1980. Today a nightly ceremony of goose-stepping guards from both sides of the border, wearing their respective national uniforms and silly hats, strut and parade in each other's faces, giving stiff-armed salutes in front of the gawping crowds of visitors that gather to watch the buffoonery of it. But there was none of this when I passed through. I only wished there had been; I could have used a little light cabaret entertainment after the long saga crossing the frontier.

I presented my passport to the junior Indian customs officer. He seemed astounded at the notion I was attempting to take an Indian-made and -registered vehicle out of the country, and hurried away to his superior. I was expecting this and had been practising my story.

The main man appeared and after a cursory glance at us invited me into his office saying, 'Please be seating,' followed by, 'Not possible motorcycle of India go over Pakistan side.' I produced the vehicle export permit that had taken a day of cajoling from the customs and excise office in New Delhi, with its red wax stamp of the Indian national emblem and its flourish of unreadable signatures.

He became momentarily muddled at this seemingly important document and we had tea while he painstakingly read through the details again. We drank more tea and ate stale biscuits while he told me I could not take the Enfield out of India without 'Foreign monies exchange proof form in rupee value of foreign currency with signatures duly noted'. With a flourish I pulled out the form, signed and sealed in more red wax – somewhere in India there is a factory making tons of this stuff – but he was still not very happy.

I was clearly a risky problem for him; if this was in any way a cunning scheme to illegally export one of India's national assets, then a long-awaited promotion might be at risk. Years of tedious toil in remote outposts patiently accumulating seniority could be in danger of being lost. If a punctuation mark on one of these documents had been tampered with, his career prospects might be set back a decade and he may become permanently exiled in no man's land, between two hostile countries at a boondock border post. I needed to tread with care.

We had more tea while I tactfully explained the importance of Indian-manufactured motorbikes being exported to a world of motorcycle enthusiasts and dealerships, if only they could get their hands on them. And how vitally important my contribution was to the economy of India and its transition to a modern vehicle-manufacturing nation. India was then still a Soviet-model economy with heavily subsidised and protected fixed price markets.

He started to waver a bit, and I pressed home the point, showing him the acting assistant deputy secretary of the Reserve Bank of India's signature, in royal blue ink under the red wax seal, which in my stressed imagination had started to resemble a bloodshot eye.

He played his final card: with a smile he leaned back and said, 'I'm thinking you are having all permissions in proper order, but I must tell you Pakistan side will not allow entry; you are needful of form Pk 5983/EL/901 in recent date or must pay Pakistan side 10,000 rupees cash monies for transit deposit, only refundable on exit, on form Pk 5983/TD/902' in triplicate copy' – or something similar.

He knew his stuff; he was a babu to his sandal straps. Triumphantly I showed him the transit letter from the Pakistan embassy in Delhi, stamped and signed down to the divisional seventh secretary's chai wallah. He began to relax, saying, 'You are in pukka order, please be taking more tea.' I was free to go; we shook hands: it seemed only proper after such a lengthy diplomatic tea session. With the junior customs officer leading the way, I was escorted to the gate, where the guard lifted the boom and ushered me out of India into no man's land, where today's daily ritual of goose-stepping masochistic nonsense is nightly performed.

At Pakistan immigration I presented my passport and transit permit to the officer. He perused the permit, issued on the New Delhi Pakistan High Commission letterhead, signed by the seventh secretary, and said, 'Where did you get this?' 'From your embassy in Delhi,' I said. 'I see,' said the bemused officer. 'Allows one week transit,' he replied. I could just get through in that time, but it meant riding hard each day and missing the sights along the way.

Once again I was told to wait as he went off to see his superior. I started preparing my story should I be refused entry. The top man appeared and invited me into his office. He read the transit permit and scrutinised my passport, noticing I was born in Preston. 'You are Preston wallah jihaan?' 'Ji,' I said. 'Leyland near Preston.' 'My brother living Preston; please be taking some tea.' The biscuits were fresh too.

With a bursting bladder I was in Pakistan at last. I'd got out of India astride one of its national assets, a 350cc single-cylinder four-stroke Indian Enfield Bullet motorcycle in gunmetal-grey paintwork, and shiny chrome bits. A machine unchanged since WW2, when they were used by British army dispatch riders. Obsolete in England, where they were first manufactured for three decades, and mechanically obsolete a decade before that. Would it be up to the task? Would I? Nine thousand kilometres of potholed dangerous roads lay ahead. It was worrying. As I rode from the border towards Lahore I began humming the Irving Berlin tune 'There May Be Trouble Ahead'. There was, and I would have to face the music and dance.

If I'd known then what Jimmy Carter was planning in the White House while I was riding through Pakistan, and what a merry dance it would cause me, I would have turned around there and then and begged to be let back into India. I have no real opinion of Jimmy's term as president; I hadn't been following President Carter's manoeuvrings, and he hadn't kept me in the loop either. I'm sure Jimmy was a true Southern gentleman and all-round good old boy. All I know is that James Earl Carter was to cause me more stress than every president before or since.

I rode slowly through the familiar rural countryside, with its toiling farmers at their bullock-drawn ploughs, past villages and rustic dwellings just as poor as those on the Indian side, into Lahore, the once great historic capital city of the Punjab and past seat of the Moghul Empire. Its many redbrick Mughal and Raj-era fortifications and once grand public buildings were succumbing to the harsh climate and lack of maintenance. Why did I care? I needed to find a room for the night, preferably with an attached toilet. I rode into the centre of the city and slowly rode along the once famous central mall.

Lahore

The Enfield's wheel chain had been scraping the chain guard for some miles and I needed to adjust the chain tension. I stopped at the roadside in front of the Lahore Museum for a smoke and a think. Then I got out the spanners and tensioned the chain, winding the rear wheel back to the next notch: new chain always stretches. As I worked, a horn-blaring mob of buses, taxis, trucks, motorbikes and pony tongas flowed around me. I don't know if any other feringhees have ever repaired a motorcycle alongside the old Mughal cannon known as Zam-zammah since 1980, but it would be no surprise if I am still the only one.

The job finished, I put the tools back in the pannier and took a closer look at the great cannon mounted on its wood-and-brass carriage in the centre of the road. It is a fine old piece of the gunmaker's trade. Zam-zammah was made famous in English literature by Rudyard Kipling in *Kim,* his classic novel of the 'Great Game', as the Raj-era espionage on the northern Indian frontier was known. Kipling opened his greatest novel with the young hero, Kim, the orphan son of an Irish soldier and an Indian mother – as follows:

He sat in defiance of municipal orders, astride the gun Zam-zammah on her brick platform opposite the old Ajaib-Gher – The Wonder House, as the Natives call the Lahore Museum. Who hold Zam-zammah hold the Punjab; for the great green-bronze piece is always first of the conqueror's loot.

In the Urdu language Zam-zammah means 'Lion's Roar'. It changed hands many times in battles and was used in tandem with a twin cannon lost while being shipped across the Indus River. First used in local battles by the Afghan Durranis, it was later captured by the Sikhs and brought to Lahore by the Sikh maharaja Ranjit Singh as a trophy of his conquests.

A teenage lad approached and asked about the bike. It was a model he hadn't seen before. He offered to shake hands but my hands were covered in grimy chain oil so I declined; he noticed my grimed state and, grinning, we shook hands and I offered him a cigarette. I explained it was an Indian version of the old English Royal Enfield bullet, manufactured in Madras and found throughout India. And I was riding through Pakistan and on to England. At this he became quite excited, and as we chatted I asked where a cheap hotel might be found.

In Pakistan in 1980 all motorcycles and cars were imported, mostly from Japan and China. It was one of the big differences between the two countries. Thirty-five years after independence, India had built a broad industrial manufacturing base, while Pakistan relied almost entirely on imports, especially from China.

My biker friend gave me directions to the Salvation Army guest house; thanking him, I rode off to it, leaving him to clean his oil-stained hand. It was a good place to stay: quiet – by Lahore standards – clean and cheap, and I could park the bike inside the gated compound. After the tensions of the frontier, a simple room and a cold shower were all I needed. After a wash with petrol to de-grease hands and a quick brush-up, I set off, walking at dusk down the Grand Trunk Road through central Lahore, where it is called 'the Mall', to find somewhere to eat. I settled on a dimly lit diner with curry-stained plastic tablecloths, a level just above the bare wooden tables of the roadside dabas I was used to, wondering if I was a bit underdressed for the standard.

Dining in the eateries of India and Pakistan is not quite the leisured pastime we expect when eating out in the West; it's more of a sit-down, bolt-it-down, money-down and down-the-road experience.

In the bush mining camps of outback Australia we called it troffing. Troffing over with, and tired – more through the day's tensions than the distance travelled – I was in bed twenty minutes later, passport and money belt tucked under my pillow, the Enfield parked under my window.

The muezzin's call woke me before dawn, reminding me I had crossed a border, and made sure I stayed awake, but at least I got my laundry done before breakfast. I spent the morning in the excellent Lahore Museum, established by Rudyard Kipling's father, who was its first curator. Afterwards I went exploring the narrow streets and alleys of the famous Lahore bazaar. I had no money to spare for souvenirs, or room on the bike to carry any, so it was window shopping only, followed by a visit to the majestic old fort mosque adjacent. In the afternoon I spent a couple of hours walking in the welcome cool and shady green botanic gardens. As evening came it was time for an early troff and to make my preparations for the ride south next day.

From Lahore I would be parting company with the Grand Trunk Road; its path from Lahore runs north to Peshawar, then through the Khyber Pass to Afghanistan, where I had travelled by public bus in 1974, but it was impossible to travel through there in 1980. The GT Road had been my companion since Delhi and I felt sad to be leaving it. The GT Road is mentioned in many historic traveller accounts and literary works including those of Rudyard Kipling. Kipling described it in his novel *Kim*:

Look! Look again! chumars, bankers and tinkers, barbers and bunnias, pilgrims and potters all the world going and coming. And truly the Grand Trunk Road is a wonderful spectacle. It runs straight, bearing without crowding India's traffic for fifteen hundred miles – such a river of life as nowhere else exists in the world.

We had come far together, and I had felt comfortable riding my Enfield along the historic highway where millions had gone before and much history had been made. Famous generals had often travelled it, including Alexander on his favourite horse Bucephalus, and countless invaders, emperors, viceroys and kings riding on elephant back, and numerous other travellers on smaller quests such as mine. It has been marched over for centuries by conquering armies and not long ago the British army, as Rudyard Kipling described in his poem 'Route Marchin':

We're marchin' on relief over Injia's sunny plains,
A little front o' Christmas-time an' just be'ind the Rains;
Ho! get away you bullock-man, you've 'eard the bugle blowed,
There's a regiment a-comin' down the Grand Trunk Road;
With its best foot first
And the road a-sliding past,
An' every bloomin' campin'-ground exactly like the last;
While the Big Drum says,
With 'is 'rowdy-dowdy-dow!'—
'Kiko kissywarsti don't you hamsher argy jow?'

We're marchin' on relief over Injia's coral strand,
Eight 'undred fightin' Englishmen, the Colonel, and the Band;
Ho! get away you bullock-man, you've 'eard the bugle blowed,
There's a regiment a-comin' down the Grand Trunk Road;
With its best foot first
And the road a-sliding past,
An' every bloomin' campin'-ground exactly like the last;
While the Big Drum says,
With 'is 'rowdy-dowdy-dow!'—
'Kiko kissywarsti don't you hamsher argy jow?'

But from Lahore south I knew nothing of the roads ahead; with only my cheap school atlas from the fortune teller's stall as a guide, I set off not long after the muezzin's early call woke me. It was a long, hard day's ride but gladly warm and dry, as we rode through the green Punjab fields past timeless village bazaars. I stopped when I felt the need for a rest and a fresh chapatti at dusty roadside dabas – traditional food and chai refreshment stops for travellers.

Wherever I stopped for a smoke and a chai, we became a curiosity and a small crowd would gather; there was nothing like us in Pakistan. I had no idea each day where I would be that night or where I would sleep. This didn't bother me. I have never cared when or where I would arrive; it always worked out. I had only one rule about when to stop – always before dark. The local traffic of trucks, buses, and especially bullock carts - showed no lights, these combined with potholes large enough to swallow us made night riding far too risky.

My first night south from Lahore was spent at a dak bungalow near Muzaffargarh south-west of Multan. I passed through the city of Multan, preferring to keep out of the dusty, choking air of big cities and stay at the dak bungalows of smaller towns.

Across the Indus at Sukkur

The dak bungalows of India and Pakistan were established in Mughal times, though their origins go back to the Persian Empire. They were extended throughout the Indian subcontinent during British rule. They served as permanent horse stables and way stations between larger settlements. Government officers on tours of duty to the remoter parts of their territory could stay at the dak bungalows as they patrolled their districts. Food and water for their needs and their horses was maintained. A 'khansamah' was permanently in residence to look after the travellers' needs and maintain the bungalow.

Private travellers could also stay if the rooms were not in use by officials; an advance booking system was in place, without which, especially in India, you could not stay. In the remoter parts of Pakistan you could turn up and try your luck; if no officials were in residence or expected then you could stay. First you sought out the khansamah (caretaker) or the district officer. If these gentlemen were not too repelled by your appearance, you were welcome.

At the Rohri dak bungalow I arrived just after sunset and was asked if I wanted a meal. I had no idea what it would be. Later that night I was served the best rogan ghosh (goat meat in tomato and onion curry) I have had before or since. The elderly khansamah – or so he seemed – slept on the veranda wrapped in blankets alongside the Enfield to make sure it was safe (thank you, sir). This extra service for a cost of two rupees for the room and whatever profit he made from the dinner and breakfast that cost just twenty rupees plus a tip.

In remoter districts facilities were basic, thin mattresses on hard beds often a knotted rope charpoy, a wooden almira (clothes stand) usually stood in one corner, a rough dining table and chairs made by the village carpenter, and a wooden wash stand with a galvanised wash basin comprised the usual furnishings. Running water could not be expected in most of them. You provided your own bed linen, in my case a cotton sheet and sleeping bag. If you were an experienced traveller you checked in the corners and under the bed for snakes and scorpions before retiring for the night.

At isolated dak bungalows, meals were available on request provided you arrived in good time to order; there was no menu, it depended entirely on what was available in the village bazaar. Meals were often cooked by the khansamah's wife, whom you would never see, and served by the khansamah in your room or on the veranda. It was all still very pukka when I rode through Sindh and Baluchistan thirty-six years after the last British district officers had packed their trunks and left for the home-counties.

Most khansamahs liked having a foreign guest, as they could make a little cash serving meals, a valuable perk of the job for the poor pay. During British times many khansamahs had once served in the Indian army as naiks or lance naiks (sergeants or corporals), perhaps with a disability from their service days. They had interesting stories to tell of their service days, but they were becoming rare when I passed through. The wages were poor but a job and a good home for their family plus a service pension meant security.

The architecture of the bungalows varied with local custom and available materials throughout the subcontinent. Timber-framed weatherboard and corrugated iron were usual in remote forested hill stations, kutcha earth walls or mud brick bungalows in arid treeless regions. The Baluchistan type was straight out of the days of the Raj. Near the top of the 12ft-high ceiling was a hole in a wall where a rope once passed through, fixed to a wooden board hinged from the ceiling, known as a punkah fan. The rope ended on the veranda, where a punkah wallah was employed to sit all night pulling the rope up and down whenever an officer was sleeping or dining.

The punkah fan would creak back and forth hour after hour, stirring the hot night air. Many travellers experienced waking in a lather of sweat to find the punkah wallah asleep at his post. Electricity had come since then and ceiling fans were over the beds: a big improvement but only when the power was on. During my travels the nights were cool enough to need a blanket.

Dak bungalow curry would have been familiar to any travelling government officer a century ago. The recipe has its roots in the Raj era, where the dish was first conjured in the dak bungalows throughout the hill stations of India and Pakistan.

This is an original recipe that would have been familiar to the travelling officers on the circuit of government business in the nineteenth century.

2kg boneless chicken thighs or goat meat.
60ml mustard oil; you can substitute but mustard oil is grown in India.
3 onions, sliced
1 large thumb of ginger
1tsp sugar
5 garlic cloves
2 tomatoes chopped
2tsp coriander seeds
5 whole dry red chillies
100g plain yoghurt
1tsp turmeric powder
3tbsp coriander powder
1tsp garam masala

Make a paste of the ginger, garlic, onion, tomatoes, sugar, coriander seeds and whole dry red chillies by blending the ingredients into a rough paste using mortar and pestle for authenticity, or blender if you can't be arsed. Make the marinade by mixing the paste with the coriander powder and garam masala powder, plain yoghurt, turmeric powder and 2tbs mustard oil. Marinade the chicken with the mix and leave in the refrigerator or – to maintain authenticity – in the snow for four hours.

Heat 2tbsp mustard oil and add in the marinated chicken, adding a dash of salt to taste. Cover and cook for thirty minutes over low heat until the chicken is falling apart under the pressure of a fork. Garnish with coriander and serve with hot rotis or naan – a traditional curry of Raj era history.

The Sukkur Barrage

I left Rohri well fed after the universal dak bungalow breakfast of onion and chilli omelette, chapattis and chai. I said goodbye to the khansamah who had kindly kept night guard over the Enfield and added a tip above the usual food and accommodation costs for his conscientious service. I never saw his wife, but there were small children playing in the garden, or perhaps grandchildren. It seems funny now but that night in the irrigation engineering officer's dak bungalow is one of my best memories of the whole journey. The welcome shelter after a long day in the saddle, the cool, star-filled night sky, the excellent dinner on the veranda under the hissing glow of a tilly lamp hung from a rafter as the moths circled. And, listening to the frogs croaking in the canal as I fell asleep, it still seems special.

Away early, riding in the cool morning mist, I crossed the Indus at the Sukkur Barrage. Built to irrigate the surrounding arid lands for agriculture, the barrage was completed in 1932 and is the largest irrigation structure of its kind in the world. It was started during the British era in 1923, known then as the Lloyd Barrage, to alleviate the regular famines in the low-rainfall Sindh District. The barrage enabled water to be channelled through a 6,166-mile network of canals. It was the largest irrigated crop system in the world when built, and more than five million acres (20,000km²) of unproductive land was turned into arable land through irrigation.

It was a hugely complex engineering project, so successful that today the land irrigated by the system still provides most of Pakistan's grain crop. The barrage has sixty-six spans, each sixty feet wide; each span has a steel gate weighing fifty tons. It was fifty years old when I crossed in 1980 and still in good working condition, but its fabric has deteriorated significantly in recent times.

There have been other problems too; the structure of the barrage, though still sound, has had insufficient maintenance over many decades, due to unstable politics, government changes and local corruption. The engineering problems are easier to overcome than the social difficulties. Unplanned settlements have been built on the banks of the irrigation canals, often illegally connected to the electricity grid, making removal of these informal settlements politically difficult. Crops have been sown on embankments, preventing access for maintenance. Political pressure groups and corrupt officials prevent remedial work and expansion of the system; the whole of the Sukkur irrigation system has become a political hot potato.

Northern Sindh is notorious for its heat, even in March, when I travelled, and I was glad I had not left it any later. I nearly fainted with heatstroke when I stopped for fuel at midday in Jacobabad, a town famous as the hottest place in Pakistan. The highest temperature recorded there was 52.8°C. I think it was the day I was there. If there's a hotter town in the world, I don't want to visit it.

Baluchistan roads

Jacobabad is where the arid desert terrain of Baluchistan begins as you travel west, leaving behind the greener lands irrigated by the Sukkur Barrage. It looked rough and rundown when I passed through – today it is a university city – but back then many of its houses were still built traditionally of kutcha. Kutcha is a mixture of earth cow or buffalo dung mixed with straw as a binder and applied as a plaster over a frame of branches and twigs. It is also made into sun-dried mud bricks plastered over with kutcha. Many of the single story house walls showed cracks due to the fierce heat and the fact the region is often affected by earth tremors.

Roofs are built by applying layers of kutcha over a supporting timber frame or, where timber is unavailable, by forming a domed roof of sun-baked kutcha, transferring the weight of the roof onto thick outer kutcha walls. Kutcha building is similar to the wattle and daub technique used by the early settlers of America and Australia to build shelters. It is still used today by poorer citizens to build their homes across the arid regions of India and Pakistan, and was once widespread in Iran, Turkey and central Asia.

Jacobabad was a town of high purdah wall compounds, with dwellings hidden within them; the narrow winding alleys were jammed with donkey carts. Pony tongas, camel drays and honking three-wheeled buses also added to the congestion. Occasionally there was the shadowy image of black-shrouded women flitting through the narrow lanes into the mud-walled courtyards.

Jacobabad is the eastern gateway to the Baluchistan desert and onwards to all points west. My ride through the Baluchistan desert was the hardest motorcycling I've ever done. The roads were mostly unsealed, and often it was only by following the wheel ruts of other vehicles through the sand dunes and dry nullahs that gave any indication there was even a road at all.

There was no turning back now; I had just enough money to get me through to England. If I turned round now and sold the bike on the Karachi black market it wouldn't bring enough money for an air ticket to Europe, I had no choice: it was head down and go for it on a wheel and a prayer.

Near the top of a hill on the Bolan Pass road I was surprised to see a European with a bicycle at a chai dhaba. I turned around and pulled in to see who this could be and what he could be doing here, on one of the most remote roads in the world, riding a bicycle. I can't remember his name but he was a Frenchman on a round-the-world ride. He had no map or much idea of where he was in Pakistan, and had never heard of the Bolan Pass. I explained it was an ancient caravan and invasion route from Afghanistan and central Asia into India, once used by various historical identities such as Mahmud of Ghazni, Alexander's generals, various British armies and one Captain Francis Burton, spy, explorer, diplomat and polymath extraordinaire – and us.

He had ridden from France through Europe, Turkey and Iran. We celebrated our meeting in this wild place with tea and chapattis; there was little else. The dhaba's proprietor, if he was at all surprised by two feringhees stopping for lunch, didn't show it. My fellow traveller had no cigarettes left so I gave him a pack, and we swapped information on what lay ahead, before wishing each other bon voyage. He was heading away from danger; I was heading into it, but I didn't know that then.

On my second day's ride from Lahore, near Muzaffargarh, I had also met another motorcyclist at a roadside dhaba. I saw a BMW bike parked up and stopped to investigate this rare machine in this unlikely place. A tall, slim man with a sun-weathered face beckoned me over to a rough table, where he was drinking chai while a crowd of idlers watched the unusual event. I took a seat and ordered chai as we swapped stories while the crowd increased expectantly; in these rural villages, entertainment is limited.

Mark was an Egyptian Australian from Sydney riding a BMW boxer twin and was heading to Egypt. He had started his ride in Singapore. I still recall his first names: 'Call me Mark or Abdul,' he said. He was a Coptic Christian born in Cairo and raised in the Sydney Coptic community. Tall and lean, with infectious optimism, he was already banishing my doubts on what difficulties might lie ahead. I guessed him to be about thirty. He was good company in the few days we rode together.

The Enfield was only comfortably safe at 40mph on these potholed roads; on his BMW along the straight stretches through Punjab and Sindh Mark was well ahead of me. We met up again at the Baluchi village of Nushki. I arrived mid-afternoon, riding down the main street looking for fuel; I filled up at every opportunity in case petrol was unavailable further on. Mark heard the unmistakable sound of the Enfield's single cylinder bopping past the dak bungalow; knowing it could only be me, he raced out on his Beemer and caught up with me.

He persuaded me to turn round and stay overnight, though I had intended to ride further that day. He had taken a room at the dak bungalow. I was happy to have a shorter day, escape the afternoon heat and be in mutual biker company. Mark had developed a bad case of Baluchi belly and had been resting all afternoon, hoping it would ease up. It's no fun riding on potholed rough tracks with a bad case of diarrhoea, as I already knew.

We spent the rest of the afternoon dozing on our charpoys in the hot bare room. When evening came we dined on the veranda of a grim dhaba next to the fuel stop on the main street, the only place serving any food, where the battered Bedford buses stopped for refreshments. The passengers hung out the windows staring at the strange Inglesies, as all foreigners are known in Baluchistan. The 'restaurant' had a one-meal menu of channa dhal and chapattis – the chickpea staple diet of rural Baluchistan. We shared our dinner with the persistent flies, washing it down with black garam chai; the local water couldn't be trusted unless boiled and that wasn't foolproof.

An extended family of Afghan nomads was passing through the settlement as we sat watching the sun set. A tall, black-turbaned, bearded tribesman was herding a flock of fat-tailed sheep with the help of two unsmiling Afghan hunting dogs prowling behind, keeping the sheep in close order. Two dromedaries carrying their possessions – black felt tents, pots, kettles, blankets, water containers – were being led by a turbaned elder, with bandoliers of ammunition around his chest. An occupied baby cot was roped on the side of the lead camel; the baby's mother walked alongside. A baby camel trotted alongside its mother on knobbly legs that looked as if they might collapse. It was a desert caravan unchanged but for modern weapons since Alexander and his homesick armies passed through Baluchistan on their long march from Hind to Babylon.

The women in these parts didn't cover their faces, as the women in Punjab and Sindh did. They wore colourful clothes and traditional jewellery in the form of nose rings, and ankle bangles: family heirlooms of many generations – an ageless part of the desert culture of their ancestors. It would still have been familiar to the long-gone British district officers, as well as Alexander's soldiers. After our dinner we sat drinking lukewarm Cokes, later we walked around the little settlement as it cooled into night, to the bemused stares of the turbaned tribesmen.

Our room had two rope charpoys with wafer-thin cotton mattress; a small table in-between was the only other furnishing. There was no running water, just a small annex with a brick floor and a drain hole in one corner; you sluiced yourself with a pan from earthenware pots filled from a well in the parched garden, where some dusty hens scratched at the sun-baked ground and a few withered plants were just about surviving. I had taken my bath earlier, while the day was still warm, but the water was icy. Our bikes were parked under the iron-barred window, where we could see who passed. I slept next to the window, where I could look out whenever I woke, and as far as we knew no one came by.

In the morning Mark felt worse and had been up half the night visiting the outside khazi. I had also not slept too well and had paid a midnight visit to the outhouse. We set out together after breakfast of chapattis, eggs and tea, hoping to reach Nok Kundi by evening. Mark rode ahead, making faster time on his bigger bike. We arranged to meet at Dalbandin for a rest stop before continuing on. When I caught him up at a Dalbandin dhaba at midday he was too sick to go any further. I left him drinking chai while I went to find the dak bungalow and got us a room, then went back and showed him the way to it.

Mark was suffering from a severe case of diarrhoea, which seemed to be worsening. I left him resting in the room and went to buy bottles of Coke at the chai stall, and some diarrhoea medicine at the small dispensary on the main street. By now we had realised the water everywhere was contaminated; neither of us was of a mind to eat out later. I bought biscuits and chapattis to see us through till morning. We had an early dinner of chapattis and Cokes, then crashed out, grateful for the shelter of our small room and the khansamah who kept a watch over our bikes while we slept.

Late in the afternoon a man arrived at the door and introduced himself as a Christian resident of the town and invited us to the only church in the settlement. Mark was too sick and I made an excuse of tiredness. I still regret not going with the Baluchi Christian to visit his church – a rare thing in these parts – and I have wondered since if there are enough Christians left there for it to still exist.

In the morning Mark said he could ride no further and had decided to put his bike on the train that came through once a week from Quetta to Teheran; he had found out from the khansamah it was due in two days, and went to the station to buy a ticket. His bike would go in the guard's van. I couldn't stay: I only had two days left on my transit permit and didn't want any trouble at the border. We had a last breakfast together; he walked out to the main road to see me ride off and I never saw him again. I should have taken the train too, as he suggested, and saved myself a lot of stress and unforeseen difficulty – we are all wise in hindsight.

I stopped for petrol on the main street at Dalbandin's only bowser, then bought chapattis at the bakery and rode out slowly through the small desert settlement, and in less than a minute I was back on the rutted sand track that was the main road to Iran. A few local buses even more battered-looking than those of Nepal were the only other traffic. The adulterated low-octane petrol – all that was found in these small settlements – never bothered the Enfield; it seemed happy with whatever was available.

Dalbandin was the only settlement between Nushki and Nok Kundi nearer the Iranian border, but it was just a dusty village with a petrol bowser, police post, rail siding and a few poorly stocked shops and chai dhabas. As I rode away I pondered on the lives of the district officers once posted to these outposts of empire, imagining some newly appointed assistant D.O. playing chess against himself and reading back copies of *The Times*, delivered once a month by a camel train from Quetta in the flickering light of a Tilley lamp, waiting for the khansamah to cook dinner as the punkah wallah pulled at his rope. I was thinking too much, but I had once lived in similar circumstances of isolation with no electricity in the highlands of Papua New Guinea, but in my case had to cook my own dinners.

An ancient Bedford truck with its cargo of turbaned tribesmen passed by, some of them carrying even more ancient weapons, including the old Lee Enfield. I wondered if these might once have been captured from a bygone frontier skirmish with a British patrol, or stolen from an arsenal in a raid on one of the frontier garrisons, which was not unknown. But more likely they were bought in Darra Adam Khel, the gunmaking town on the north-west frontier of Pakistan, where you can still buy working replicas of almost any gun ever made. Some of the older Lee Enfields in circulation hereabouts may even have come from the original Royal Enfield factory in north London, where the original R.E. motorcycles were also once made.

With bandoliers of ammunition strapped around their chests, the tribesmen sat on the roofs of trucks and buses, staring down at me with unsmiling faces as I rode past in the eddying dust cloud. And I worried I would be a challenge for a bit of target practice, as I zig-zagged and sped up to lengthen the range between us, feeling exposed and my mind full of doubts. The verse from Rudyard Kipling's well known poem 'Arithmetic on the Frontier' came into my mind, and a shiver ran down my spine.

> A scrimmage in a Border Station —
> A canter down some dark defile —
> Two thousand pounds of education
> Drops to a ten-rupee Jezail —
> The Crammer's boast, the Squadron's pride,
> Shot like a rabbit in a ride!

(Jezail: a long-barrelled muzzle loader used by Afghan and Pashtun snipers in nineteenth-century wars against the British.)

It wasn't long before I had to make my first toilet stop one of many that day. It was only 100 miles to Nok Kundi but averaging at best 20mph on the rutted sand track I had a good six hours of rough riding ahead before reaching the settlement of Nok Kundi. Soon enough I had to make another stop: the rough potholed track through the hills and sand dunes was loosening my bowels, and so it continued. Whenever I felt the pressure I slowed looking for a suitable place to stop. I would ride behind a sand hill, out of sight from any traffic. In these parts many carried a gun; it was not advisable for a traveller to be caught with their trousers down.

Continuing I passed nomadic herder families driving sheep and goats to or from traditional grazing lands or to small rural markets somewhere over the horizons in the expanse of prehistoric desert. They appeared in the distance as a hazy mirage, and as we came together I slowed and left the road, weaving my route through the dunes, giving them room to pass to avoid startling their animals. It could have been biblical if it hadn't been for the weapons they carried slung over a shoulder.

I was getting weaker but there was no choice other than carry on; I had to be out of Pakistan the next day. It became a day of toilet stops, and increased heat as the day wore on, though it was still only early spring. The road took many different ways to the only destination, one as good as another to a traveller who didn't know the shortest route. But all these were just vague tracks meandering between low hills in what seemed wilderness. I lost the way several times and had to ride around over the baked earth till I found wheel tracks to follow.

Occasionally, away from the main track, a pair of sand grouse would rise in alarm at the unfamiliar sound of the Enfield's exhaust note, disappearing in a clatter around the nearest sand hill, and I wondered what they found to eat in such a barren place. There are over 430 species of birds in Baluchistan, despite the barrenness of much of the landscape. There has been a tradition of falconry here since ancient times and today many wealthy Arabs from the Gulf States come to hunt with their falcons, sand grouse and bustard being commonly hunted birds.

I fell off once when the Enfield found a pothole full of what in Australia we called bulldust, so fine it appears to be solid ground but gives way to the least pressure; the forks bottomed out and developed a front-wheel wobble I couldn't control in my weakened state. I was only going slowly so I let the bike fall and rolled away. The Enfield lay in the dust, back wheel spinning, till I got on my feet as quick as I could and killed the engine: some petrol had spilled from the jerrycan and I feared it might ignite on the hot exhaust pipe. With a struggle I lifted the heavy bike upright, and onto its side stand, then I dropped my pants and squatted by the trackside, uncaring if I were seen.

I checked over the bike. It was fine: it was made of tough steel; not a single piece of plastic adorned its sturdy frame. I now noticed that the water container strapped onto the rear carrier had leaked and I had lost most of my water. It had happened well before the spill as there was no water stain on the track. I had bought the canister in the Lahore bazaar: the best I could find, but it had split a seam already.

In the late 1970s Pakistan's physicists and engineers were secretly working on their nuclear programme. Now I wondered how Pakistan would manage to build a nuclear reactor that didn't leak if they couldn't make a bloody water bottle that didn't. What goes through your mind in times of stress is strange. Now I had a minor problem: I was only managing about 15mph along the potholed track and had another five hours of hard riding if all went well, and only a mouthful of water left.

Carrying on after a reflective smoke, I came to a side track with a signpost showing an arrow and some Urdu script I couldn't read. I could see a kutcha house some way down it behind a high purdah wall, and decided to go and ask for water as I didn't know if any more lay ahead and it was getting hotter by the hour. I knocked on the wall's gate and shouted but no one answered. The house looked deserted. I walked round the outside of the compound wall and found two large earthen jars of water in the shade of an awning by an open well.

I didn't like helping myself with no one there to ask, but I had little choice, and whoever lived there had a good well. I half-filled the plastic canister, tying it on the carrier with the split seam at the top, then had a good drink of the earthy brew and left a few rupees and a note to say I'd stopped for water. I have wondered since who lived there and where they were that day, and whether they ever had the note translated and wondered who the Inglesie was who stopped by for a drink. Whoever lived there, I thank you: you saved me from a terrible ordeal.

I made it to Nok Khundi late in the afternoon, collapsing tired but relieved on the charpoy as soon as the khansamah let me into the dak bungalow. While I lay sweating on the hard bed, he went off to report my presence at the police station. A few minutes later a police officer in a flowing blue Baluchi turban arrived, checked my passport and asked my business. Satisfied I was only staying the night and passing through, he ordered tea to be brought and we chatted a while before he left me to rest. I didn't eat till the morning, too tired to bother going to the bazaar, but the black tea was as welcome as a good beer. It was another night of many visits to the outside khazi.

After a breakfast of chapattis and fried egg, I paid my bill and made another visit to the toilet. I still had a supply of toilet paper from Lahore and I stuffed a new wad of it in the seat of my underpants just in case the road ahead was as rough as it was behind.

I stopped in the main street to top up at the petrol bowser, then set out for the border at Qila Safed. I had passed the worst of the desert track and the road began to improve as I neared the frontier post. I arrived soon after it opened, and after surprisingly brief formalities was passed through. No one bothered to check the date on my transit permit: I could easily have spent a few more days in Pakistan but it was too late now. Unfortunately they took the permit off me, though I asked if I could keep it as a souvenir, then they waved me through – glad to see me gone, no doubt; perhaps it's still there, filed away in a dusty filing cabinet, to this day.

Eastern Iran

At Taftan I produced my British passport and got an entry stamp with none of the aggravation I was expecting as a citizen of the Little Satan. They noted the registration number of the Enfield in my passport and I was free to enter. I would have preferred to enter on my Australian passport, but this would have meant getting a visa back in Delhi and I was well over visiting yet another embassy and waiting days for it. So I entered Iran on my British passport as no visa was required for the Little Sataners; an unforeseen complication would arise later as a result.

The first large town from the border was Zahedan, a wild and windswept outpost of sand-blown streets with a population of mostly ethnic Iranian Baluchi. But at least the roads were sealed with bitumen from here on westwards. As I rode towards Zahedan from the frontier post, the trucks going toward Pakistan were flashing their headlights, their drivers waving at me; after three or four passed I realised I was riding on the wrong side of the road: Iran drives on the right, Pakistan on the left.

The truck drivers had all crossed over to avoid running me down; in return for their courtesy I had been giving them two-fingered obverse victory salutes for driving at me: how embarrassing is that? They were saving my life while I was being very rude. I here offer my sincere apologies to the truck drivers heading east that April morning, who saved my life. I have thought about you since, and wished you safe journeys.

The basic but reliable and safe dak bungalows of Pakistan and Baluchistan were no more now. I had only my blue plastic tarpaulin from the Delhi bazaar to serve as a shelter. At the municipal campsite in Zahedan that afternoon, I tied the tarp to the handlebars and rear carrier, then stretched it down to the ground and pegged it out. It made a small covered space 4ft wide and 8ft long with open ends with just enough room for me to sleep with my possessions alongside. My camp prepared, I went out looking for food.

Walking down the main street of Zahedan, I came to the medical college and decided to try my luck finding a canteen where I could get a meal and maybe find English-speaking students to enquire about the road ahead. It seemed like a good idea at the time: don't they always? As I was walking onto the campus I came on a gathering of students demonstrating and chanting slogans. Coming closer, I noticed a police presence at the rear of the crowd; seconds later I heard loud bangs. Suddenly tear gas canisters landed among the crowd just as I reached it.

It was not the end to the day I'd imagined: instead of dining on lamb kebabs and saffron rice in the university's refectory, making enquiries on the sights ahead among polite minds, I was running for my life with a crowd of rebellious students. More shots were fired and I thought: not tear gas this time. There was a general panic as the police surged forward, and we ran as fast as we could. It occurred to me in a flash of clarity that if I were arrested I would be perceived as a foreign spy agitating against the Khomeini regime, and I sped up looking over my shoulder to see if the police were gaining.

Back on the main road I headed fast back to the campsite, where I arrived breathless and in need of the toilet. Then I crawled under the tarpaulin and into my sleeping bag, exhausted, hungry, but still alive and ready to suffer another day. It wasn't the most restful night's sleep and I was visited again by the mongoose.

I woke about midnight from a bad dream where a giant mongoose was chasing me down the road riding on the Enfield and it was gaining on us; no matter how urgently I twisted the throttle, the bike wouldn't go any faster. I woke up just as it was about to pounce, and lay wondering what I was doing there. I lit a smoke and tried to relax but I needed the campsite khazi again: not a pleasant experience, just a hole in the concrete floor with a concrete block wall on three sides, no roof and no door; the only light the moon above.

Morning couldn't come fast enough and at the first grey inkling of it I was up packed and toileted, with a fresh wad in place. I rode out of town through the sandy streets as soon as I got petrol and naan bread. From Zahedan the main road was smooth bitumen and mostly straight as an arrow; mirages danced in the hazy distance, disappearing as I got closer. I could throttle up to 60mph on the smooth pothole-free surface. It was the fastest speed we'd ever travelled at. The Enfield was happy at this speed but if I went any faster it showed its displeasure and the front wheel began wobbling.

I began to enjoy the ride; after the trials of the rough Baluchistan roads it was easy cruising, with a welcome feel of sun on my back in the early chill. The Enfield throbbed along hour after hour all day without a missed beat, its single thumping cylinder making a comforting bupp, bupp, bupp as it echoed off the surface of the smooth black bitumin. It sounded like a happy cylinder, and I too was happy leaving Zahedan and its riotous students far behind.

It was a long day in the saddle but without incident, the Enfield cruising without a care, the heat haze making the oncoming traffic shimmer against the washed-out skyline. I stopped every two hours to relieve cold stiff joints and loose bowels, and to have a smoke and stretch my legs, taking a bite of my hardening bread, and to change the wad of toilet paper when necessary.

At the Zahedan campsite I had first met a party of Swiss travellers in a VW combi van who had also travelled through Baluchistan from India; at my first road break stop they passed me and waved. Carrying on, I passed them having a roadside stop, and so it went most of the morning. Two nights later we met again at the campsite in Kerman.

After making my camp I went over for a chat with them; they asked me if I'd heard the news. What news, I wondered. I didn't have a radio but they did and had heard on the BBC World Service of the attempted rescue of the American embassy hostages, who had been held prisoners in Teheran for over five months.

We didn't know the details of the American raid but we understood that for us this was serious news and we were now in the thick of it. The Swiss party advised me to get out of Iran as fast as possible. I wasn't to know it then but the Iranian police and every citizen were on the lookout for Americans who may have been left behind in the chaos of the American withdrawal.

I knew of the hostage situation; everyone knew all too well of it. It had been a major news item for months in every country of the world. When I had entered Iran the crisis had been a political stalemate for months. Negotiations had continued between the two countries through neutral intermediaries; it had looked like it would remain so indefinitely. Since I left India I had had no news of the crisis; no complimentary newspapers were delivered with my breakfasts at the dak bungalows in Pakistan.

As I lay under the tarpaulin that night I considered what might lie ahead, and it all seemed bad. I had to decide what was best; there were only two options: turn around and head back to the bad roads of Baluchistan and a long painful ride to Pakistan, and then what? It wasn't an option. Or an equally long ride the full length of Iran to the Turkish border on a wheel and a prayer. It was another night of fitful sleep as I mulled it over during waking moments. I was up at dawn and as I crouched over the hole in the khazi I heard the kettle whistling in the Swiss combi van as they brewed up for breakfast. I went straight over and scrounged a coffee.

The Swiss were planning to go all out, taking turns at driving round the clock till they reached the Turkish border. The best I could manage was five, maybe six, hundred kilometres a day, and then only if the Enfield held up and my diarrhoea didn't worsen. I estimated it would take at least five days to reach Turkey. There was nothing I could do now other than hope I would not be mistaken for an American, and put all my faith in the Enfield's three and a half galloping horses.

Operation Eagle Claw

Following a breakdown in negotiations with the Khomeini regime in Teheran, President James Earl Carter ordered his military advisors to come up with a plan for a top-secret hostage rescue mission. On the evening of 24 April 1980, eight RH-53D helicopters took off from the aircraft carrier USS *Nimitz* in the Persian Gulf. The next morning, six of the eight helicopters rendezvoused with several US C-130 refuelling planes at a remote stretch of road in the Great Dasht e Lut desert of eastern Iran, which they planned to use as an airstrip they had codenamed 'Desert One'.

The name chosen for the rescue mission was 'Operation Eagle Claw'. I don't know who coined that one up, but it sounds about right for such a wild and desperate adventure. Due to a combination of bad luck, mechanical failure of helicopters, freak dust storms, poor intelligence, bad planning and some very gung-ho egos, the outcome was a disaster. It resulted in the deaths of eight American servicemen, one Iranian civilian and the loss of two American aircraft, and a loss of prestige in the Middle East.

Two of the helicopters never even got as far as the Desert One rendezvous. One had avionics failures halfway there and returned to USS *Nimitz*. The other developed a fracture in one of its main rotor blades and was abandoned in the desert. Its crew was retrieved by another helicopter, which then continued on to Desert One. The helicopters had to fly under strict radio silence for the entire flight, preventing them from keeping in contact with each other as a combined unit.

The flights ran into a severe sandstorm, making visual flying impossible, and due to the order for radio silence the pilots could not keep in touch to give advance warning to each other. Flying solely on instruments, they arrived separately at Desert One behind schedule. The strict order for radio silence had prevented the pilots asking permission to fly at a higher level above the sandstorm, forcing them to fly the whole distance at dangerously low levels with no visibility.

The rescue plan called for a minimum of six helicopters to be available to rescue all the hostages, but, of the six that made it to the rendezvous at 'Desert One', one helicopter developed a hydraulics problem and had to fly in on its secondary system.

The helicopter crew wanted to continue, but, owing to the risk of a hydraulic system failure with no backup, the squadron's flight commander decided to ground the helicopter, forcing the operation commander, Col. Beckwith, to abort the mission as it became clear that with the loss of the two other helicopters the mission couldn't succeed in evacuating all the hostages. As the remaining helicopters refuelled from the C-130 aircraft and prepared to fly back to the *Nimitz*, one of them collided with a parked C-130 tanker aircraft, crashing in flames. In the collision and subsequent fire, eight servicemen were killed and several more injured. The rest of the force then withdrew, leaving their dead behind.

We didn't know any of these details as we drank our breakfast coffees at the campsite discussing our options, but I knew the raid was serious news, and Murphy's Law had dropped me in the thick of it. I calculated later that at the time the disaster at Desert One was happening I was lying under my tarpaulin alongside the Enfield near the ancient citadel town of Bam, my only worry was wondering if I had contracted rabies.

I said goodbye to the Swiss travellers, watching with envy as they drove away in the relative safety and warmth of their VW combi van with its home comforts of kettle and coffee jug, and supplies of chocolate and alcohol, and with their politically neutral passports I envied them. Before they left, one of them gave me his old Swiss army surplus jacket.

I hadn't needed much warm clothing in India and Pakistan, but it was getting colder each day on the journey west. I thanked him for his thoughtful gift; he had noticed how badly equipped I was and offered me his old army camouflage jacket, or perhaps he just didn't want to appear like a fleeing American soldier. I was just very glad of the well-patched jacket.

I was used to travelling alone and had done a lot of it in past years, but now I felt very alone as I watched the combi van head off into the hazy distance and disappear from sight. There was nothing for it now but to ride west as fast as the Enfield would safely go, for as long each day as my Baluchi belly would allow. I fuelled up on the main street, feeling like every eye was on me, bought fresh naan bread at a nearby stall, then kicked the Enfield into life, said the biker's prayer and headed warily down the road. The Swiss had long disappeared over the horizon, and I never saw them again.

It was a cold morning but with the extra Swiss army jacket over my thinner Australian army jacket I was at least warmer than I had been. I had no proper gloves and was wearing my thick trekking socks on my hands, a woollen Indian balaclava under my cheap Indian helmet covered most of my face. A pair of Delhi bazaar leather and metal aviator style glasses completed my uniform, and made me look like a despatch rider from a film of WW2. Not such a far-fetched notion, as the original Royal Enfield Bullet 350cc was used extensively by the British Army Dispatch Corps during WW2.

The miles began slipping behind and as the sun rose higher I slowly warmed up in the saddle. I stopped about every two hours to stretch my cramped legs and give my throttle hand a chance to uncramp, and seek a convenient ditch to relieve my Baluchi belly, followed by a quick smoke, a hasty nibble of Naan-e Songsak – Iranian bread – then back in the saddle and away.

In the early afternoon I stopped for fuel at the small town of Anar; after paying the attendant he suddenly locked his garage door jumped on his scooter and took off in a bit of a hurry. I didn't give it any thought and sat on the forecourt wall having a smoke before continuing. As I was about to leave, checking my pack and fuel can were securely fastened, a pickup truck came spinning into the forecourt. Out jumped four armed police officers and surrounded me.

Under the muzzles of their rifles I was questioned in broken English by an officer. Then he ordered me to mount my bike and follow the pickup as the armed police in the back kept me under surveillance, fingers on triggers, muzzles pointing at me. I worried that one bad jolt from a pothole in the road and one of the triggers would be pulled and I would be brown bread on the dusty street of a boondock Iranian town. It was a nervous ride through dusty litter strewn streets, and I was never more relieved to be taken into a police station. In the walled courtyard I lifted the Enfield onto its centre stand, as the gate we'd entered through was shut and bolted. I was trying to look cool and in control, while sweat ran down my back under the layers of the army surplus clothes that I suddenly felt made me look suspicious.

I was marched down a corridor to a bare room at the end furnished with a desk and chairs and told to sit and wait; an armed police officer stood at the open door. After what seemed an age a man in civilian clothes came in with the police officer who had questioned me and asked for my papers. I had entered Iran on my British passport as this required no entry visa. I now made the mistake of showing them my Australian passport. What made me do this was the fact that Australia had normal relations with Iran – a more neutral country – while Britain was the ally of America the Iranians called Little Deputy Satan, while America was Big Sheriff Satan.

I had been thinking about this all morning and decided that if I were stopped and it were discovered I had two passports they would think me a spy. Two passports here were very suspicious; dual nationality was unrecognised by Iran. So I had hidden my British passport under my toolkit at the bottom of a pannier and kept my politically neutral Australian passport handy in my inside pocket. He began turning the pages, looking for the Iran entry stamp, and I realised I had blundered. They asked me where I had entered Iran. I bluffed as calmly as I could while the clammy sweat – I was still wearing both jackets – ran down my back.

I lied that the immigration officer at Mojave had not bothered stamping my passport but merely looked at it. I only got away with the lie because this was a boondock police post in a small town where there was little notion of the procedures at border posts. I was sweating on them not searching my panniers, while desperately thinking of an excuse if they did find my satanic passport. I would just say I got them mixed up and hope for the best; they couldn't hang me for it, could they?

I was asked for all my other documents: bike registration, drivers licence etc. I showed these things but they were unconvinced I had ridden from India on the Enfield. Then I remembered the Indian Automobile Association membership card from the time warped office in Delhi and showed them it; things slowly warmed up. We went back outside and I pointed to the yellow India AA badge proudly mounted on the handlebars, proof I had ridden from Delhi. It was enough to convince them. My neutral Australian passport was accepted. The gamble had paid off. I was free to go, but first we had some tea and cigarettes to show there were no hard feelings.

As we drank our tea they discussed the crisis, warning me not to go down any side roads or into small villages or stop at any demonstrations, and especially to avoid mosques or religious gatherings. I thought it wise not to mention the Zahedan episode, being tear-gassed and shot at, afraid to be thought of as a touring agitator. They warned me to avoid the cities of Qom and Teheran, and not to camp in sight of the road, and to get out of Iran as fast as possible as it was very dangerous for a foreigner on the roads. I had been slightly worried before this; now I was really worried.

The village mullahs were often uneducated and thought all Westerners to be American and related to Satan; rural villages had to be avoided, but food and fuel stops still had to be made. The British were even less liked than Americans, seen as lackeys of US policy with no real power of their own, attached to America as its deputy sheriff. I didn't need telling twice: things were tricky and I was caught in the middle of it.

The Caravansaries of Persia

Throughout history Persia has been a land many travellers have passed through, a branch of the great Silk Road between Constantinople and the ancient cities of the Middle East through Persia to Central Asia, and beyond to India and China: a crossroads for merchant travellers and invading armies. All along its ancient routes caravansaries were established where travellers could obtain food and shelter, with fodder for their pack camels and horses.

Today's equivalent of Persia's old caravansaries are the less romantic municipal campsites. It was usual to find campsites with basic facilities on the edge of all large towns, the caravansaries of modern-day travellers, run by local government with a caretaker on site to collect payment.

During the power of the Persian Empire, caravansaries were spaced at intervals of a day's march between towns and important villages along the Persian Empire's Royal Road, a 2,500-kilometre highway between Sardis on the Aegean Sea in modern-day Turkey to Susa in southern Iran. Herodotus wrote of it 'Royal stations exist along its whole length, and excellent caravansaries; and throughout, it traverses an inhabited tract, and is free from danger.' The police obviously didn't have need of tear gas back then.

Though municipal campsites have replaced the ancient caravansaries, the purpose is much the same: a place for a traveller to rest and spend the night, safe from brigands and wolves, with food and water and news of the roads ahead. Except there was no food available; since the Iranian revolution and the hostage crisis overland travellers had stopped coming, and many campsites were closed.

During the flower-power '60s and '70s a steady flow of ganja-fuelled hippies travelled along the ancient silk roads between Europe and India, keeping both campsites and local drug dealers in business. But by the early 1980s the overlanding hippy had become a rarity. The Soviet army had entered Afghanistan in December 1979; as Afghan mujahidin and the Taliban became active, the overland journey through Afghanistan became too dangerous.

The ragged army of hippies travelling from Istanbul to Kathmandu in clapped-out magic buses in their bell-bottom denims, cheesecloth shirts and John Lennon glasses, with flowers and nits in their hair, had suddenly ended. One of the peculiarities of twentieth-century travel was over, replaced by punks and rappers whose idea of travel was a trip down the M1 from their suburbs to Glastonbury, and who just didn't get the overland vibe, man.

The flower children who had once gathered around the campsite fires along the silk roads of Persia, passing around joints and sharing each other's saliva, twanging guitars and singing 'Mr. Tambourine Man', were relegated to a short-lived history: long-haired ghosts of a time gone by. It was the end of their era, and I was thankful for that.

I saw a camping road sign and steered onto the deserted campsite in looming darkness; afraid to use my torch so as not to make my presence known, I tiredly I set up camp, and then crawled under the plastic tarpaulin for a smoke where the glow of the cig wasn't visible. I was becoming a bit paranoid. Once during the night, as I lay awake with my head out of the tarp watching the shooting stars flash across the heavens, I thought I heard a familiar song. Was it the ghosts of past hippies singing 'Lucy in the Sky with Diamonds' or just my restless imaginings? A nagging thought I couldn't shake off was rabies: could I have contracted it? I tried remembering what the symptoms were and how long before they manifested. They were stressful nights under star-filled skies dreaming of mongooses and riotous mobs.

I was up as the first hint of dawn arrived; there was no pleasure lingering in my bag on the rock-hard ground under a plastic sheet and a layer of dew. The nights had become very cold; my army surplus sleeping bag was not up to the task, and I would wake stiff, cold and cramped, then be quickly packed and away in under ten minutes. It became routine.

I would ride slowly down the main street of the first town I came to, sometimes still in semi-darkness, looking for a bakery, where fresh hot naan bread was baked in a traditional clay oven. If the proprietors of these bakeries were surprised by a foreigner arriving on a motorbike just after dawn, they never showed it, and were always happy to sell me bread. And just as well, as it was more or less all I ate in Iran. Then I was set up for another day in the saddle.

I avoided anywhere a crowd was to be seen; I didn't need another tear gassing or gun pointed at me. I kept to myself as much as was possible. I would eat one naan fresh and hot from the oven for breakfast, if possible with a glass of tea, often available from a nearby stall. Two naans went into a pannier for the day ahead and then the ride began.

To this day, if I go to a Pakistani or Indian restaurant, I always ask for naan bread. It's my favourite and brings back the memories after all the years. Odd that a piece of baked dough can give you that 'good to be alive' feeling.

Benzene in Iran was almost free and available everywhere. I would pull up by a bowser, where a boy would fill the tank. I tried not to speak, and was usually taken for an Iranian; I was sunburned and dark-haired, dressed in drab clothes, a balaclava and aviator glasses. I was barely visible and didn't look out of place. The fuel was so cheap I handed over a small note and didn't wait for the change: better to be gone than risk being pointed out as a foreigner.

Each day slipped by much the same: the roads were good and uncrowded. Big trucks heading towards Baluchistan from Turkey and Bulgaria were the main traffic, and I was puzzled about what they carried and where in Pakistan they were going.

At the Iran border I had seen these trucks from Eastern Europe queuing at the customs post to enter Pakistan. It was a long haul from Europe, and for those trucks to be there meant they were going to cross Baluchistan; there was nowhere else they could deliver a cargo to. Some had passed me and I had followed truck tracks when the route became confused in the dunes and nullahs. They were often modern European makes: MAN and Volvos, not like the rattling tinsel-decorated old British Bedfords that ruled the roads throughout Pakistan.

At this time Pakistan had an active nuclear programme and was building up its nuclear facilities. I wondered if these trucks could be carrying materials or nuclear equipment into Pakistan, from the Soviet Union and its European satellite states.

After three days I became less concerned about my safety and began stopping around midday for a meal at one of the benzene trucking stops. I tried to find one with a foreign truck or two parked there, figuring I would be taken for another European truck driver who couldn't speak the language. No one spoke to me or gave me as much as a glance. These roadhouses had large trays of rice and mutton dishes on the counter and little else, but it was all I needed. I would point to what I wanted and take some extra naan to save me looking for food later wherever I camped that night.

My biggest regret was the historic cities and ancient sights I was missing as a result of this mad run for the border. Iran has a wealth of ancient sites, from the stunning architecture of Isphahan to ancient medieval mud brick towns such as Bam and Kerman. I had also had to rush through Pakistan because of the seven-day transit visa. The journey had turned into an endurance race, rather than the once-in-a-lifetime motorcycle trip I naively imagined when I bought the Enfield in Delhi.

Once again on the next campsite I was warned by the caretaker to stay out of towns and especially not to go near Teheran or Qom. I looked at my school atlas map and planned a route south, skirting Isphahan to Kermanshah. From there I hoped to make the border in two more days.

It was all I wanted now: the long hours of riding, food snatched on the go at roadside laybys, the desolate campsites and their foul toilets were grating on my nerves. The fitful, sleepless nights were also beginning to exhaust me. I had woken once from a dream where I was being chased down the road by a giant mongoose, and it was outpacing the bike. It was all beginning to tell and I longed for the Turkish food waiting over the border, where I could eat at leisure, followed by a warm bed and hot shower in a hotel with no mongoose.

One saving grace was the excellent road surfaces on the highways since Zahedan. The deposed Shah Pahlavi had spent most of his country's oil money on himself and his secret security police, army and hangers on while he was in power, but he had also spent money on the highways, so he could quickly send troops to troublesome regions if needed. These roads seemed all the more wonderful after the bulldust and indistinct potholed sand tracks of Baluchistan.

The highway was mostly free of private cars; the traffic was trucks and public buses. I rode for hours with only an occasional truck or bus to be overtaken. Sometimes one would overtake me, pumping out a backwash of diesel fumes with no regard for a motorcyclist. I had no rights on these roads.

I was often faced with a headwind, and the 3.5-horsepower one-pot engine would struggle to keep up a good speed. Sometimes I tucked in behind a truck, riding in its slipstream to help the engine. It was a risk riding close behind, but it took some strain off me and the bike. The downside was the exhaust fumes; they blackened my clothes and my face and lungs, but I was past caring of my appearance or well-being. I just wanted to reach the border, and wondered if the Swiss had already done so and were enjoying the comforts of Turkish food.

I made a detour to avoid Teheran and Qom, on the advice of the police who had detained me. It added many miles, looping south via Kermanshah, but had to be done. I was making good progress on the long, open roads, stopping only for fuel and a quick feed at roadhouses. I tried to avoid the loathsome toilets full of turds and flies that could be smelled coming a mile down the road, looking instead for a side track or culvert to make use of.

Most Iranians are well aware of the government's line of propaganda against the West, but are afraid of the secret police network. If I was spoken to in English, I was careful to let them know I was from Australia. Most Iranians had little knowledge of Australia and didn't know it was an ally of the US.

From Kermanshah I planned to reach Tabriz for my last night stop and then arrive at the Turkish border early the following morning. It was all going smoothly enough, in a desperate sort of way, but it started raining lightly on the last afternoon. Not far from Tabriz the rear wheel suddenly started dragging and wobbling. I had got my first puncture. I steered into the roadside just in time as the truck driving too close behind me roared past. I was on the main Tabriz highway and there was a lot more traffic than in eastern Iran. A flyover bridge crossed the highway a little further on in the rain I pushed the bike along to the shelter of it.

I was lucky it was a rear-wheel puncture and not a front-wheel blowout as that would probably have spilled me into the road at 50mph and under the truck driving too close behind. But rear-wheel punctures are more trouble to mend. I was tired, wet and cold; I was not in the hot desert now, the weather had got progressively colder as I travelled west.

I had bought tools and tyre levers in Delhi, a puncture kit, hand pump and spare inner tube. With an hour before dark I started the tedious task of fixing the puncture, but at least I was under shelter. Fortunately, the Enfield had a centre stand. With my rucksack balanced on the front wheel guard and the bike on the centre stand, the back wheel was counterbalanced off the ground.

I started removing the chain, first loosening the tensioner bolts to allow enough slack to slip the chain of the sprocket. Then the rear brake rod had to be disconnected from the brake drum arm; with the axle bolt loosened I dropped the wheel out of its slots. The inner tube valve was unscrewed and pushed in, and tyre levers were applied.

With an effort I stretched the tyre off the rim. The punctured tube was pulled out, air pumped into it and I found the puncture hole.

Feeling inside the tyre, I removed a small wire tack and began putting the spare tube in place. The main problem now was getting the tyre back onto the rim without nipping the tube with the tyre levers and putting another hole in it. This carefully done, I lifted the wheel into its axle slots and tightened the axle bolt, reattached the brake rod to the drum lever arm and put the chain on the sprocket. The wheel alignment was equalised between the chain stays, and finally the chain tensioned to one-inch vertical movement. It had needed doing before but I was going to wait till I was over the border.

I attached the hand pump to the tube valve and began pumping as hard as I could in my tired state, till I guessed the pressure was somewhere near the handbook's recommendation, judged by sitting on the bike and seeing how firm the tyre felt. I patched the old tube, and then packed all the tools into the panniers. I was damp, cold and miserable, my hands covered in chain oil and road grime.

It had started raining heavier, and I decided it was too unsafe to continue riding in these conditions in my exhausted state, with speeding trucks throwing up curtains of spray. It had taken two hours to mend the puncture and darkness had fallen. I cleaned my hands with petrol from my gallon jerrycan and took stock of my situation.

I was cold and had started to shiver: the first sign of hypothermia. I was well aware the next stage of hypothermia was muddled thinking and confusion. Riding around looking for a campsite in my present state would be folly. There was nothing for it than to set up camp under the bridge as far back from the road as possible to avoid the spray. It was the most miserable camp I had made since I set off from Delhi. I was tired, hungry and dispirited. Trucks and buses were flashing by just metres away, their exhausts echoing as they passed under the bridge. I would just have to lie here, in my sleeping bag, keeping as warm and dry as I could, under the tarpaulin, eating my last scraps of bread, and thinking of better days to come.

To this day if I am camping somewhere noisy or stuck in some dingy hotel room with the traffic roaring past the window, I think of that cold, wet night under a freeway bridge on the road to Tabriz and my discomforts seem as nothing.

I lay in the bag on my oil-stained foam mat under the tarpaulin, road spray occasionally reaching me as a larger truck sped past. At least it was warm enough in my sleeping bag wearing most of my clothes. I had a lot of time to think as sleep wouldn't come with the traffic noise and headlights. I thought of the border, how close I was now, how tomorrow should see me through and into Turkey. I lay thinking about soft beds and clean hotel rooms with hot showers and a proper toilet, and a belly full of Turkish food, with the possibility of beer in that alcohol tolerant country.

In spite of my miserable situation, I dozed off, for I woke up suddenly with a beam of light in my face, unable to see and momentarily confused by the flashing lights of passing traffic. I remembered where I was and then realised there was a police car and from its window a torch was being shone in my face. My spirits dropped and fears of 'not this again' overcame me. Would I be taken to a police station at gunpoint again, and have to go through all the explaining, or worse still be detained, all within a few hours of the border.

I got out of the sleeping bag and put on my boots, then started to explain I had got a puncture; the inner tube was hanging over the handlebars with the patch on it. I showed them this evidence: one of them had some English and they began to understand. Out came the Australian passport and the Indian AA membership card. I pointed out the yellow badge on the front bars. To my relief they didn't arrest me; they just told me to pack and leave immediately. I wasn't welcome on their patch.

It was almost midnight. The traffic had reduced to a few trucks, and the rain to a light drizzle. Feeling relief at not being detained, I hurriedly packed my bag, tarpaulin and inner tube into the panniers. Not sure where to find the road through Tabriz towards Turkey, I asked them for directions and was told to follow them. With a police escort I was led through Tabriz and put on the road to the border. As

I rode away from town; the rain stopped and some stars emerged. Things were looking up.

I rode till the first benzene station appeared, its lights visible a mile ahead in the darkness. I was on the main trucking highway to Turkey and the roadhouse was a welcome find. The service station was a night stop for cross-border trucks and buses, and hot food was available. Feeling less under threat now, I sat down for a 1 am meal of bread and rice and welcome hot tea. Then I went looking for the dreaded khazi and found a quiet area with picnic tables. Wheeling the Enfield around to it, I set up camp under a concrete table furthest from the building and lay down under the tarp to wait for dawn.

I woke with the cold off and on, and as soon as first light came I was up and dressed in all my clothes, with my kit packed onto the bike I went back into the café. The friendly staff made me a breakfast of eggs, naan bread yoghurt and tea, my most relaxed meal since I crossed from Pakistan. I made my last visit to an Iranian toilet – nothing had changed there – bought extra naan for the ride and checked the tyre pressures. Then I kicked the start lever and we pulled out of the roadhouse just as a watery sun broke through the cloud, and began riding into the cold misty dawn along the wet highway to Turkey.

Despite the damp and cold my spirits were high with the border so close. Slowly the rising sun began to filter through the mist warming me and lifting my mood. The border was congested with trucks queuing to cross into Turkey. I joined the quieter car and bus line; I was nervous about being stopped after all that had happened previously, but I got through immigration without difficulty. At the customs post when my turn came the Enfield drew the attention of a rather nasty official. Everything was in order paper-wise – neither Iran nor Turkey required a vehicle carnet, and the evidence of import was already written in Farsi in my passport.

Now came a tricky moment; the official was, I guess, a motorcyclist and he wanted a ride. Not on the pillion: he wanted to take the bike for a run himself, I flatly refused. It wouldn't take much for him to have an accident and end my trip right there, or perhaps not bring it back at all. What could I say if he didn't? So I put my foot down and said no way, mate. There was an unpleasant standoff; he told me to wait there and went back in the office. I waited for an hour with no sign of him. What now, I wondered. I went into the office; his colleague said he had gone for lunch and I would have to wait till he returned.

Back outside, I decided it was time to act. He had seen me once, and I was at the end of my patience with Iranian officialdom. It was time for the great escape. Silently pushing the Enfield away from the customs building, I waited till a big truck was setting off for the Turkish side. I kicked the Enfield into life. It didn't let me down, starting first time: it wanted out as much as I did. As the truck drove away I rode alongside on the blind side, shielded from the customs building; as the boom gate rose to let the truck through I was off and racing. As soon as we got clear I rode fast through no man's land ahead of the truck and into the Turkish immigration post. Looking back, to my relief no one was coming after me.

Turkish Food and Hot Baths

I passed through Turkish immigration without a hitch and into the customs shed; they wrote the Enfield's registration number into my passport, stamped it and that was that: I was free to go – easy as falling off a bike. At last I was out of the reach of Iranian officials and gun-toting police, and into friendly Turkey. It had been an anxious few minutes. If my journey were a form of escapism from the hot monotony of roofing work in Pilbara mining towns, then crossing from Iran into Turkey seemed to symbolise the escapism.

If I had been detained leaving Iran illegally, it was likely I would have been arrested and perhaps the Enfield forfeited. Maybe I would have been held a long time in a dismal cell with a squat hole in the corner shared with some even longer-forgotten grey-haired hippies. I breathed a sigh of relief that I was clear of Iran in a country not dominated by religious zealots and secret police watching everywhere.

It was a moment for celebrations, but I had no one to hug and nothing to drink, so I just shouted 'Freeeee!' to the bright sky and opened the throttle. The Enfield's one-pot clamour resounded in my ears like Hector Berlioz's *Symphonie fantastique* – well, you get the drift – it was a moment of relief. I thought it best to put some distance between me and the Iran border. In my febrile mind there was a possibility the Iranian customs might phone their Turkish counterparts and have me detained, so down the road I went as fast as the Enfield's three and a half horses would gallop.

Dogubayazit was the first town I stopped at, a faintly grubby eastern

Turkey/Kurdish town of begrimed houses and mostly empty streets of hungry looking stray dogs, with a frontier feel and nothing to linger for. I fuelled up, found a café and had a quick meal of corba and bread, and, feeling better, decided to move on rather than stay the night. There was still time to reach Erzurum before dark, and I felt I was still too close to the border. If the police were looking for a foreigner on a motorbike on the run from Iran I wouldn't take much finding in a small town of few hotels. I had become a bit paranoid, but Erzurum was the bright lights of eastern Turkey and I needed some comforts.

It was colder still on the high Anatolian plateau and I had to slow down to reduce the wind chill as I rode west. I was shivering with first-stage hypothermia when I arrived in Erzurum after dark. I cruised the dark streets, looking for somewhere cheap and cheerful, and, seeing a lit *hoteli* sign over the door of a suitably neglected building, I parked and went up the steps into a dim foyer of peeling paint and worn carpets. A potbellied man in a flat cap and stained waistcoat sat behind a desk, cigarette dangling from his lip; a pigeon was cooing in a large wire cage in the corner. I felt an instant familiarity: I could have been in Wigan.

He beckoned me over. 'Yes, have room, good, peace, hot water, big bed.' I asked where I could leave the Enfield. 'Here' – pointing to a space in the corner of the foyer next to the pigeon, and called his son to help me drag the Enfield up the steps and through the door into the foyer, where I set it on its stand as the pigeon cooed encouragement. You just don't get that service from the night desk manager at the Hilton.

It was still winter in eastern Turkey and guests were few; the hoteli had all I needed: hot water, a large bed in a quiet room and a management for whom nothing was too much trouble. I like travelling in Turkey: the drivers are mad, but the hospitable people and excellent food can't be bettered. When I explained where I had ridden from, they were not surprised or impressed. Perhaps people did this all the time, just not during American military invasions. I had got the timing wrong, that's all. I had a long hot shower, then went out to the café the manager recommended and had the best meal since the dak bungalow curry at Rohri, with its chorus of frogs and whirring moths.

There were other travellers in Iran at this time: the Swiss party, who informed me of the American rescue attempt. Mark was somewhere in Iran, travelling on the train to Teheran, during it all, and I have wondered since how he fared in that rioting city. There must have been others in far-flung villages who perhaps still didn't know of the raid. What I did know was that only one traveller was riding through Iran on an Indian Enfield Bullet that week – more fool me.

Jimmy Carter had been forced into taking action to bring the hostage crisis to an end. Negotiations had stalled and the Khomeini regime was playing it for all it was worth, embarrassing America internationally. The American public had been demanding he take action for months; a second-term election was getting close so Carter had to act. Had Operation Eagle Claw succeeded, he would likely have won a second term. When Operation Eagle Claw failed, he lost his chance.

Perhaps I'm being cynical but that I believe is what it was about. Ronald Reagan won the election by a landslide. The regime under Ayatollah Khomeini decided they had made their point and it would be wiser not to push their luck further. Reagan had been talking tough, and was an unknown quantity. As soon as he took office the hostages were released. How it would have turned out had the Iranians continued to hold the hostages under Reagans presidency, we will never know.

Looking back we can see how the operation was doomed before it ever left the deck of the USS *Nimitz*. There is a wealth of detail about it on the internet, and a book telling the story, including the profiles of all the main players involved and how gung-ho those players were. Operation Eagle Claw is still used as a training exercise for American special forces – as an example of how not to plan and carry out an airborne raid.

It was so complicated operationally and logistically it's surprising it got as far as it did into the Iranian desert. At the time it happened

I was camped about 400km south of the road used as the runway at Desert One. As I had lain in my sleeping bag watching shooting stars and plagued by dreams of a giant mongoose, I was unmindful that not far away helicopters were crashing and burning in the desert over the horizon.

But all's well that ends well. Jimmy Carter didn't get me killed and I never developed rabies – two times lucky. I have forgiven the mongoose: it was only being playful – I think. But I could so easily have been collateral damage, as the Americans say.

The failure of 'Eagle Claw' had many repercussions. It became the clarion call that led to the creation of the 160th S.O.A.R., the helicopter-borne special forces unit of the United States Army, and the establishment of the United States Special Operations Command, whose purpose was to deal with incidents where American overseas interests were under threat. Navy SEALs and other special units were brought under the oversight of the new command and trained to deal with emergency responses to critical incidents hostile to American interests.

There is some irony in that it was US Navy SEALs that took out Osama bin Laden in his bolthole in Abbottabad, Pakistan.* The SEALs had been strengthened and better trained largely as a result of the failure of Operation Eagle Claw. In a roundabout way, Jimmy Carter had contributed to taking out America's most wanted thirty years later – and not all that far from where the Eagle had landed all those years ago in April 1980 – and the worst week of my life was about to start.

---

* In 2005 following the Kashmir earthquake I worked for the IFRC based in Mansehra Pakistan. I drove along the main street of Abbottabad many times, a few metres down a side road lived bin Laden in his bolthole unknown to the world.

Anatolia

In the morning I pumped more air into the rear tyre, checked the wheel axle nuts, and chain tension, under the watchful eye of the pigeon in the hoteli's foyer. Then the manager helped me manhandle the Enfield down the steps onto the roadside. I love Turkish hotels – Best Western, take note. I said goodbye and thank you, the pigeon's coos fading as I rode away. My route by necessity had to be the shortest one; I was not certain my diminishing funds would even be enough to finish the journey.

From Erzurum, the road over the Anatolian high country was mostly bitumen, with some gravelled sections under repair and in places very narrow, with little room for passing. Sivas was my destination for the day. It was a very cold day with snow on the tops of hills; I was glad the sun was shining, but snow clouds were looming ahead. The country looked barren and undeveloped, mostly rough grazing for the angora goats that are native to Anatolia and take their name from Turkey's capital, Ankara. I was feeling colder as the day wore on in my inadequate clothing; my hands had gone numb gripping the bars and I had to stop frequently to warm them over the exhaust pipe.

Some miles from Sivas it started snowing. Feeling very cold and tired, I decided to stop at the first place that offered any shelter for the night. On a high, bleak stretch of road a benzene sign appeared through the drifting snow and I pulled in to refuel and warm my hands. Next door was a wooden-built café with wood smoke rising from its chimney. Sensing hot tea, I nosed through the battered door. A fire was blazing in a clay hearth, and a large blackened kettle and pots of lentil soup were hanging on iron hooks from the oak lintel above it, and I ordered tea and soup.

A group of men in the uniform of the rural Anatolian labourer – threadbare jackets, flat caps, mufflers and waistcoats – looking for all the world like the Lancashire mill town men of pre-war Britain from an L.S. Lowry painting, all sipping glasses of black tea and smoking around the cosy fire. An old grandmother was doling out soup into chipped bowls. It conjured a scene slightly reminiscent of *The Peasant Wedding* by Bruegel the Elder. I regretted having no film left to record the welcome sight, but was too cold to care long about that.

I stood dripping snow; my hands had hardly any feeling left in them. The jolly proprietor almost dragged me to the hearth and produced a chair. The rural labourers shuffled aside, making space for me by the fire. A glass of tea was put in my hands and I started to thaw out. After a bowl of corba soup and bread, I asked about the whereabouts of the nearest cheap hoteli.

When it was realised I needed somewhere to sleep, I was shown a boarded loft room above the café with a roughly made wooden bed and plenty of worn and darned angora wool blankets. It would do just fine. I wouldn't need to ride another mile in the increasing snow and darkening night. After two more hot bowls of lentil corba with lemon wedges, olives and tomatoes and plentiful black, sugary tea I headed to bed, leaving my wet clothes drying above the fire, and slept till daylight. There was even a porcelain pot under the bed so I needn't brave the falling snow to the outside throne room.

Breakfast was eggs, bread, cheese and olives and all the tea my bladder could manage. The Enfield had spent a comfortable night in the woodshed. In spite of the sub-zero night it came to life after a few extra kicks with its regular beat. It hadn't let me down yet through the dank chaotic Jawahar tunnel in Kashmir, the potholed badlands of Baluchistan or the hot dusty expanses of desert roads in Iran. Would it keep its good record in the cold and damp of the Anatolian plateau?

Before leaving the garage I took the opportunity to do some checks, putting the correct air pressure in the tyres and topping up the oil, then we were set to go.

The snow had stopped during the night; all around the landscape was covered in a thick layer of the white stuff lying still and silent under a cold grey blue sky. It looked beautiful but I would have swapped it for some Baluchistan sun. I delayed my start, sipping black, sweet tea by the fire till enough traffic had passed to clear a track through the snow that I could more safely ride on. But I couldn't sit drinking tea all day, so, wearing every item of my wardrobe and two pairs of socks on my hands, I reluctantly left the warm, hospitable café for the cold road west. Ankara was my intended destination but unless the snow held off I was unsure I would reach it.

I had about 300 miles of slush-covered road ahead. Some patches had turned to ice where traffic had turned the snow to mush and it had frozen during the night. The miles only slowly receded; it was too dangerous to ride fast. Occasionally a flock of angora goats would look up from the grey land as they pawed the ground. Browsing on what? I couldn't tell as I passed by. The angora domesticated goat originated in central Anatolia, though they are bred for their fleece in other countries. The fleece from angora goats is known as mohair or pashmina. Unlike sheep, Angoras can be shorn twice a year, and are bred for their white coat, though darker fleeces are also bred.

I stopped at Sorgun for an early lunch of corba and bread. Corba had become my daily staple. It was cheap, tasty and healthy, and came with as much fresh bread as you could eat; as soon as you half emptied the basket more bread was put into it. On my tight budget it solved my food needs perfectly. While riding I decided to have a rest day at Ankara. I had been on the go without a break for weeks due to deadlines, revolutions and raids. Ankara was the first city I had the chance to stop at since I left Lahore in Pakistan, after bypassing the cities of Iran on police advice. I got to Ankara without incident by evening, shivering with cold after a stop at Kirikkali for more corba and tea.

Riding through the darkening cobbled streets of the older city, I saw the welcoming sign of a hoteli and stopped. It looked a bit up-market after the Erzurum pigeon fancier's inn but after my previous night in a bare wooden room with no washing facilities I splurged on a room with a bath and a window looking over the old citadel. It also had a basement car park, where I left the Enfield under the guard of an all-night watchman for a small tip and some cigarettes.

I had a long soak in the water-stained enamelled bath and the water was hot and plentiful. As I soaked the grime away, I thought of the lonely dak bungalows in the wild Baluchistan outposts, with their earthen pots of icy water to pour over yourself if you could suffer to. And of all the stinking Iranian campsite toilets where trying to wash was a whole different kind of torture.

Rugged up in my best kit I went out later to find a café for dinner, looking forward to an early night in a warm room in a big, comfortable bed: things were becoming more civilised the further west I travelled. In a side street near the citadel I found what I wanted. A small family-run café with cauldrons of Turkish stews sitting on the counter for the diner to choose from, pointing to whatever took your fancy, and the choices were all good.

I had been eating a vegetarian diet almost exclusively since I'd left Australia nearly three months earlier. The last thing I wanted was to be struck down again with food poisoning. The Nepali, Indian, Pakistani and Iranian standards of food hygiene in the cheap eateries I relied on couldn't be trusted to serve meat dishes uncontaminated by salmonella or worse. Though eggs, cheese and tinned fish had been on my menu, I hadn't trusted meat. Being vegetarian in Nepal and India is no problem there are plenty of vegetarian eateries. In Pakistan there is little vegetarian choice. I had weakened at the Rohri dak bungalow, where I was served a goat rogan ghosh – and very good it was, even if it may have been the cause of my Baluchi belly. But that was more likely due to contaminated well water, the only source available from Jacobabad to Zahedan.

I stayed with the tried and tested, I had a long way to ride yet and the Baluchi belly that dogged me all the way across the Baluchi deserts and all through Iran was still lingering. I didn't want to risk meat dishes, which might have worsened it. I ordered more corba with a dish of green capsicums stuffed with rice and beans in a broth of tomatoes, onion and lentils, accompanied by the customary basket of home-baked bread and complimentary glasses of black tea. Turkish food, especially in rural villages and small towns, is always excellent and I was not disappointed here.

The next morning I returned there for breakfast, then began to explore the old city and its narrow medieval cobbled streets. It was a nice change to be walking instead of spending hours in a cramped riding position hunched forward to minimise the pressure of the headwinds I often encountered.

After the Ottoman defeat in the First World War, Turkey's capital, Constantinople (Istanbul), and western Anatolia were occupied by the Allies, leaving the Turks a territory in central Anatolia. The new leader of the Turkish nationalist movement was Mustafa Kemal (Atatürk), the same colonel whose timely arrival with infantry at Sari Bair on Gallipoli had saved Turkey from Allied occupation, and so denied the Allies from capturing Constantinople and bringing Bulgaria and Romania into the war on the Allied side.

Atatürk established the headquarters of his resistance movement at Angora (Ankara) in 1920. After independence following the Treaty of Lausanne (1923), the Turkish nationalists restructured the diminished Ottoman Empire into the Republic of Turkey on 29 October 1923. Angora replaced Constantinople as the Turkish capital; the city's name was changed to Ankara.

Over the course of history, Ankara was occupied by the Hittites, Phrygians, Hellenes, Romans, Byzantines and Ottomans. It is a great city to live in if you're an archaeologist. The historical centre lies on a hill on the left bank of the Ankara Çayı. On its summit lie the ruins of the old citadel with many well preserved Roman and Ottoman architectural sights throughout the city, including a 20 BC temple to Augustus.

The Greeks of Pontos came about 300 BC, developing the city as a trading centre between the Black Sea ports and Crimea, Assyria, Cyprus, Lebanon, Georgia, Armenia and Persia, then known as Ἄγκυρα (Ánkyra meaning anchor in Greek). In 278 BC, central Anatolia was occupied by the Galatians, a local Celtic tribe, and the Celtic language continued to be spoken for many centuries. At the end of the fourth century AD, St Jerome, a native of Dalmatia, witnessed that the language spoken around Ankara was similar to that spoken in the north-west of the Roman world at Trier.-

Ancyra was the junction where the roads of northern Anatolia running north to south and the imperial road running east to west intersected. A succession of emperors and armies had all come this way. In the second half of the third century AD, Ánkyra was invaded by the Goths from the west and later by the Arabs. The town was a western outpost of the Palmyra empress Zenobia of Syria, who took advantage of the disorder in the Roman Empire to set up her own state. It was reincorporated into the Roman Empire under Emperor Aurelian in AD 272.

There is a lot of archaeology to see and museums to visit; too many for a day trip. My first stop was Ankara citadel, whose foundations were laid by the Galatians and completed by the Romans. The Byzantines and Seljuks made restorations and additions. The citadel is the oldest part of Ankara, with many examples of traditional architecture. Restored Turkish houses within the citadel have been converted into restaurants and more lately boutique hotels. The Roman theatre lies just outside the castle; many Roman statues found there are exhibited in the Museum of Anatolian Civilizations. The Temple of Augustus was built following the Roman conquest of central Anatolia.

The Roman baths have all the features of a classical bath house: a frigidarium (cold room), tepidarium (warm room) and a caldarium (hot room). The baths were built during the reign of Emperor Caracalla in the early third century AD in honour of Asclepios, the god of medicine. Only the basement and first floors remain, but no matter: I had my own bath with copious hot water and I definitely didn't need the frigidarium.

There are many museums but the Museum of Anatolian Civilizations was all I had time for, situated at the entrance of Ankara Castle. Originally a fifteenth-century bedesten (covered bazaar), now restored and housing a large collection of Palaeolithic, Neolithic, Hatti, Hittite, Phrygian, Urartian and Roman works of art, there is also a section dedicated to Lydian treasures. I was weakening by late afternoon and passing an outdoor quadrangle where Ankarians were sitting with what looked suspiciously like glasses of beer I approached hopefully.

There were no spare tables but, noticing my need, the waiter ushered me to a stool at a table of young drinkers and I was soon in possession of a stein of Efes beer in the style of German lager. When my drinking pals realised I was an English speaker I was roped in to the role of teacher as they practised their English. They were students studying engineering at the polytechnic, as I once had in what seemed like another life. The late afternoon passed pleasantly in the last rays of sun; as it got too cold to sit longer, I wished them good luck with their upcoming exams and headed for a long, hot soak and another belly-busting indulgence and early bed, in preparation for the morrow's ride.

Ankara can't be seen in a day or a month, but I'd enjoyed walking the streets and being a tourist for a day, instead of a biker on a mad mission of my own foolish making. I made a mental note to come again to Ankara in the future and explore the region, but just like Kashmir all these years later I still haven't – perhaps next year.

I allowed myself a lie-in and another hot bath before leaving; there was no saying when the next would be. Then, after a quick check of the Enfield's chain tension and a spark plug clean and reset, I packed my kit, pilfered a roll of toilet paper; well, I was on a budget, and my case of Baluchi belly showed no sign it was cured. Then I roared out of the basement engine echoing loudly – well, not quite roaring: 350cc Enfields don't roar, they bupp, bupp, bupp – and in minutes I was back on the highway and bupping west.

As I rode I contemplated those who had also once travelled this ancient route: emperors, generals, kings and consuls, sultans, Mongol warlords, caliphs from Baghdad, bishops from Byzantium and every other variety of uninvited invaders. All of them could be pigeonholed into either a mercenary, missionary or misfit, and I realised that here I was in the latter category. Alexander had ridden through on his favourite horse, Bucephalus, and now it was our turn, a three-and-a-half-horsepower Indian-made motorbike with a ten-and-a-half-stone misfit riding it. I thought of nicknaming the Enfield 'Bucephalus 3.5' but it would have been pretentious and rather poor form; let sleeping horses lie.

The day was cold but the snow held off and after the usual stops for bowel relief, and to warm my hands on the exhaust pipe by the roadside, the day threw up no greater challenges. In late afternoon we sighted the famed Bosporus. I'd been looking forward to this milestone for weeks, sometimes doubting it would happen. The bridge over the historic waterway was the biggest engineering feat I had seen since the Sukkur Barrage, where I'd crossed the equally historic Indus River that had once been crossed by the great general on Bucephalus..

Xerxes, Darius, Mandrocles of Samos...

Alexander the Great, Venus Williams and Tiger Woods

The plans for a bridge over the Bosporus dates to antiquity. Herodotus in his *Histories* tells us that Mandrocles of Samos engineered a pontoon bridge across the Bosporus in 513 BC, to link Asia to Europe, allowing Darius to pursue the fleeing Scythians and march his army into the Balkans to sack Macedon. Leonardo da Vinci designed a parabolic arch bridge for Sultan Bayezid II in 1502 but it was never built. The first permanent bridge was proposed to the Ottoman Sultan Abdul Hamid II by the Bosporus Railroad Company in 1900, for a rail link between the continents of Asia and Europe.

In 1957, nearly two and a half thousand years after Mr Mandrocles' first effort, the prevarication ended. Prime Minister Menderes decided a bridge was needed, but it wasn't till a contract was signed with the British structural engineers Freeman Fox & Partners in 1968 that work began. And the designers of the Humber Bridge, Severn Bridge, and Forth Road Bridge – Gilbert Roberts, William Brown and Michael Parsons – sharpened their pencils.

Construction began in February 1970. The Cleveland Bridge Company (England) manufactured the steelwork. Turkish engineering company Enka won the contract to build it; it was opened on 30 October 1973 by President Fahri Korutürk on the fiftieth anniversary of the founding of the Republic of Turkey, at a cost of US$200 million ($1.13 billion in 2020 funny money).

Much was made of it being the first bridge between Europe and Asia since the pontoon bridge of Xerxes in 480 BC. But Xerxes' bridge of boats had spanned the Dardanelles, halfway down the Gallipoli peninsula, and not the Bosporus. Mandrocles' bridge for Emperor Darius was the first over the Bosporus, almost 2,500 years ago.

But we aren't done yet: there is much more to the history of this two-and-a-half-millennia-late silver medallist.

Trivia time

On 15 May 2005 (as I was driving through Abbottabad past O.B.L.'s retirement villa), the USA's Venus Williams played a game of tennis against Turkish player İpek Şenoğlu on the bridge, sponsored as the first tennis match played on two continents simultaneously. The game lasted five minutes to promote the Women's Tennis Association Istanbul Cup; afterwards they both hit a ball into the Bosporus to symbolise the game. Well, why shouldn't they? Go the Sisterhood.

Not to be outdone following this historic sporting event, and to uphold male pride, on 17 July 2005 British Formula One driver David Coulthard drove his Red Bull racing car across the bridge from the European side to the Asian side, executed a power-slide turn of burning rubber at the toll barriers, and raced back to the European side – just because he could. Coulthard's stunt was caught by the surveillance cameras; he was fined 20 euros for evading the toll booths. I bet that hurt.

And we are not done yet – on 5 November 2013, Tiger Woods was delivered to the bridge by helicopter to make some golf drives, hitting several mighty efforts with his No 1 from the Asian side to the European side - the first to hike a golf ball between two continents - while the traffic was stopped for an hour. I bet that made him popular. It isn't known if he hit any into the water.

Xerxes, Darius, Mandrocles, Alexander, Venus Williams, Davy Coulthard, Tiger Woods: what renown, what history. Where will it end? where do we find such men and women? And we aren't done yet.

On a lesser note, I also have a modest place among it all. For as far as I know, in April 1980 I became the only person to cross the bridge from the Asian to the European side riding a three-and-a-half-horsepower gunmetal-grey Indian Enfield motorcycle – and, in the unlikely event anyone else has done so since, I'm sure I'm the only one to have ridden across with a wad of stolen toilet paper up their ass.

Istanbul

I moved into the slow lane – it was the safest place for such as us – pulled up at the toll booth and handed over some Turkish lire, then we began to ride slowly across. I wanted to make this moment last; it had been a long time coming. I had thought about it often and sometimes wondered if I would ever reach this milestone, and I would certainly never do it again. It felt symbolic of the journey crossing from one continent to another, even the sun was shining.

A strong wind was coming down the Bosporus strait from the Black Sea, and I had to lean to my right at an uncomfortably steep angle to keep upright. It was a satisfying feeling, looking at the western shore as it came slowly closer and the European continent loomed, though the mosques and minarets on the skyline still spoke of Asia. After riding from India through Pakistan, Baluchistan and Iran, I was leaving Asia geographically, but the actual Turkish border with Greece was still 250km further away at Edirne.

The Turkish boundary with Greece was established by the Treaty of Lausanne (1923). Under the agreement, most of the Greek-speaking community of western Turkey were forced to resettle in Greece, while many Turkish-speaking residents of Thrace were resettled in Turkey, some of them to the Gallipoli peninsula, where they fished and farmed for a livelihood.

On the European side I headed for the travellers' quarter of Sultan Ahmet and found a room in a backstreet pensione, and while no one was watching I wheeled the Enfield inside it. No private bath here, as

Buddhist Shrines on the trail to Mt Everest

View from Bung to Gudel or is it Gudel to Bung?
Traditional shingle roofs are rare these days

Lancashire Landing cemetery looking toward Cape Helles memorial to the
missing. Commemorating the 20,956 men with no known graves who died during
the Gallipoli campaign

Breakfast stop on the Grand Trunk road to Kashmir at a chai dhaba

Memorial to the youngest British casualty Skew Bridge cemetry

The 1980 Polish expedition base camp on the Khumbu glacial moraine. The first successful winter ascent of Mt Everest

Everest from Kala Pather summit

Rice Farming families in the Arun valley working in their fields

All that remains of the lighter abandonded at Gully beach during the evacuation when general Maude left his kit behind in the confusion

Mowing the Taj Mahal lawns by bullock power

Arun Valley sisters outside their village school 1980

Making a puja and leaving coin to the toothache Goddess
is cheaper than a dentist

Tibetan Lady wearing her antique coral
jewellery of many hereditary generations

Traditional Tibetan dress still worn by older generations in the Solu Khumbu

Women Porters carrying steel roof sheets to Namache Bazaar market. These loads weigh up to 50kg. Men sometimes carry 80 or 100kg. Porters are paid by weight carried

I'd had last night, but I had got my lire's worth, while I'd had it. I had neither enough time nor money to spend long in Istanbul, but in two days I could see some sights. At the top of my list was Haghia Sophia, the Blue Mosque and the Basilica Cistern. If dank, dim cavernous subterranean feats of ancient reservoir engineering aren't your thing, then skip the next section.

The subterranean Basilica cistern (reservoir) was built during the reign of Emperor Constantine in the fourth century AD to provide Constantinople with a reserve water supply against times of drought or siege. The Basilica Cistern is the largest of hundreds of cisterns beneath Istanbul. It stands near the Haghia Sophia at Sultan Ahmet. Following the Ottoman conquest the cistern fell into disuse and was built over and largely forgotten until rediscovered to a wider world by the Frenchman, Petrus Gyllius, in 1545. Petrus enquired about the origins of live fish for sale in a local market and was shown an access shaft to the underground reservoir, where local families used small coracles for catching fish.

The name Basilica Cistern derives from the old public square of Constantinople. Before the site was converted into a cistern, a Basilica stood there. According to ancient historians, Emperor Constantine built the original cistern. It was enlarged later by Emperor Justinian after the Nika riots of AD 532, which destroyed much of the old city. It is claimed that 7,000 slaves were employed in its construction. The Great Cistern provided a water supply and filtration system to the Great Palace of Constantinople, and continued providing water to the Topkapi Palace after the Ottoman conquest of 1453.

The subterranean chamber measures almost 9,000 square metres – and was once capable of holding 80,000 cubic metres of water. The roof is supported by 336 marble columns, 9m in height, arranged in twelve rows of twenty-eight spaced 4.9m apart. The capitals of the columns are of the Ionic and Corinthian styles; a few Doric columns are also found.

One of the columns is engraved with a carving of a hen's eye and teardrops. This column is thought to have come from the Triumphal

Arch of Theodosius I, as it resembles other columns found there from the fourth century AD (379–395), once erected in the 'Forum Tauri' Square. One theory suggests that the tears pay tribute to the hundreds of slaves who died during its construction. But I doubt Justinian would have cared much for the memory of his dead slaves, especially after the Nika riots that destroyed half the city.

Most columns are thought to have been salvaged from the ruins of older buildings – a process called 'spoliation' – and brought to Constantinople from various outposts of the Roman Empire. The evidence for this is seen in the varying types of marble and granite originating from different quarries, and the differing architectural ages of the columns, Doric, Ionic and Corinthian all being used, from different eras of Greek architecture.

Fifty stone steps descend into the cool dripping, dark cavern. The cistern is enclosed by a wall of hard burned brick known as firebrick, up to four metres thick. Some of the original waterproof cement rendering still survives. I ran my hands over the columns and render with pleasure; perhaps the last hands to have touched the same spot belonged to the artisans who made or erected it. I have a weakness for hand-crafted ancient artefacts.

I don't want to bore those who have persevered this far by going into the history of cement, but, that said, it was first used by the Romans, then lost to history as an unrecorded manufacturing technique, and only reinvented 2,000 years later by the Yorkshireman Joseph Aspdin in 1824 – they can be a bit slow in Yorkshire. The Great Cistern is one of the oldest surviving examples of Roman cement-building technology.

The Great Cistern's water supply came from the Eğrikapı aquifer in the Belgrade Forest, north of the city, named during the Balkan Wars when Serbian POWs were brought there as slaves to maintain the city water source. If ever a city were built by slaves, it must be Constantinople – Istanbul. Water was channelled into the cistern via the 970m Valens Aqueduct and the 115m Mağlova Aqueduct, built by Emperor Justinian.

The cistern had the capacity to store 80,000 tons of water, though only a metre depth is kept in it now, home to carp and goldfish that keep the water clean and free from worms. The weight of the cistern's roof and the forum above it is transferred onto the ancient columns by vaulted brick arches. A masterpiece of the engineers' and stonemasons' skills; let us say the same of the work of the many slaves who died in its construction.

The cistern had many restorations over the centuries, the first during Ottoman rule in the reign of Ahmed III in 1723. The second major repair was in the nineteenth century, during the reign of Sultan Abdul Hamid II (1876–1909). In recent times, some cracked masonry and damaged columns were repaired in 1968, when 50,000 tons of mud and debris were also removed, and walkways built to replace the punts previously used by tourists to see the cistern.

In one corner, the pedestals of two columns supporting artfully carved Medusa heads can be found; one is set on its side, the other upside down. I ran my hands over their slimy, cold, coiled, coiffured snake hairstyles: what history. Whose long-dead, anonymous hands carved these goddesses' heads, and from where in the Roman world did they come from to spend eternity in this dank, dripping cistern? Their origins are unknown; it is thought they were brought there from a site of the late Roman period, possibly salvaged from earthquake destroyed temples. There is no evidence they were used as column pedestals before they were brought here.

Popular reason says that the Medusas' heads are inverted to deny the power of the gorgon's gaze. However, it is more likely that both were placed to support the columns because this would better suit the height of the column to the vaulted roof; this is my theory, anyway, purely a practical engineering reason, though superstitious theories have more appeal, even to a cynic like myself. A gorgon would love this dark, dripping cavern, and some defence against its fatal gaze would be needed.

A gorgon is a female god, the word deriving from the ancient Greek *Gorgós*, meaning dreadful. While descriptions of gorgons vary in early

Greek literature, the term refers to any of the three sisters whose hair was formed of living snakes, and whose horrifying gaze turned those gazed upon to stone. Two of the Gorgon sisters were immortal, Stheno and Euryale, but their sister Medusa was not, and was slain by Perseus. I like the ring of the Gorgon Sisters; it sounds like a '70s Tamla Mo-town act. I'm surprised the name was never used for one.

If ancient subterranean reservoirs are your passion and I can't think why they wouldn't be, then the Basilica Cistern must rank high on your Istanbul bucket list, not to be missed for the treasures of the ancient world. But for many it is a sideshow to the countless other architectural attractions of Istanbul. Whether or not you are a cistern admirer or prefer your antiquity less dark and damp, you should not miss this classic engineering feat of antiquity, even at the risk of being turned to stone. If this is not enough to tempt you down the steps, there is a souvenir shop below selling Medusa snake-head tea towels and bottle openers.

Emerging into the light, I went for lunch to the nearby café on the forum once famous throughout Hippydom as the 'Istanbul Pudding Shop'. When I first passed through Istanbul in 1974, it was the hangout of choice, known all along the hippy trail from Istanbul to Kathmandu. I had lunch there, pondering the idiosyncrasy of this old hippy HQ overlooking the old Roman hippodrome.

Its famous noticeboard once provided such an array of travel information and contacts it took half a day to read them. Its time has passed, though there are still some yellowing photos on its walls of those heady smoke-filled days, man. I recalled a hirsute American hippy in 1974 who sat at a table with a briefcase of forged student cards for an hour every lunch time. For two dollars you could buy a student card stamped from any university requested, giving you a discount on bus and train tickets and most European cultural sites. The most popular were Oxford and Cambridge cards, but he hadn't got a stamp for Preston Polytechnic. But the hippies have long gone, like red phone boxes their passing is regretted but no real loss. Nostalgic lunch over, I walked to the Galata Bridge.

I couldn't resist the chestnuts roasted on vendors charcoal fires along the bridge. Sitting on a bench eating chestnuts, I watched the bustle passing, noticing how it had changed since my visit in 1974: few beggars now; then there had been many. The bridge was still lined with men and women of pension age fishing for sprats to supplement their larder and sell to pedestrians and tourists. They smelled delicious fried on portable gas stoves and served in crusty rolls, but I was too full of chestnuts.

I walked through the famous spice bazaar into the historic Kapali Carsi – the covered bazaar. Its vaulted brick domes supported on hundreds of masonry columns. It is easy to get lost in its labyrinthine alleyways, though there are numerous entrances so a way out is never far. The bazaar of over 4,000 shops and sixty-six alleyways can trace its history to 1453, the early years of the Ottoman Empire, built on the site of an earlier market from Byzantine times.

I wandered through the alleys, avoiding eye contact with the infamous carpet sellers. It is no place for idle loitering; should you hesitate you will be ushered into a shop, and before you can say 'just looking, mate' will find yourself sat on a three-legged stool in front of a stack of carpets. Or admiring the workmanship of a scimitar, or a set of brass knuckledusters, or some other thing you're too old for. The idea is to keep on moving; window gazing is a sales opportunity. And you will need the negotiating skills of a secretary of state to get a bargain. Once a price is agreed you are bound by honour to buy; the more glasses of free tea you accept, the more your honour is on the line. I escaped into the street, hand on wallet like the miser my limited funds dictated.

I worked through the cobbled backstreets to Haghia Sophia, once the largest church in the world, completed in AD 537 on the site of two previous churches destroyed in riots – If there is one ancient city that can claim to have been founded by rioting mobs, it must be Istanbul.

Haghia Sophia

If the Basilica Cistern is the must see of subterranean sights, Haghia Sophia is the above-ground T-shirt to have. Starting religious life as Christendom's finest cathedral, it became Islam's biggest mosque on the fall of Constantinople to the Ottomans in 1453. Today it is a museum of ancient mosaic art and religious icons, a testament to the architectural, engineering and craftsmanship of the anonymous lives who built it in ancient times.

If we read the history books we are told that Aya Sofya – to give it its Turkish name – was built by the Roman emperor Justinian. Let me say, as one who started work at the age of fifteen on construction sites, that Justinian never laid a brick in his life. Emperors, presidents, pontiffs and prime ministers don't labour in the hot sun on construction sites; they get others to do it.

Justinian simply cut the ribbon and went down in history as its builder. An habitual lie: it was built by anonymous craftsmen and slaves; Justinian simply paid the bills out of the taxes he imposed on pain of death on the population. A great many of the real builders died at their labours, yet not a mention of them or an engraved stone to their mighty efforts is found.

It is no different today. Australians say Jørn Utzon built the Sydney Opera House – well, those in Sydney, at least, though Melbourne's citizens would be hard pressed to tell you his name. What they don't know is that I had a modest hand in it too, along with thousands of others. Where's our historic legacy? A bit of respect, please, you recorders of history. If every undistinguished politician can be immortalised with their name on every town hall foundation stone, then those who pay the wages and pensions of these timeservers should be remembered for their contributions.

Thousands of skilled craftsmen from Europe, the Middle East and Asia left their vision and workmanship on the walls, columns and soaring dome of the Aya Sofya for us to see and wonder at. I feel pity for those who find magnificent ancient buildings, or equally great modern feats of engineering, of little interest, though I can understand the envy of those whose work revolves around the boring grind of marketing design-your-own-coffee-cup websites.

For many, the great works of antiquity must seem overbearing. They are, however, missing the point in not admiring such great works, as it is likely we all had an ancestor who worked on such feats. So I feel some pity those who prefer developing melanomas on litter-kissed beaches, among lumpy red lookalikes, to gazing at the dappled light filtering through stained glass windows in the cool interior of such great works as Aya Sofya.

There is something mystical about running a hand over the worn smooth patina of a long-dead artisan's work on a fluted marble column, wondering how it was quarried without a power source other than horses and men, then transported from its quarry and carved to such perfection before being lifted into position in an age without machinery – or an engineering office of nerds, sipping coffee from designer cups while sweating over Microsoft Engineer Version 20.20.

In night classes at technical college I was taught to plot the geometric design of a classical Grecian pedestal, column and capital scroll, using only ruler, compass, divider, pencil and paper. In the 1960s we had no computers and weren't allowed to use a calculator; we used the tools the Greek mathematicians and architects had when they first formulated the geometry and design of columns and scrolls, as had been done by the anonymous artisans in the quarries of the ancient world.

During my introduction to the mysteries of Grecian column

design and engineering in the 1960s, I was sadly more interested in getting night class over with and out to the Globe Hotel across the road for what we apprentices called 'a swift one' – a pint of lukewarm Thwaite's bitter. If we got out early there would be time for two before the bus home. Any more and there was a risk the conductor wouldn't let me on, and that meant a six-mile walk. It's all a long time ago but some of what I learned from John and Joe still lingers in my mind.

So I will take the opportunity to say thank you, Joe Lindley and John Cross, Harris College of Engineering Technology, Preston, Lancashire – an industrial town of the cotton days of the early nineteenth century, an odd place in which to have been taught Grecian column design. Thanks, Joe and John, for your efforts teaching knucklehead apprentices some geometry of the classical era. I didn't get it at the time but I do now – it's about continuity. But try telling that to today's information technology nerds; they'd only want to get out early for several swift shooters.

The guidebook tells us that for the best part of a thousand years Aya Sofya was the largest enclosed space in the world. Consider what this means: it's a sobering thought. It means architectural and engineering technology practice stood still or declined for a millennium. Today this great building is still one of the world's largest covered spaces.

The great Byzantium Cathedral suffered many sacrileges during its 900-year life as a church. The worst was in 1204, when the Catholic knights of the Fourth Crusade sacked the city, removing everything that could be carried away on hundreds of mules. As a finishing touch, they seated a prostitute on the Orthodox patriarch's throne. I'm not sure what religious purpose this served.

The cathedral was born out of the Nika riots of AD 532, when the population rose against Emperor Justinian's excessive taxation, destroyed half the city and burned down the original church on the site. Unruly behaviour has been part of the city's history ever since. Justinian's revenge was brutal and most of the rioters were killed. The result was more deaths and taxes. I wonder if that is where the old saying 'the only certainties in life are death and taxes' comes from.

In 1452 the Seljuk Turks were at the city gates under Sultan Mehmet II. The guidebook tells us Mehmet built the Rumeli Hisari fortress – actually he didn't, his slaves did, but let's not go there again. Mehmet was in control of all shipping entering the straits from the Black Sea, blocking access into the city and controlling all trade into the Sea of Marmara and the Mediterranean.

He had positioning his navy in the Sea of Marmara, blocking access from the south and preventing Emperor Constantine's allies reaching the city by sea. With the city cut off from supplies and allies, the bombardment of the city's land walls began – these comprised a strong defence line built between the Marmara and the Golden Horn channel. For this purpose, Mehmet had hired artillery mercenaries and ballistic weapons experts from Christian Europe.

Constantine positioned a massive iron chain across the Golden Horn at its mouth, preventing Mehmet's navy from entering the strait. In the books it tells us Mehmet hauled his ships over the hills of Galata, launching them above the chain blockade (actually his slaves did this, but try telling that to a historian). Then attacks began on the city by a cannonade from his ships. The population panicked and began defecting as the bombardment of the land walls began.

Orban, a Hungarian metallurgist, had offered his services to Emperor Constantine, who declined to pay the fee demanded for constructing huge cannons to defend the city. In the best mercenary tradition, Orban then offered his services to Sultan Mehmet, claiming his cannons could breach 'the walls of Babylon itself'. Mehmet paid up and Orban cast the giant cannons in three months at Adrianople; the massive guns were dragged to Constantinople by a team of sixty oxen.

The largest cannons ever built were brought into position and began bombarding the city walls. Over seven weeks, 7,000 defenders held the siege at bay, until, on 29 May, the cannonade succeeded in breaching the walls between the Edirnekapi and Topkapi gates and 60,000 Ottoman attackers poured into the city; its inhabitants were slaughtered wherever they were found.

It is claimed Orban and his gun crew were killed during the siege when one of his cannons exploded, or just maybe Mehmet didn't want him sneaking off to build bigger cannons for another conqueror, just my thoughts. Constantine XI, the last Byzantine emperor, was killed among his 7,000 defenders on the land walls of Constantinople. His body was never found among the thousands of dead.

Legend has it that, as the Ottomans entered the great Cathedral of Haghia Sophia, the Greek Orthodox patriarch who was conducting mass vaporised into the walls, and will not reappear until the church is once more in Greek Orthodox control; it's been a long time already.

During the siege the Byzantine Christians were forced to beg for military aid from the Catholic powers in Rome in a last-ditch attempt to save the city for Christendom, but it was too late coming. Diehard Orthodox clergy pronounced they would rather see the turban of the Turk than the mitre of a Catholic cardinal in the great church, and got their wish when the city fell to Mehmet on 29 May 1453. Mehmet held his first Islamic service a week later; the great church was now a mosque.

The Gallipoli Battlefields

After two days slogging through Istanbul's damp streets, it was time to saddle up. I wanted time to visit some of the Commonwealth War Graves Commission (CWGC) monuments, cemeteries and the landing sites of the WW1 Gallipoli campaign. I set out early in light rain but as I turned south along the Gallipoli peninsula the day brightened up and my tatty army surplus jacket had dried out by the time I stopped for a sardine lunch at Gallipoli town. The sun kept shining and I arrived in late afternoon at the small port of Eceabat (Maidos during the Gallipoli campaign), the fishing village on the European shore of the Cannakale Strait, known to the Allies in WW1 as the Dardanelles Strait.

Ever since I had read Moorehead's book *Gallipoli* in a small village in the highlands of Papua New Guinea I had wanted to see where the Anzacs and British seaborne forces had come ashore under intensive Turkish fire on 25 April 1915.

The Dardanelles has been a trade route since antiquity. In mythology, Jason and his crew in the *Argo* passed through the straits in their quest for the Golden Fleece. In Greek myth, Leander swam across the Hellespont for his nightly liaisons with the goddess Hero, a feat copied by Lord Byron. Byron swam across the Dardanelles (Hellespont) on 3 May 1810. Born with a club foot, Byron found a freedom swimming that he didn't when walking. Byron claimed his swim across the Hellespont was his greatest achievement.

'Swimming the Hellespont' — Lord Byron.

If, in the month of dark December,
Leander, who was nightly wont
(What maid will not the tale remember?)
To cross thy stream, broad Hellespont!

If, when the wintry tempest roared,
He sped to Hero, nothing loath,
And thus of old thy current poured,
Fair Venus! how I pity both!

For me, degenerate modern wretch,
Though in the genial month of May,
My dripping limbs I faintly stretch,
And think I've done a feat today.

But since he crossed the rapid tide,
According to the doubtful story,
To woo -and -Lord knows what beside,
And swam for Love, as I for Glory;

'Twere hard to say who fared the best:
Sad mortals! thus the gods still plague you!
He lost his labour, I my jest;
For he was drowned, and I've the ague.

Herodotus tells us that in 480 BC Xerxes ordered his engineers to build a bridge across the Hellespont at Abydos, for his army to cross from Persia into Greece, a feat repeated by Alexander the Great in the opposite direction to invade Persia in 334 BC. Alexander's army carried on to India to cross the Indus in 326 BC, where at great loss he defeated King Porus.

It was after this Pyrrhic victory that Alexander's Macedonian army, homesick and tired of wars, refused to march further east. Alexander reluctantly ordered his now-diminished yet conquering army to set out on the journey back to Babylon through the Punjab and Sindh, recrossing the Indus and marching along the Makran coast of Baluchistan, not far south of my own route through that desert land, many of his weakened men dying of exhaustion and thirst along the way, as I imagined I might have done if the Enfield had broken down and I'd had no water left.

According to Herodotus, Xerxes' pontoon bridge across the Hellespont was destroyed by an untimely storm. In a fit of rage Xerxes had the engineers responsible beheaded. Xerxes was said to have thrown iron fetters into the strait, and ordered it be given 300 lashes and had it branded with red-hot irons as his soldiers shouted insults at the water. Herodotus wrote this was 'a presumptuous way to address the Hellespont'.

Today a regular flow of visitors use Eceabat as a base for touring the WW1 battle sites, monuments and Commonwealth war cemeteries at Anzac and Cape Helles. During the annual remembrance service on 25 April, commemorating the date of the first landings, the hotels in Cannakale, on the Asian side of the straits and Eceabat, are fully booked with Australian and New Zealand backpackers who have made the sites a place of pilgrimage. But it wasn't so in 1980; no backpacker hostels existed then. And there were no guided tours or information boards nor any signage to the many locations of interest as there are today. I found a small pensioni on a potholed backstreet where I was able to park the Enfield in the sunny courtyard.

Early the next morning at the small village of Kilitbahir on the road to Cape Helles I stopped for breakfast at the only café, warming up by the stove among Turkish workers having a tea break. To questions of why I was there I explained I came to visit the WW1 cemeteries and battlefields, and I was on my way to Cape Helles Memorial to the Missing at Seddülbahir. Very few foreign visitors came to Gallipoli in 1980, even fewer riding a motorcycle, and I was a curiosity. In broken English an older man told me to wait, and I settled in for another glass of tea. He returned with a plate of cheese, olives, tomatoes and bread, refusing any payment. I was always shown great hospitality on the Gallipoli peninsula, and throughout Turkey.

The Gallipoli campaign was a war between empires; the British Empire was at the peak of its power but about to start a long decline and withdrawal from its far-flung territories. The partly dismembered Ottoman Empire was already in its death throws after a series of military defeats in the Balkans. The Austro-Hungarian Empire, also in decline, and being challenged by Russia. The actions that took place at Gallipoli would lead to further weakening of the Ottoman Empire and then its reformation as a unified Turkish state and modern nation. In April 1915 neither empire foresaw the effects on their fortunes shaped by the tragic events that took place there.

I continued riding through the peaceful farmlands to the Cape Helles Memorial to the Missing (those with no known grave). As you stand looking upon the thousands of names engraved on the memorial, the enormity and futility of so many young lives lost has its effect. The long list of regimental names on the tablets reminds us that the men who died here came from just about every corner of the British Isles and its far dominions, to lose their lives in a cause that few understood the political complexities of.

In the 1960s I was at school in Lancashire, whose industrial towns and farming villages had sent thousands of young men to be killed here, hundreds on the first day alone. At Cape Helles Memorial I was only half a mile from where they had fought their way ashore through the barbed-wire entanglements upon which they died in hundreds, easy targets for the Turkish snipers dug in on the cliffs above. Many were killed before they reached the beach, shot in open landing boats by sustained fire from the Turkish marksmen on the cliffs, others drowned weighed down by their equipment as they abandoned the boats to avoid the accuracy of the Turkish riflemen.

Looking upon the names of the Lancashire men engraved on the monument and its perimeter panels, I began to wonder why generations of Lancashire school children were not aware of their sacrifice. During my school days I never heard the name Gallipoli. It wasn't taught at school. I was taught instead of Clive and the Battle of Plassey, of General Wolfe's victory at Quebec, and Baden Powell at Mafeking: high points of empire but none of the blunders such as Gallipoli.

Only in Australia did I become aware of the sacrifices that took place on these shores and among these hills and ravines. Though the Gallipoli front was a secondary campaign to the Western Front, the fighting was every bit as desperate as the battles of the Somme. Yet, in contrast to Flanders fields and the Somme, very few visitors from Britain tour the lonely cemeteries of Gallipoli. Though for those that do it is an interesting place, culturally, geographically and for historic military interest.

There are twenty-eight plaques on the Cape Helles monument bearing the names of the men and boys of the Lancashire Fusiliers who perished on the beaches, and among the hills and gullies hereabouts, three times more than any other regiment honoured there. Lancashire lost so many men and boys that some towns didn't recover for many years.

I walked slowly around the obelisk, reading the names of the naval ships and their companies, whose dead are also honoured here. Many young sailors were killed on that first day, shot dead at the oars in the landing crafts as they rowed their open boats packed full of soldiers to the beaches into a hail of rifle fire. Many soldiers never got ashore, shot in the boats: easy targets for Turkish snipers on the heights overlooking the beaches.

Research in recent times has cast doubt whether there were machine guns at the Cape Helles landings on 25 April 1915, but accounts of survivors claim there were two, no one can be certain of it now. What is not disputed was the accuracy and discipline of the Turkish rifle fire. It was so heavy and continuous that it may have been taken for machine guns. The Turks had placed heavy wire entanglements submerged in the shallows that proved difficult to surmount causing many casualties as they waded in from the grounded boats fifty yards offshore. Many of those that did get ashore became trapped against wire entanglements on the beach. Lines of bodies began piling up before the wire; the wire cutters the men carried proved worthless against the heavy-gauge Turkish wire.

I left the Enfield at the café in Seddülbahir village; the owner offering to look after it. The day was warm and it was nice to be out of the saddle, walking along the track to Lancashire Landing Cemetery, through the fields of young wheat where once the bullets and shells flew thick, but now so quiet. A farm tractor passed; the driver acknowledged me, knowing where I was going and why I was there.

The first grave I came to along the track was that of Lieutenant Colonel Doughty-Wylie VC, staff officer, 9th Division, the division allocated to General Hamilton by Lord Kitchener, chief of the British army. Doughty-Wylie's grave is the only known individual grave of a British soldier at Cape Helles. He had gathered the survivors of the Munster Fusiliers, Dublin Fusiliers and Hampshire Regiment, who were pinned down by intensive Turkish rifle fire, with most of their officers killed.

Doughty-Wylie had been awarded the Imperial Ottoman Order of Medijedieh, for his service to the Turkish wounded when he was working with the Red Cross during the Balkan Wars of 1912–1913. As a fluent Turkish speaker, he was attached as intelligence officer on the troop transport ship *River Clyde*. From the ship he observed the failure of the British troops under intense Turkish fire to make progress inland from Ertuğrul Koyu (Cove). On the morning of 26 April, along with Captain Garth Walford, Royal Field Artillery, and Major Beckwith of the Hampshires, they gathered the scattered survivors and led a charge into Seddülbahir.

The village was taken, but Doughty-Wylie knew the beach would not be safe until Eskitabya fort was also taken. At the head of a bayonet charge, he led his men up the hill and captured the fort. It is said that, because of his love for the Turkish people, he carried only a walking stick into action, not wanting to take up arms against them. Doughty-Wylie and Capt. Walford, who was also killed, were awarded posthumous Victoria Crosses.

His leadership and bravery were testified to by many that day; his death, according to witnesses, had been avoidable if he had been in the habit of taking cover. He was standing upright to observe Turkish positions with his orderly when they were both killed by snipers. Earlier in the action his cap had been shot off the top of his head. Captain Nightingale of the Munster Fusiliers saw it happen and described the colonel as calm and unflinching. Doughty-Wylie has been criticised by historians for being reckless of his safety at a time when officers were sorely needed.

In theory, as a staff officer he should have been watching from the rear, reporting back to the higher command, organising the reserves, sending and receiving messages and making tactical plans. The situation had gone beyond observing: actions were needed. He had led from the front and paid with his life. It was following the taking of the fort as he stood to observe the retreating Turks' new positions that he was shot and killed.

He was buried where he fell by Lieutenant Colonel Lancey Williams, who had come up with reinforcements. Williams described it: 'I found him on the top of the hill by the fort, we just buried him where he lay and I said the Lord's Prayer over his grave. I am firmly of the opinion that Doughty-Wylie realised he would be killed in this war and went singing cheerily to his death.' There we have the account from one of his own: he died leading the men who later honoured him as a hero.

A strange event was witnessed on 17 November 1915, a small boat brought ashore the only woman to visit Gallipoli during the whole of the campaign. Covered by a veil, she walked through Seddülbahir and on to Doughty-Wylie's grave, where she laid a wreath. Was it was his wife, Lillian? It was known that Doughty-Wylie kept a correspondence with Gertrude Bell from 1913 until his death. Bell was an English writer, traveller, political officer and archaeologist who explored in Syria, Mesopotamia, Asia Minor and Arabia. Was the black-shrouded visitor Gertrude Bell or his wife? It has never been confirmed.

Further on, the track forked left to Lancashire Landing Cemetery. The Lancashire Fusiliers had been tasked with coming ashore on W Beach, the most strongly defended beach at Cape Helles. I wanted to visit as many of the CWGC sites as possible in the little time I had, but I had come to Lancashire Landing Cemetery first. Having been born in Lancashire, it was my first priority. Now I stood at the cemetery gate, feeling the heaviness that comes on at these cemeteries for all the lives cut short. After some minutes quietly looking, I went in, walking along the headstones and reading the names of those who it had been possible to identify.

The CWGC keeps all its cemeteries well maintained. The Turkish people respect the monuments and cemeteries; I never saw vandalism, graffiti or even litter. It says much, especially when you see the litter lying around the war memorials of Britain's towns. Why these values survive in Turkey and other countries where I have visited CWGC cemeteries, yet have declined in Britain, I don't know.

As a carpenter, I notice the detail in these monuments: the traditional joinery of the oak gates, with mortised and tenoned rails and stiles, opening on smoothly working band-and-gudgeon hinges; the neatly fitting masonry of the perimeter retaining walls and Altar of Sacrifice. Weather-worn and cracked headstones are replaced with new by local artisans. The retaining walls and drainage channels kept clear of debris, the headstones still legible despite where lichens and mosses thrive. I left school on my fifteenth birthday for my first job as an apprentice joiner; when you have done an apprenticeship in that, your eye for detail is well developed. It was satisfying to see that skilled craftsmanship was still valued in these cemeteries and monuments.

I felt both pride and sadness as I walked along the rows of headstones: pride for the way all these men are not forgotten, their graves not forlorn, and sadness for the lives cut short. There is egalitarianism in a war cemetery as nowhere else, with the spirit of sacrifice and comradeship of these young men to their countries, to each other and to their families left behind. If we are not moved by these cemeteries, we are without feeling; I doubt such a person exists. No one else was there that April day, the silence broken only by birdsong, and a goat bell nearby.

I spent an hour walking the rows of headstones naming the 1,252 soldiers and sailors who could be identified, stopping occasionally to read an inscription, such as for Lancashire Fusilier R. Steel, aged 16: 'Thy will is just to thee we leave them now in trust.' You sense his father's faith, grief and trust at his choice of those few words, not only for his son but for them all, as the word 'them' testifies, as you also can for the epithet chosen by the grieving mother of Gunner A. Mackie, aged 20: 'Tread gently over a soldiers grave a mothers love lies there.' Chosen, you feel, not just for her son but for them all.

With feelings of sadness but also respect for all these young men who gave their lives for their country and what they believed was their duty in a faraway place unknown to most of them, I said my goodbye and closed the gate. The gates are necessary to keep goats and sheep from grazing on the shrubs and flowers surrounding the graves.

The battlefields have become wheat farms and grazing lands now, peaceful and still under the wide sky, and never very far from the sea. I noticed how similar the countryside was to the fields and farms of the Lancashire countryside I grew up in. I felt they were lying in a place that would have seemed familiar to them. Then I set off along the quiet lane towards Alçitepe. Known as Krithia in 1915, it had been the first day's objective for the British force. But it was never achieved in the whole campaign; thousands died in the three battles for it.

I was looking for a way onto W Beach. After a short walk, a small track branched off left, I followed it past some ruined buildings from when the area was a Turkish military base. Two barking dogs eyed me. I passed, keeping to the right side of the track as far from them as possible. The sheepdogs here have a fierce reputation.

The track petered out into a goat path. I followed it where the sheep and goats had forced a way through the scrub evident from the wool left on the thorns. It was decision time: go back or go on. I could see no easy way through but was reluctant to go back. I pushed through bushes and around stunted scrub oak till I saw a glimpse of the sea and made my way towards it. A cliff appeared but too steep to climb down without fatal consequences if I slipped. There was no one around here to find me and no one knew where I was if I did fall.

They say caution is the better part of valour, and I opted for it and turned around. These lonely cliffs had seen the meaning of real valour; any small risks I took would be unworthy of this place. I went back to a narrow goat path running parallel to the coastline. Following it, the undergrowth thinned out enough to find a way through to a view of the sea. I picked a way along to the path the goats used to descend it.

I followed the path down a short way to the sea. I was on W beach in the stillness where so many of those whose graves I had walked among had died; others had sheltered under the cliffs I had just come down, where Turkish snipers had shot many of them down. I felt a relief having got down to the beach, and a heaviness knowing that I stood at the site of many deaths of brave young men from many parts of Britain, and my own corner of England.

I felt a need to sit quietly for a while the silence and what seemed overbearing stillness having its effect. There were no distractions save for a gentle lapping of waves on the shingle, nothing to take thoughts away from where so many had died, so many the sea became red with their blood, as the accounts of witnesses waiting their turn to disembark the ships had observed.

I felt a sensation of being in a place where something terrible had once happened, yet the normality and peace was real, with only birds and a goat bell making any sound. The only other sound I made walking on the beach, and when I stood still only the sound of small waves lapping on the shingle. The rusting remains of piers jutting into the sea were still visible, and the stranded skeleton of a landing vessel, its rusting iron ribs in the shape of a boat, still lay half buried in the sand.

W Beach

German officers had been covertly attached to the Ottoman land forces at the Dardanelles, though it was no real secret. Sir Louis Mallet, the British ambassador in Istanbul, had been sending back reports on the Turkish defensive positions for months. The Turkish defences extended to all the cliffs and shores of the Hellespont beaches but especially W, X and V Beaches. The German advisors had plenty of time to plan the fortifications on the cliffs, and artillery bunkers hidden inland.

From the heights overlooking the 300m-long arc of W Beach, interlocking fields of rifle fire claimed many lives. Barbed-wire entanglements secured in the shallows and more above the shoreline prevented the men getting into cover. Land mines had also been buried on the beach. Both Turks and Germans considered it impossible for a successful landing of troops in small boats, yet this was carried out by weight of numbers, albeit with great losses.

W Beach landing plan called for the 1st Battalion Lancashire Fusiliers to go ashore in strings of four cutters towed by steam pinnaces. Once cut free in the shallows, they were rowed to the beach by ratings under the command of midshipmen, most of them in their teens. A platoon of the Anson Battalion, Division (Royal Navy) was attached to them; the 1st Essex Regiment was held in reserve.

As the cutters from HMS *Implacable* and HMS *Euryalus* neared the shore, the Turkish riflemen dug in on the cliffs opened a concentrated rifle fire. Many never got ashore and were killed in the boats; others jumped into the sea when it was seen that staying in the boats meant certain death. Some men drowned under the weight of packs and ammunition; others were shot as they got stuck on the barbed-wire barricades. Caught on the wire, they were easy targets for snipers: many that got ashore never got further than the wire. Despite these odds, some got through to the first line of Turkish trenches taking them at great loss.

Captain Richard Willis ('Walking Stick Willis') left this account of what happened to the picket boat he came ashore on. Willis won the VC for his actions during the landings.

The sea was like glass, but as the picket boats drew off to get into formation our boats heeled over dangerously, and one of the men remarked to the Cox, 'I listed to get killed, not to get drowned'. As the tows got to a safe distance from the ships the shelling began again, the guns lifting their fire as we approached the shore. When the water began to get shallow the picket boats called out 'Slip', for the tow ropes to be cast off, and we began to approach the shore under the oars of the naval ratings. There were five to each boat. Not a sign of life was to be seen on the Peninsula in front of us. It might have been a deserted land we were nearing in our little boats. Then crack! The stroke oar of my boat fell forward to the angry astonishment of his mates. The signal for the massacre had been given: rapid fire, machine guns and deadly accurate sniping opened from the cliffs above, and soon the casualties included the rest of the crew and many men. The timing of the ambush was perfect; we were completely exposed and helpless in our slow-moving boats, just target practice for the concealed Turks, and within a few minutes only half of the thirty men in my boat were left alive. We were now 100 yards from the shore, and I gave the order 'Overboard'. We scrambled out into some four feet of water, and some of the boats with their cargo of dead and wounded floated away on the currents, still under fire from the snipers. With this unpromising start the advance began. Many were hit in the sea, and no response was possible, for the enemy was in trenches well above our heads.

The soldiers detailed for W beach landing were the 1st Battalion Lancashire Fusiliers. By 7:30 am they had won six Victoria Crosses. There was so much sacrifice that the men selected for decorations were chosen by a ballot of survivors. The action became a huge point of pride in the town of Bury, the battalion HQ. The press soon coined the phrase – 'The six VCs before breakfast action'. The men awarded VCs were Captain Cuthbert Bromley, Corporal John Grimshaw, Private William Keneally, Sergeant Alfred Richards, Sergeant Frank Stubbs and Captain Richard Willis, quoted above.

As Sergeant Richards led his platoon through the wire entanglements and across fifty yards of beach, he was hit by a burst of fire, his leg almost severed by bullets: this is one argument for at least one machine gun being at W Beach. Dragging his leg, he crawled forward, urging his men on till they overran the first trenches; he was evacuated and his leg amputated.

Private Keneally was less fortunate. He had shown exceptional bravery, his VC celebrated by all in his home town of Wigan. He was killed later in the Battle of Krithia at Gully Ravine on 28 June aged twenty-eight. His family were not notified of his death until four months later; privates in 1915 didn't get the privilege of having their kin informed, as officers did, even if they were a VC winner. Born in Wexford, Ireland, his family moved to Lancashire when his father left the army. Keneally went into the Wigan coal mines at age thirteen; they were hardier people then.

Lieutenant General Sir Ian Hamilton, the overall Allied commander at Gallipoli, later ordered W Beach be renamed Lancashire Landing in honour of the lives lost and heavy casualties there, saying, 'No finer feat of arms has been achieved by the British Soldier than the storming of these beaches.'

Every year since 1916 on Gallipoli Sunday, the nearest Sunday to 25 April, a commemoration service is held in the Lancashire Fusiliers' regimental town of Bury. If you ask in a Lancashire pub beyond the town what Bury is famous for, they will tell you the weekly market and the best black puddings in England. Perhaps one in a hundred will know of the six VCs before breakfast or the landing of the Lancashire Fusiliers at Cape Helles.

After my return I visited Bury, taking a pine cone from Skew Bridge cemetery to lay at the war memorial. Not knowing Bury, I asked at the tourist information office where the war memorial was. They couldn't tell me, and hadn't heard of Gallipoli, Cape Helles or the six VCs. It was 200 metres away; how easily we forget. Compare this to Australia and New Zealand's teaching of the Gallipoli campaign, where every child is taught its significance. There is much to be proud of in Lancashire's military history. Lancashire is still a favourite recruiting ground for the British army, often the only meaningful job many of its young men will get.

Lancashire today would be unrecognisable to the Fusiliers who fought at Gallipoli. It was once a crucible of the Industrial Revolution and one of the largest manufacturing counties in Britain. It was why the Keneally family moved there from Ireland. Many Irish and Scottish were still doing so when I was growing up. My hometown, Leyland, was once known worldwide for its trucks and buses. But it's changed since I left school: dead-end jobs and few opportunities for its school leavers.

A force under Captain Thomas Frankland, 2nd Royal Fusiliers, had landed at X Beach better sheltered from Turkish rifle fire. Seizing the opportunity, he led them forward, outflanking the Turkish positions. From W Beach, the Lancashire Fusiliers fought their way through the Turkish defences to join up with the Royal Fusiliers at X Beach and take the objective of Hill 114 at a heavy cost in lives.

The guns of the *Euryalus* had also caused casualties among the Fusiliers as they fought their way through the defences to link up with the 2nd Royal Fusiliers. Later in the afternoon, the 1st Essex Regiment was landed to reinforce the decimated ranks of the Lancashire Fusiliers. When they had embarked in Egypt, the battalion's strength was 1,029; by the end of the first day it was just 410.

W Beach became the main supply beach for the duration of the Cape Helles campaign. It was one of three stormed that day by the 29th Division; V Beach landing also suffered heavy casualties. As the weeks went by, W Beach developed into a small port: four piers were built, allowing small boats to take off casualties and bring in supplies from the ships anchored out of range of Turkish artillery.

Casualty dressing stations and command bunkers were dug into the cliffs. Mule and horse lines, stables and farrier workshops were established; blacksmiths and weapons repair workshops sprang up, carpenters' workshops were built to repair carts and horse wagons needed for transporting ammunition, water and food to the front lines. W Beach became a busy HQ for the Cape Helles campaign and remained in constant use until the withdrawal on 9 January 1916.

I sat a while at the base of the cliffs, having a reflective think. I had ridden a long way and faced a few challenges along some dangerous roads to get here, a place I had wanted to visit for a long time. It was still and silent as I rested trying to imagine how it must have been on that fateful April day. Today the beach is still little used other than by a few Turkish holidaymakers; nearby is a small hotel used by foreign visitors to the memorials and cemeteries, but none of this existed in 1980, not even a small pensioni in the nearby farming and fishing village at Seddülbahir.

A small fishing boat a few hundred metres off the beach was puttering along, leaving wisps of exhaust smoke lingering on the flat blue sea as they sailed past the barnacle-encrusted remains of the WW1 piers that are still exposed at low tide. Some of the old Turkish trenches and sniper pits that caused many casualties can still be found, though most have become grown over. Several eroded remains of the dugouts used as command posts and casualty clinics were still visible. It is easy to imagine the carnage of that day as you look up from the beach; the advantage held by the Turkish defenders is clear to see.

Time was passing. It was late afternoon, mild and warm as the sun began its course to the western horizon, too late in the day to walk the clifftops thoroughly. I had two hours of daylight left, and I didn't want to be on the roads after dark; the dogs that run free at night to guard the sheep here have a reputation. I carried on along the deserted beach till I found a way up the cliff back towards Cape Helles Memorial. I passed some old defences overlooking V Beach and the remains of Turkish artillery batteries built after WW1 against a future attack, the big guns now rusting on their stocks.

A quick walk around the gun batteries and bunkers was all I had time for before walking back past Lancashire Landing Cemetery. I didn't go through the gate again; I had done that. And, with a heavier feeling than when I'd arrived, I walked back past Doughty-Wylie's lonely grave, wondering why he was there alone and not lying in Lancashire Landing Cemetery among some of the men he led to capture the fort less than a mile away.

At the village of Seddülbahir I refilled my water bottle and sat having a drink. A dog the size of a Great Dane was patrolling the village square. It approached me, but I was wary of it. It seemed friendly but I didn't pat it; the mongoose was still a fresh memory. It was old and a little mangy, with a lifeless pelt, matted with sheep droppings. It smelled even worse than it looked; its muzzle displayed a lifetime of battle scars. I took a tin of sardines from the pannier and emptied them onto the pavement. It ate them leisurely, as though it had been taught good manners, then laid its scarred muzzle across my foot and dozed off; it could recognise a spineless foreigner.

Time was getting on. I slowly eased my foot from under the monster's head, still unsure just how friendly the big mongrel was, then it was time to set off. The light was fading and the road was full of potholes. How many half-wild dogs lay ahead waiting for an unsuspecting traveller? I reflected on my timidity; the Fusiliers would not have been intimidated by a few sheepdogs, but they had been armed. It had been a long day. I was tired but I had made it onto W Beach and paid my respects at Lancashire Landing Cemetery and Cape Helles Memorial to the Missing.

Y Beach

The landing at Y Beach was an afterthought by General Hamilton, the overall commander. Y Beach was further north along the west coast, closer to Krithia (modern-day Alçitepe) – and the objective of the first day at the rear of the Turkish defences. It is a narrow beach overlooked by steeps cliffs; the only way off it was up a steep gully. The Turks had left it undefended owing to its difficult terrain and limited size to support a big landing. Two thousand men landed at 5:45 from the Plymouth Battalion RND, under Lieutenant Colonel Godfrey Matthews, and 1st Battalion, King's Own Scottish Borderers, under Lieutenant Colonel Archibald Koe, and a company of the South Wales Borderers.

Matthews found no defenders; with his adjutant and some men they walked inland to within 300 yards (270m) of Krithia village. It was there for the taking. When Matthews arrived back at Y Beach, there was a dispute with Koe over what to do next. Matthews wanted to advance, capture Krithia then turn south to link up with the other beaches. Koe wanted to stay at Y Beach till reinforcements arrived. Neither knew of the bloodbaths at W and V Beaches. Matthews and Koe argued over who was senior officer in command. They stayed in place till 15:00, when Matthews agreed with Koe to dig in. Their trenches were only half dug when the Turks counter-attacked.

The fighting lasted all night and following morning as the Turks tried to drive them off the cliff into the sea, but they held on. By dawn the 2,000-man force had taken 697 casualties. Colonel Koe was mortally wounded. Matthews asked for reinforcements but got no reply from General Hunter-Weston. When boats were sent in to take off the wounded on the second day, an unauthorised withdrawal began. The beach was abandoned at 23:30 on 26 April. A good opportunity was lost due to poor communications and muddled orders. The Allies would never get this close to Krithia again during the whole campaign.

Next day in the afternoon of 27 April, a launch returned to Y Beach in search of any wounded left behind. The senior officer walked around the battlefield for two hours, without seeing anyone; the Turks had moved south to the other beaches. Hamilton had asked Hunter-Weston if he wanted to send more men to Y Beach while it was still held by Matthews, but Hunter-Weston wouldn't change his plan and Hamilton didn't want to overrule his senior commander and take the decision that could have seen Krithia in British hands on the first day. The objective had been lost.

Later on the rainy night of 12th May under cover of darkness, Gurkha and Punjabi forces climbed the cliffs above Y Beach and overran the Turkish defenders at a cost of hundreds of lives. To this day, the area above Y Beach is known as 'Gurkha's Bluff' in honour of those killed taking it.

Gully Beach

At Gully Beach are the remains of a well begun by Joseph Murray RN Division at the bottom of Gully Ravine, to provide water for the troops and mules. At this well the soldiers filled their canteens and jars before loading them on mules for the haul up Gully Ravine to the forward lines. The quote is from Joseph's memoir.

> I and an Engineer moved back about thirty yards where we began sinking a well. I was put in charge... it was a soft job, we thought, and our well began to take shape. The soil was easily dug for the first four or five feet and we had room to get rid of it away from the top. After four days work on the well and not finding a single drop of water even at fifteen feet, we were given a new job.

Just who finished the well Joseph doesn't say but the remains of it are there all these years later.

A major battle at Gully Ravine took place on 28 June, with huge losses on both sides. The assault went well enough for the 29th Division's sector on the left flank of the gully, supported by heavy artillery barrage. On the right flank along Fir Tree Spur the 156th Brigade found themselves up against well-defended positions. There had been insufficient artillery support on their sector; as the forward troops advanced they were slaughtered by machine guns as they charged the Turkish positions. On Gully Spur at the top of the ravine a Turkish strong point was causing heavy casualties.

The 156th had only just arrived and not yet seen action; they paid a heavy price to learn. The brigade was commanded by Brigadier General Scott-Moncrieff, a veteran of the Boer War. The first and second waves of troops on the right flank had been decimated, but Moncrieff was ordered to continue the advance against the machine guns at any cost. He called up his reserve battalion, the 7th Scottish Rifles, leading them forward in the footsteps of the 8th Scottish, who had lost half their strength in the earlier attack.

A few minutes later the 7th were also being slaughtered, losing twenty-five of their twenty-six officers and over 400 men. Moncrieff knew that certain death lay ahead after seeing what had gone before; he led his reserve battalion into the Turkish machine guns and was killed with them. Three futile charges against entrenched machine guns had been repelled with great slaughter. Hunter-Weston, the commander of the Cape Helles theatre, who ordered Moncrieff to attack 'at any cost', was heard to comment that 'he was glad to have blooded the new pups'. It was a reference to foxhunting: he had been a master of hounds. The deaths of enlisted men meant little to him; his battle tactics never changed: always senseless charges in full daylight against entrenched machine gun positions.

But it wasn't foxes the British were up against. It was a determined Ottoman army holding the best defensive positions on high ground, ably led by Turkish and German officers and armed with German machine guns. British casualties at Gully Ravine were mounting: after two days, on 30 June, they had reached nearly 4,000. Turkish losses according to official accounts were over 16,000. Even today Gully Ravine continues to expose their bones with every torrent of rain that rushes down it.

There is a small museum at Alçitepe – Krithia – with a collection of relics from the battle unearthed over the years by farmers' ploughs and amateur archaeologists. Rusted rifles, grenades, ammunition, jam tin bombs, rum jars, tobacco tins, dead men's uniforms and personal effects – fob watches, pipes, toothbrushes, combs, false teeth and, most poignant of all, faded photos of their families, taken before the soldiers left home. How often had they looked at those photos and prayed they would see them again.

Ariburnu

Like the landings at Cape Helles the Anzac landing went wrong before they had reached the beach. They came ashore 2km further north than the planned landing point; it has never been established why they were off course. One theory is that a marker buoy had come loose and drifted north showing the wrong place to land. It's a poor explanation and unlikely. Another is that the ships from which they disembarked were anchored too far north: again, unlikely. The best theory is that strong currents took them north as they came in. Instead of meeting light opposition, they came ashore where it was stronger, at Ariburnu.

There are twenty-one CWGC cemeteries in the Anzac theatre, beginning with Shell Green at the south of Anzac Cove and continuing north to 7th Field Ambulance and Hill 60 Cemeteries. Further north, Lala Baba, Green Hill, Hill 10 and Azmak Cemeteries surround the Suvla Bay theatre.

The soldiers and sailors buried there walked and often crawled under heavy loads up the hills and ravines immediately inland. You can get a slight sense of what it must have once been like walking the roads and overgrown goat paths. We are too far removed now in time and understanding to get a true feel of what took place here. Modern society would never accept such needless deaths on the whims of ambitious politicians and bungling generals now.

The soldiers contended with dysentery, thirst, wounds, fly-blown food and lice-infested clothes. They watched their friends dying, unable to help, burying them in mass graves; when there wasn't time to dig graves, they doused the dead with petrol and burned them. Perhaps they got two or three hours' sleep a night. They were always alert, tense and ready for an attack.

Their experience of war was related more to the time of Alexander than today's wars of laser-guided missiles and remote-control drones. We can never understand what it was really like, and, at risk of sounding obvious, they were hardier people then, used to going without comforts; even necessities like water were scarce. And a great many of the wounded died of thirst where they lay.

These verses by Captain Sorley, written in September 1914 and found in his pocket after his death on 13 October 1915, would have struck a chord to the men fighting on Gallipoli. Sorley was killed by a sniper at the final offensive of the Battle of Loos, aged twenty. It is not nice poetry; he never meant it to be: Sorley was writing from first-hand experience that would have been familiar to everyone on the Western Front.

Sorley has no known grave and is commemorated on the CWGC Memorial at Loos.

A Hundred thousand million mites we go
Wheeling and tacking o'er the eternal plain,
Some black with death—and some are white with woe.
Who sent us forth? Who takes us home again?
And there is sound of hymns of praise—to whom?
And curses—on whom curses?—snap the air.
And there is hope goes hand in hand with gloom,
And blood and indignation and despair.
A hundred thousand million mites we sway
Writhing and tossing on the eternal plain,
Some black with death--but most are bright with Day!
Who sent us forth? Who brings us home again?

Captain Sorley, like the tens of thousands who died at Gallipoli, was never brought home again.

Sorley was the antithesis of Rupert Brooke: not for him the romance of war. Instead he wrote of misused power, the nationalism and misery of it all, and the vermin-infested conditions. He saw and lived the reality. Brooke never saw action; he died two days before the Gallipoli landings, of blood poisoning from an infected mosquito bite, as his hero Alexander the Great had in 323 BC in Babylon.

Brookes yearned for death or glory on the shores of the Dardanelles, where Xerxes and Alexander had made military history; it was denied him by a mosquito. He would never go into battle as he had dreamed on the shores of antiquity at the Hellespont. Had he done so, perhaps his verses would have changed from romance to realism, like Sorley's. But unlike Sorley he has a known grave, and found his corner of a foreign field on nearby Skyros, but I think he would have preferred Lancashire Landing or V Beach Cemetery.

The CWGC

The cemeteries are the responsibility of the CWGC. And are all well cared for by the Commission, which employs local gardeners and tradesmen to maintain all its sites. I came across some of them working in the cemeteries, pruning and planting shrubs and weeding the verges and beds. They smile and greet visitors, and are well presented and respectful. I recognise skilled and conscientious workers when I see them work, and these men are.

The CWGC was formed from the vision of Sir Fabian Ware. At age forty-five, Ware was too old to enlist; instead he commanded a medical unit of the British Red Cross. Dismayed by the number of casualties at Flanders in WW1, he began thinking of a way to ensure the final resting places of the fallen would be marked and maintained. Under his leadership, the forerunner of the CWGC was established. By 1915, it was given official recognition by the British War Office and incorporated into the British Army Graves Registration Commission.

Following the armistice at the end of WW1 the vast task of recording the names and whereabouts of the fallen began. Land for the cemeteries and memorials had to be bought. By 1918, 587,000 graves had been identified; a further 559,000 names were registered as missing with no known grave. The Commission set the highest standards for its cemeteries and memorials. Three of Britain's most distinguished architects – Sir Edwin Lutyens and Sir Herbert Baker – who had been responsible for the design of New Delhi and its public buildings, were commissioned, along with Sir Reginald Blomfield, to design the cemeteries and memorials. Rudyard Kipling advised on the memorial inscriptions.

Sir Fabian Ware asked Sir Frederic Kenyon, the director of the British Museum, to interpret the differing approaches of the architects. In his report to the Commission, he emphasised equality as the core ideology. Rank had no place; neither had ethnicity or religion. All were equal in death, laid side by side in the cemeteries, a principle abided by ever since. During the campaigns at Anzac and Cape Helles, many battlefield cemeteries were hurriedly established. In 1918, units were sent to Gallipoli, marking the graves and burying the unburied.

In the Anzac sector, the work was overseen by an Australian Gallipoli veteran, Lieutenant Cyril Hughes of Tasmania. In 1919 Hughes was appointed director of works to the Imperial War Graves Commission – now the CWGC – at Gallipoli. Hughes's labour force consisted of Turks, Greeks and White Russians, none of whom spoke much English. Hughes communicated in a mixture of Arabic, Turkish and Greek. He found that 'The fact that I'm an Australian is better still'. Hughes was impressed by his men's skills, saying, 'Thank goodness all my fellows can do about fifteen things.'

His first task was to establish a quarry at Ulgardere. According to one authority, the stone was of 'The same class as that of which the Homeric walls of Troy were built'. The stone was brought by mule cart and boat to North Beach, where an aerial ropeway was rigged to take it up the ridge to Lone Pine. As work proceeded, the first visitors began to arrive. In April 1920 Hughes wrote of one who may have been the first Anzac pilgrim. 'One old chap managed to get here from Australia looking for his son's grave; we looked after him.'

Gradually, through the early 1920s, the cemeteries and memorials were built to the specifications of the Scottish architect, Sir John Burnet. Burnet's designs differed from those used in France and Belgium. The three distinguishing features of the Gallipoli cemeteries are a walled cross instead of the free-standing cross of sacrifice, pedestal grave markers instead of headstones – more able to withstand earth tremors – and being surrounded by a sunken stone retaining wall and drain to channel away flood waters. The design has stood the test of time: they look simple and dignified, blending into the local landscape.

There are thirty-one Allied cemeteries at Gallipoli maintained by the CWGC, twenty-one in the Anzac sector. The cemeteries contain 22,000 graves; of these only 9,000 are identified burials individually named. Where it is known that a soldier is buried in a particular cemetery but his grave could not be identified, he is commemorated there by what is called a 'special memorial'. The British and Dominion 'missing' – approximately 27,000 men – are commemorated by name on five Gallipoli memorials — Cape Helles (British, Australian, Indian), Lone Pine (Australian and New Zealand), Twelve Tree Copse, Hill 60 and Chunuk Bair (New Zealand).

Besides the thirty-one CWGC cemeteries of Gallipoli, there are many more worldwide, so many that when I first saw the numbers I thought it must be a mistake. The CWGC maintain 23,000 sites in 153 countries; 1.7 million names are on its registers. Not all the 1.7 million have marked graves many lying with their brothers in arms in communal graves. Many others have no known graves or whereabouts and are commemorated on memorials to the missing. The numbers are overwhelming by today's understanding of war casualties.

After his visit to Flanders in 1922, King George V commented, 'I have many times asked myself whether there can be more potent advocates of peace upon earth through the years to come than this massed multitude of silent witnesses [the headstones] to the desolation of war.'

Such numbers of casualties would be so unacceptable today that governments would fall. Fewer soldiers die in wars today; instead, the casualties are mostly civilians; many are children. War has changed, fought from a distance by technology unimaginable in 1915. Almost no civilians were killed at Gallipoli; it was one of the last conflicts where soldiers faced each other over isolated battlefields on roughly equal terms. An honourable conflict compared to today's technological wars that target hospitals and civilians.

Shell Green

The first cemetery I visited at Brighton Beach, where the Anzacs came ashore, is Shell Green, reached half a kilometre along a track called Artillery Road inland from Brighton Beach. Shell Green takes its name from the heavy Turkish shelling of the area. It was established in 1919 following the armistice and contains over 400 burials. The remains of Australian soldiers from scattered hastily made graves were reinterred here.

Most of those lying here were killed in April and May 1915. I think Shell Green has the best outlook of them all: its gently sloping lawns look over the Aegean Sea, calm and tranquil. No one was there but myself; only songbirds in the surrounding bushes broke the silence. I sat looking at the sea beyond the perimeter wall, thinking of the Australia they had left behind and what they would make of it now. When they had left home there were fewer than five million people in Australia and it was a rural, agricultural economy. Now it has a population of twenty-five million, with most living in sprawling, suburban, skyscraper cities, a world away from what these men would have recognised.

Private Roy Facey was twenty-three when he left Western Australia for Gallipoli. Roy came to Gallipoli in 1915 in the Imperial Force of the 11th Battalion, to join his brother Albert, already serving in the battalion. Albert put in a request to transfer to Roy's company to be with his brother. The reunion never took place. On 28 June 1915, both Roy and Albert took part in an attack. In Albert's autobiography *A Fortunate Life* he wrote:

On arriving back I was told that Roy had been killed. He and his mate had been killed by the same shell. This was a terrible blow to me. I had lost a lot of my mates and seen a lot of men die, but Roy was my brother. I helped to bury Roy and fifteen of our mates who had been killed on the twenty-eighth. We put them in a grave side by side on the edge of a clearing we called Shell Green. Roy was in pieces when they found him. We put him together as best we could — I can remember carrying a leg — it was terrible.

Albert Facey, *A Fortunate Life*, 1984, p 273.

The story of Albert Facey's life is simply amazing, and what a hard one it was, yet no harder than many others in the rural Australia of his time. The deprivations and setbacks of all that a hard life threw at them can hardly be imagined today. Albert's life story has become a standard text in Australian history lessons.

Lone Pine

A further half-kilometre up Artillery Road is Lone Pine Cemetery, with the remains of 986 soldiers, sailors and marines. Lone Pine is a name legendary throughout Australia; I doubt a child over twelve hasn't heard of it or know where it is. Contrast this with the British sites – Skew Bridge, V Beach or Lancashire Landing Cemeteries – you will be lucky to find one in a hundred who know of any of them. Australia hasn't forgotten its Gallipoli fallen. I hope it never does.

Where Lone Pine Memorial stands today, a single pine tree stood on 25 April 1915. The original tree was shot to splinters within days of the landing. But not before the troops coined the name Lone Pine. Soon, Lone Pine entered Australia's military history as the site of one of the hardest-fought actions of the entire campaign.

On the afternoon of 6 August 1915 at 5:25 an artillery barrage from Royal Navy warships and shore batteries in the Anzac area began shelling the Turkish positions. At 5:30 the barrage ceased and, leaping from their trenches in the Anzac lines, the men of the New South Wales 1st Brigade (1st, 2nd, 3rd and 4th Battalions) charged across the area into heavy Turkish gunfire. As they reached the first trenches, instead of finding them open, they were covered over by logs and sods of earth.

Some ran on and reached the Turkish communication trenches; others broke through the cover, dropping into the dark pits beneath. The artillery bombardment had caused the Turks to move back to safer positions; others fled before the first rush of the Australians. By dark, most of the enemy's front line was taken and pickets posted in the Turkish communication trenches. The Engineers began digging trenches across no man's land for reinforcements to come up without being fired on. Lone Pine was taken but the real battle was still to begin.

Lone Pine was a critical position and the Turks had not expected or been prepared for the surprise attack; Turkish commanders quickly gave orders to retake it. For the next three days and nights the Turks attacked Australian positions in the trenches and tunnels around Lone Pine. The casualties mounted till the position was congested with wounded and dead, as Private Gammage described:

> The wounded bodies of both Turks and our own were piled up 3 and 4 deep the bombs simply poured in but as fast as our men went down another would take his place. Besides our own wounded the Turkish wounded lying in our trench were cut to pieces with their own bombs. We had no time to think of our wounded their pleas for mercy were not heeded. Some poor fellows lay for 30 hours waiting for help and many died still waiting.
>
> Private John Gammage, 1st Battalion, quoted in Les Carlyon, *Gallipoli*, 2001, p 360.

Lieutenant Frederick Tubb, 7th Battalion, of Longwood, Victoria, was holding a position with eight others. As Turkish hand grenades were thrown into their trench, Tubb and his men threw them back or smothered them with greatcoats taken from Turkish dead. Hand-to-hand fighting took place as the Turks broke through. Tubb was on the parapet firing his revolver, but the men catching the bombs were becoming casualties. Corporal Frederick Wright, 7th Battalion, of Melbourne, caught one that burst, killing him. Corporal Harry Webb had both hands blown off before walking out of the action for medical help; he too died. Four other men of Tubb's contingent were killed or wounded.

Only Tubb, wounded in his arm and head, and Corporals William Dunstan of Ballarat and Alexander Burton of Euroa, were left. When an explosion breached the Australians sandbags, Tubb drove the Turks out while Dunstan and Burton worked to rebuild the wall. Then another bomb came over, killing Burton and blinding Dunstan, just as the position was reinforced and the Turks fell back.

Burton, Tubb, Dunstan and four other Australians were awarded the Victoria Cross at Lone Pine. The Battle of Lone Pine between 6 and 9 August resulted in 2,000 Australian casualties. Turkish losses were estimated at 7,000. The action had been planned as a diversion to keep Turkish reserves at Lone Pine and away from the main objective of taking Chunuk Bair by New Zealand, British, Indian and Gurkha units. However, Chunuk Bair was held by the Turks in a stand made famous by the arrival of Colonel Kemal (Atatürk). Lone Pine was a victory for the Australians but at a great cost.

Because of the losses there, it was decided to build Australia's foremost memorial in the Anzac sector at this spot. The Turkish name for Lone Pine is Kanli Sirt – Bloody Ridge. In 1918, an unnamed British visitor attached to the Graves Registration Unit came up the ridge and saw the sad evidence of the Battle of Lone Pine.

On the tumbled soil of the trenches lay the bare white bones, piled or clustered so thickly in places that we had to tread upon them as we passed.

Visitor to Lone Pine in December 1918, quoted in John North, *Gallipoli: The Fading Vision*, 1936, p 219.

Charles Bean, Australia's official war correspondent, reported the action as follows:

The attack at Lone Pine

Until the last only one doubt obsessed the regimental officers — whether the men, sick with diarrhoea and strained with lack of sleep and heavy work, could sustain prolonged fighting and marching. But, as the battalions marched to the starting-point and settled themselves to wait for the signal, their officers – as often afterwards in France – watched with intense interest the evidence of qualities which, till the end of the war, never ceased to surprise even those who knew the Australian soldier best. Whatever their present feelings, the actual filling and dumping of their packs, the march through the trenches, and the imminence of the advance after months of trench life, provided an excitement which put new vitality into the troops. As they waited in the crowded bays, there was not the least sign of nervousness in face, speech, or action. The prevailing thought was: 'It's the turn of the 1st Brigade to show what they can do.' The men chafed each other dryly, after the manner of spectators waiting to see a football match. Some belated messenger hurried along the trench to find his platoon, and in passing, recognized a friend. 'Au revoir, Bill.' He nodded, 'meet you over there.' 'So long, Tom,' was the answer; 'see you again in half-an-hour.' In the opening in the main tunnel – B5, leading forward from the old firing line to the new underground line – stood Major King, whistle in one hand, watch in the other. At the corresponding opening in the underground line was Major McConaghy of the 3rd, ready to repeat the signal for the attack – three blasts of the whistle. Watches had been twice compared and corrected, and while the officers gave a few last hints to their men they kept an eye on the minute-hand as though they were starting a boat race. 'Five twenty-seven – get ready to go over the parapet,' said a young officer crouched in the corner of one fire-step, glancing at his wrist-watch. Almost immediately the order came: 'Pull down the top bags in that recess.' The men of the second line on the fire-step crouched higher against the wall. Those of the third, on the floor of the trench, took a firmer foothold for their spring. A whistle sounded and was repeated shrilly along the front. In a scatter of falling bags and earth the young officer and his men scrambled from the bay. Rifle-shots rang out from the enemy's trenches, gradually growing into a heavy fusillade. One of the men leaving that particular bay fell back, shot through the mouth. From every section of the Pimple, and from the holes of the forward line, troops were similarly scrambling; the sunny square of the daisy Patch and the scrub south of it were full of figures running forward.

Charles Bean, *The Story of Anzac*, Vol 2, 1924, pp 502–503.

Sergeant Lawrence was in the thick of it:

One mass of dead bodies

The whole way across it is just one mass of dead bodies, bags of bombs, bales of sandbags, rifles, shovels and all the hundred and one things that had to be rushed across to the enemy trenches. The undergrowth has been cut down, like mown hay, simply stalks left standing, by the rifle fire, whilst the earth itself appears just as though one had taken a huge rake and scratched it all over. Here and there it is torn up where a shell has landed. Right beside me, within a space of fifteen feet, I can count fourteen of our boy's stone dead. Ah! It is a piteous sight. Men and boys who yesterday were full of joy and life, now lying there, cold – cold – dead – their eyes glassy, their faces sallow and covered with dust – soulless – gone – somebody's son, somebody's boy – now merely a thing. Thank God that their loved ones cannot see them now – dead, with the blood congealed or oozing out. God, what a sight. The major is standing next to me and he says 'Well we have won'. Great God – won – that means victory and all those bodies within arm's reach – then may I never witness a defeat. Just where we have broken into their tunnel there is one of our boys lying with his head and shoulders hanging into the hole; the blood is drip, drip, drip into the trench. I sit watching it – I'm fascinated; the major has just sat down too on the step into the tunnel and it is dripping on his back. I wonder who this poor devil was. I will look at his identity disc. It is under his chin and his face hangs downwards into the trench. Each time I lift his head it falls back; it is heavy and full of dirt and Ugh, the blood is on my hands – a momentary shudder – but one is used to these sights now, and I simply wipe my hands upon the dirt in the trench. Lying right against the trench (I could get him if it was worthwhile) lies another; his back is towards me, and he is on his side. From the back of his head down his neck runs a congealed line of dark red, but that is not what I notice; it is his hands. They are clasped before him just as though he was in prayer. I wonder what the prayer was. I wonder if it will be answered, but surely it must. Surely the prayer of one who died so worthily (he was right on the parapet of the Turkish trench) could not fail to be answered.

Sir Ronald East, The Gallipoli Diary of Sergeant Lawrence, 1983, p 68.

These quotations are from the writings and dairies of those who fought or interviewed the survivors and are kept in the archives of the Australian War Museum Canberra.

Johnston's Jolly Cemetery

The morning cool had gone and the heat building as I continued up Artillery Road to the small '4th Battalion Parade Ground Cemetery', holding the remains of 116 men. Nearby is Johnston's Jolly on Pine Ridge (Kanli Sirt) Named for the commander of the 2nd Australian Division Artillery, Brigadier General George Johnston, it was reached by Australian soldiers on the morning of the landing, 25 April. The field-guns of Johnston's artillery were said by the troops to be 'jollying up' the Turkish battery opposite. This position, known to the Turks as Kirmezi Sirt, or 'Red Ridge', was lost on 26 April and never retaken by the Australians.

Johnston's Jolly Cemetery was created after the war, when remains were brought there from isolated graves in the surrounding battlefield. Of the 181 burials in this cemetery, 144 are unidentified. There are special memorials to thirty-six Australians known to be buried here. Nearly all were serving in the 4th and 7th Battalions and died during the action at Lone Pine between 6 and 10 August 1915.

A little further is Courtney's and Steel's Post. One hundred and sixty men whose remains were never identified lie here among the sixty Australians, one New Zealand and four British soldiers known. After the war, the Imperial War Graves Commission (CWGC) made Courtney's and Steel's Post Cemetery at this Anzac position.

Both sides recognised the strategic importance of this ridgeline; the Anzacs knew if they controlled the ridge victory would not be far away. The Turks were equally determined to dislodge the Anzacs from their foothold and on 19 May they launched a major offensive to drive the Australians back to the sea. More than 40,000 Turks charged the Australian lines that day and, while most of the attack was repelled, a section of the forward trench at Courtney's Post was overrun in bitter hand-to-hand fighting.

Albert Jacka, 14th Battalion, of Wedderburn, Victoria, was awarded the Victoria Cross for his actions at Courtney's Post on the night of 19 May 1915, single-handedly driving back a party of Turks who had attacked his trench and killing them all.

Jacka found himself alone at the end of the trench, but he held the Turks back till reinforcements arrived. An attempt to take the Turkish position had failed, so Jacka devised a plan that would see him win this small battle and go down in the annals of Australian military history. While his fellow diggers threw diversionary bombs, Jacka worked around their rear before leaping over the parapet, attacking the Turks from behind, shooting five and bayoneting two and causing the rest to retreat. At dawn, an officer entered the trench. Jacka, greeted him, 'Well, I managed to get the beggars, sir.'

The laconic Victorian became the first Australian in the war to receive the Victoria Cross, and became a national celebrity. Jacka's image was used on recruiting posters to drum up volunteers, but, newly promoted to lance corporal, he resisted all efforts to bring him home to endorse the war effort, believing an act of bravery or medal was no reason to leave his mates. Jacka's heroics did not end at Gallipoli.

In August 1916, at Pozieres in France, he led a charge on a section of the German line, retaking it and capturing fifty enemy soldiers. His gallantry on the Western Front earned Jacka two more decorations, including the Military Cross. Many war historians believe Jacka's actions in France should have won him two more VCs.

Jacka received his long-overdue hero's reception when a cheering crowd greeted his arrival in Melbourne in October 1919. In January 1932, this war hero, who had survived bullets and hand grenades, was admitted to hospital seriously ill. On January 17, 1932, one week after his thirty-ninth birthday, Albert Jacka died. Nearly 6,000 people filed past his body as it lay in state; 50,000 people came out to attend his funeral.

Next along the ridge is Quinn's Post, where the remains of 165 Australian, thirteen New Zealand and one British soldier are buried; 294 unidentified men are also buried here. The post was named for Major Hugh Quinn, who was killed at Bomb Ridge (Bombasirti). Quinn's post marked the front line and was as far as the Anzacs advanced up the ridge before the Turkish troops were able to hold them back. The trenches were only a few metres apart here: so close they could hear each other talking.

I stopped at each cemetery on the way up, walking the perimeter to look over all the headstones. The day had become hot so I stopped for a longer rest and some water, trying to imagine what it must have been like living with the constant threats from a grenade, or sniper's bullet if you raised your head above the parapet.

Water was a constant problem on the ridge and had to be carried up from the beach; men were killed frequently by snipers as they carried water to the front line. There was never any water to wash with; that could only be done when men were relieved by reinforcements, and returned to the beach to bathe in the sea at night when snipers were less active, though full moons were just as dangerous. Throughout the conflict water was scarce and often contaminated. Dysentery and diarrhoea were always with them, causing them to grow steadily weaker.

Turkish commitment to their defences was evident at Quinn's Post following a Turkish counter-attack on 19 May. That morning 3,000 Turkish dead lay along the ridge and a further 7,000 were wounded. The Anzacs, thinking the Turks to be demoralised by the heavy losses, called out that they would be well treated if they surrendered. The response was a bomb or bullet. A message thrown into the Turkish lines brought the reply thrown back: 'You think there are no Turks left. But there are Turks, and Turks' sons!'

There were some lighter moments at Quinn's, Australian war correspondent Charles Bean reported:

Anyway, near daybreak one morning there came out of their trench at Quinn's a packet tied to a string, thrown so it lobbed near our parapet and lay outside between the trenches. Of course, our sentries waited for it to explode or fizz or burst into smoke or some such devilry. The sergeant near it looked at it very carefully through a telescope. While he was looking Turkish hands came up and waved and then a cautious head. A head our side went up too, and gradually a line of heads on each parapet; and before the sergeant knew what was happening the man next him had climbed up on to the parapet and stepped round the netting and into the deadly area between the trenches and was bringing back the packet. It was a small packet of cigarettes. In it, scrawled in indelible pencil and in badly spelt French, were the words, 'A Notre Herox Ennemis' (To our heroic enemies). 'Bully beef non.' Of course some return had to be made, and so our men threw over a tin or two of bully beef. Presently back flew a piece of paper wrapped round a stone. It read 'Bully beef non.' After that we threw some sweet biscuits and a tin of jam. Other cigarettes came back. I have seen some of them. They had on them the same pencilled writing, 'Notre Cher Enemi' or 'Femez' – probably meant for 'Prenez – A Vee Plessir': that is, 'To our dear enemy – Take with pleasure'; another reads: 'Envoyez Milk' ('Send us milk'). Then one of them waved down with his hands and shouted 'Fini'. And our men waved back, and down gradually went the two lines of smiling heads, and after a pause of a minute or two the bombs began to fly again. They had begun at half-past 8 and they lasted until about a quarter past 9. The same courtesies repeated themselves next morning.

Charles Bean, dispatch, *Commonwealth of Australia Gazette*, 13 January 1916, p 92.

From Quinn's Post it is a short walk to the 57 Regiment Turkish Memorial site. A bronze statue of a Turkish soldier, poised with rifle, faces the Anzac enemy advancing up the ridge on 25 April 1915. Behind this monument, leading up Battleship Hill, was fought one of the most if not the most decisive actions of the campaign. It was here that the courageous stand of Turkish infantry led by Colonel Mustafa Kemal stopped the Anzac advance.

The 'Ottoman Empire' had been in decline for almost a century and it was thought by the 'Entente', as the alliance of Russia, France and Britain was known, that their military superiority would quickly defeat the Ottoman infantry. When the Australians had first landed at Anzac Cove and began advancing inland, they only encountered small parties of Turkish soldiers; after putting up little resistance, they withdrew inland.

This was misinterpreted as an unwillingness to fight; however, these were just scouting patrols. The main Turkish forces had not yet been committed, being held in readiness until it was known where the main forces intended to land. At 6:30 am a report reached Colonel Kemal, commander of the Turkish 19th Division, that Anzac forces were attacking the heights of Ari Burnu. Kemal's forces were stationed at Bigali, his HQ to the east. He immediately ordered his division to march to the west coast to meet the threat. Then he set off on horseback with some junior officers in advance of the 57th Regiment, as his main force marched up behind.

At about 9:30 am Colonel Kemal arrived on Battleship Hill with his officers; the 57th Regiment was still some way behind. What happened next is well known to those who have read the history of the Anzac landings, in Colonel Kemal's own words when interviewed later he said:

Just then I saw men of a detachment who had been placed on hill Point 261 (Battleship Hill) south of Chunuk Bair to observe and cover the shore from there, running back towards, in fact fleeing towards, Chunuk Bair. Confronting these men myself, I said, 'Why are you running away?' 'Sir, the enemy', they said. 'Where'? 'Over there', they said, pointing out hill 261.

In fact a line of skirmishers of the enemy approached hill 261 and was advancing completely unopposed. Now just consider the situation. I had left my troops, so as to give them ten minutes' rest. The enemy had come to this hill. It meant the enemy was nearer to me than my troops were, and if the enemy came to where I was my troops would find themselves in a very difficult position. Then, I still don't know what it was, whether a logical appreciation or an instinctive action, I do not know. I said to the men who were running away, 'You cannot run away from the enemy.' 'We have got no ammunition', they said. 'If you haven't got any ammunition, you have your bayonets', I said, and shouting to them, I made them fix their bayonets and lie down on the ground. At the same time I sent the orderly officer beside me off to the rear to bring up to where I was at the double those men of the infantry regiment who were advancing on Chunuk Bair who could reach it in time. When the men fixed their bayonets and lay down on the ground the enemy also lay down. The moment of time that we gained was this. It was about 10.00 hours when the 57th Regiment began its attack.

This was the moment Colonel Kemal made his famous order – 'I don't order you to attack; I order you to die. In the time which passes until we die other troops and commanders can take our place.'

Interviewed after the war, Kemal said this was the most decisive moment of the day. The Anzacs had been temporarily halted; he sent at once for the advance units of the 57th Regiment. For the rest of the day Kemal's men and the soldiers of the 27th Regiment, further south at Lone Pine, held back the Anzac advance. The Anzacs had been stopped and held to the positions they would occupy for the next eight months. The myth that Turkish soldiers would not put up much resistance was disproved; they were well led and motivated, fighting for their homeland against foreign invaders.

This account of the Turkish Infantryman by a German officer who served at Gallipoli describes them:

The Turkish soldier, the 'Asker', was the Anatolian and Thracian, slightly educated, brave, trustworthy, of whom a large majority were Anatolians. Content with little, it never entered into his mind to dispute the authority of those above him. He followed his leader without question even in attack in the face of the enemy. It is the will of Allah. He is deeply religious and regards this life as the first stage to a better. In the midst of shelling, shortly before the entry of the battalion into battle, the Imam, or the battalion priest, generally held a short address. The impression left on the onlooker was always curious, particularly when at those points in the address an 'Inshallah' (we ask Allah to give it to us) rose over the thirsty plain in earnest but happy tones from hundreds of men's deep voices. One evening, as the jackals were already howling, the address appeared to me to last far too long. The battalion was urgently needed at the front, but nevertheless I did not dare to make a move. That would have been regarded as an evil action, coming from me as a Christian. The Imams were often splendid men with great and good influence on the soldiers, and in the event of all the officers being killed they took control, sometimes taking control of the battalion.

The Asker bears the heaviest wound with wonderful stoicism. One only hears a small whimper, 'Aman, aman'.

Hans Kannengiesser, *The Campaign in Gallipoli,* no date, p 146.

Kemal's star had begun to rise; his planning and tactics would be unrivalled by any other commander at Gallipoli. In October 1923 Kemal became the first president of the Turkish Republic, becoming known as Atatürk – Father of the Turks – and began the modernisation of the country after centuries of declining Ottoman rule.

Continuing up is the Nek Cemetery. All Australians with an interest in Gallipoli history know of the Nek, the small battlefield up the ridge from Quinn's where the most courageous bayonet charges of the whole campaign were made, on 7 August 1915. The Nek Cemetery lies off the ridge road past the 57th Turkish Soldiers Memorial, along a track branching off the road to Chunuk Bair. Along the track is a Turkish memorial (Sergeant Mehmet's); a little further on is the Nek Cemetery.

Charles Bean, the official Australian war historian, described the area in 1919 as 'strewn' with the human remains of the men of the Light Horse who had charged the Turkish lines on 7 August 1915 and of Turkish defenders. It was only after the end of the war under the terms of the armistice in 1918 between the Allies and Turkish government that officials from the War Graves Unit were able to return to Gallipoli to begin burying the dead, whose remains were still lying where they had fallen in 1915. These were the casualties in the action depicted in George Lambert's painting that hangs in the Australian War Memorial – *The Charge of the 3rd Light Horse Brigade at the Nek, 7 August 1915*. In total, 234 Australian Light Horsemen from Victoria and Western Australia were killed in the three charges a further 138 were wounded.

From the edge of the cemetery the coast to the north-east is seen, where the landings of the 'August Offensive' were made. On the night of 6 August the New Zealand infantry were to advance and by dawn on 7 August were meant to reach the high point of Chunuk Bair. The Australians were ordered to make a charge at the Nek, planned for the moment when the New Zealanders were to have been taking Chunuk Bair. The Turks in their trenches at the Nek were to be distracted by the New Zealand attack from their rear. But by 4:30 am the New Zealanders had been halted on Rhododendron Ridge below the summit of Chunuk Bair.

The charge at the Nek, planned for 4:30 am on 7 August, was one of a number of diversionary actions aimed to tie down Turkish troops to the Anzac position while Allied units (Australians, British, New Zealanders, Gurkhas and Indians) stormed Chunuk Bair and Hill 971.

An attack across the narrow section of land at the Nek on the heavily defended Turkish position was regarded as suicidal unless the enemy line was collapsing from the rear as planned. But now that could not happen at the appointed time. But the Light Horse was ordered to charge on the grounds that everything must be done to assist the New Zealanders making their attack on Chunuk Bair. An artillery and naval bombardment on the Turkish trenches inexplicably stopped minutes before the Light Horsemen were due to go, giving the defenders time to emerge from the bunkers and man their firing steps.

When the first wave of the 8th Light Horse rose from their trench, the Turkish soldiers had plenty of time to take up positions in the lull after the bombardment, cutting the first wave down within a few seconds. A second wave of the 8th rose and was similarly destroyed. There was then a short pause. An officer questioned the value of sending more men to certain death but the order came to press on. The 10th went forward to meet their deaths, as the 8th had done, running as swiftly and straight as possible over their dead and dying mates towards the Turkish lines and their own deaths.

A fourth wave of Western Australians also charged before the attack was finally called off. Charles Bean called this event 'one of the bravest actions in the history of war': each man in those waves after the first went forward in the full knowledge he was unlikely to survive. How the Nek looked on that morning as the day lengthened has been described in these words:

At first here and there a man raised his arm to the sky, or tried to drink from his water bottle; but, as the sun of that burning day climbed higher, such movements ceased: over the whole summit the figures lay still in the quivering heat.

Bean, *Story of Anzac*, Vol 2, p 633; this and other accounts can be found on the Australian War Memorial website.

Here is the account left by Captain L.F.S. Hore, 8th Light Horse:

And so perished the 8th Light Horse.

We had about one hundred yards to go, the first line starting from saps which are trenches in front of the firing line leading in the enemy's direction. At twenty five minutes past four we stood up on the banquettes of our trenches and in a few minutes the crackle of musketry turned into a roar. Never have I heard such an awful sound and no wonder. We knew they had three machine guns trained on the Nek and quite possibly more. Their trench must have had at least two hundred men. Judging from the number we had in ours more likely two hundred and fifty. Now a machine gun fires at top speed six hundred rounds per minute and a rifleman fifteen rounds per minute. So we had concentrated on a piece of land say two hundred yards long and one hundred yards deep no fewer than five thousand bullets per minute.

Out went the first line and we waited for our word, by the time they had gone the first forty yards they were down to a man. What could one hundred and seventy five men do against that volume of fire? We saw our fate in front of us but we were pledged to go and to their eternal credit the word being given not a man in the second line stayed in his trench. As I jumped out I looked down the line and they were all rising over the parapet. We bent low and ran as hard as we could. Ahead we could see the trench aflame with rifle fire. All round were smoke and dust kicked up by the bullets. I felt a sting on my shoulder and remember thinking it could not be a hit or it would have hurt more. It bled a lot afterward but was only a flesh wound.

I passed our first line all dead or dying it seemed and went on a bit further and flung myself down about forty yards from the Turkish trenches. I was a bit ahead of my men having got a good start and traveling lighter. I looked round and saw them all down mostly hit.

I did not know what to do, the dirt was spurting up all around like rain from a pavement in a thunderstorm. Some bigger spurts near me were either bombs or pom poms. I could notice they were much bigger. The trench ahead was a living flame, the roar of musketry not a bit diminished. I was protected by a little, a very little fold in the ground and by a dead Turk dead about six weeks. I had looked round again and reckoned I could get about six men to follow and it would have been murder to take them on.

Lastly the supports had not started and if they had, they were only one hundred and seventy five for the whole line, absolutely and totally inadequate. I made up my mind and started to shove myself backwards on the flat of my stomach. After going a few yards I felt a hard sting in my right foot but so long as my arms and chest were right I didn't mind. I passed through our dead and fell into one of the saps and managed to limp out into one of the back trenches and lay down wondering how on earth I got out of it. My three subalterns were killed and I should say about seventy per cent of my men. There were no live men near me when I started back except one who did the same as I did and I hope got back. Our Colonel was killed, one Major killed the other wounded, the only Captain (myself) wounded and ten subalterns killed and three wounded leaving two officers not hit, and about five per cent of the men. And so perished the 8th Light Horse.

Captain L F S Hore, 8th Light Horse, letter, quoted in Cameron Simpson, *Maygar's Boys: A Biographical History of the 8th Light Horse Regiment AIF 1914-19*, 1998.

The Nek Cemetery was calm and quiet, and heavy under its tragic history. It looks over a setting that, were it not a cemetery, would be a perfect place for a holiday picnic. Its sweeping aspect towards Suvla Bay, with the Aegean shimmering in the glare of the early afternoon when I arrived, was spectacular. Beyond it, the distant horizon of the Saros Gulf merged into a pale-blue sky. Had he lived, Rupert Brooke may have found inspiration here to write stirring verses of valiant charges against unwinnable positions, and the irrational slaughter of so many Adonises.

It is now a place of pilgrimage for Australians on a tour of Mediterranean Europe or Turkey: 321 men are buried here, 316 of them casualties of the heroic charges on 7 August. Four New Zealand soldiers also lie here. The only identified grave is that of Private Alexander Campbell, 12th Battalion Australia, killed on the day of the landings, 25 April. All the others who died here could not be identified and were left unburied until after the armistice.

Charles Bean described the area in 1919 as he found it:

When shortly after our visit [February 1919] Hughes [Lieutenant C E Hughes, Australian attached to the British Graves Registration Unit, Gallipoli] came to bury the missing in this area, he found and buried more than three hundred Australians in that strip the size of three tennis courts. Their graves today mark one of the bravest actions in the history of war.

Charles Bean, *Gallipoli Mission*, 1990, p 109.

It is an uneasy place to visit if you know what took place; there are few battlefields of WW1 so small yet where such big sacrifices took place.

Continuing up the ridge is Baby 700 cemetery. Except for a few hours on the first day of the landings on 25 April the hill was Turkish held territory. It is named because warships offshore had ranged the top for shelling at 700ft above sea level; it was the lesser hill of two in the area. When Charles Bean visited the site in 1919, he wrote, 'Could look towards where Tulloch fought, and know that almost certainly among the graves at their side lay the relics of Lalor and possibly those of Mordaunt Reid.' These were the Australian officers who led their men up here from the beach at dawn, their objective being Chunuk Bair. But 'Baby 700' Hill and the inland slope of Battleship Hill beyond were as far as they got; the Turks fought off all further advance.

Captain Eric Tulloch, 11th Battalion (Western Australia), with Lieutenant Mordaunt Reid, led their men onto Battleship Hill. Turkish fire pinned Tulloch's men down and after about half an hour they withdrew to Baby 700. Mordaunt Reid was seriously wounded and was never seen again. Tulloch advanced on Chunuk Bair as far as anyone came on 25 April. In 1919, Bean found an Australian water bottle with a bullet hole in it on Battleship Hill, evidence Tulloch's party had reached there.

At Baby 700 a Special Memorial states that among the 493 soldiers buried there are thought to be the remains of Captain Peter Lalor, 12th Battalion (Western Australia and Tasmania). Lalor was the grandson of Peter Lalor, one of the leaders at the Eureka stockade rebellion at Ballarat in 1854. As the last surviving officer of his battalion at Baby 700, Lalor was the officer the others looked to for leadership. He and his men fought for hours just below Baby 700. As the situation worsened, Lalor decided to advance rather than wait to be slowly picked off. He rose to lead and was heard to say, 'Come on the 12th,' then he fell forward, killed by a Turkish bullet. His grandfather would have been proud of how he continued the family tradition, leading his men against greater odds.

Anzac attack on Sari Bair – August Offensive

The failure to capture Krithia on the Cape Helles front led General Hamilton to revise his plan. Both sides had been reinforced. Hamilton's five divisions were increased to fifteen and the six original Ottoman divisions to sixteen. The new British plan was to land two fresh infantry divisions from IX Corps (General Frederick Stopford) at Suvla, five miles (eight kilometres) north of Anzac, followed by an advance on Sari Bair from the north-west.

The attack was to be made by the New Zealand and Australian Division under Major General Alexander Godley on the northern flank, advancing over rough but thinly defended territory. The division was reinforced with the 13th Western Division under Lieutenant General F.C. Shaw. The 29th Indian Infantry Brigade and the Indian Mountain Artillery Brigade, brought the strength to about 20,000 infantry.

The attack was to be directed on the right up Rhododendron Spur, the left assaulting column would divide at Aghyl Dere, half advancing across Damakjelik Spur and Azma Dere to attack Hill 971. The other half would move right up Damakjelik Spur to Hill Q. To prevent delays, a right covering force was to take Destroyer Hill, Table Top, Old No 3 Post and Bauchop's Hill.

When the covering forces had captured their objectives by an estimated 10:30 pm, the attacking columns would advance to reach the ridge an hour before dawn. Once Hill Q and Hill 971 had been captured, the left column was to dig in, and the right column to consolidate at Chunuk Bair and then capture Battleship Hill. The Australian 3rd Light Horse Brigade would attack the Nek at dawn, in support of the by New Zealand Infantry Brigade attack on Chunuk Bair. Hill 971 would be attacked by Gurkhas of the 29th Indian Brigade and the Australian 4th Infantry Brigade.

The approach to the summit was along Rhododendron Spur, which ran from the beach to the peak of Chunuk Bair. The Turks had outposts along the spur, at the Table Top, Destroyer Hill, Old No. 3 Outpost, and Bauchop's Hill to the north. These outposts would have to be taken by the four understrength regiments of the New Zealand Mounted Rifles before the main assault column could proceed up the spur to the summit.

The Auckland Mounted Rifles cleared Old No. 3 Outpost and the Wellington Mounted Rifles took Destroyer Hill and the Table Top. The Otago Mounted Rifles and Canterbury Mounted Rifles captured Bauchop's Hill, named for Colonel Arthur Bauchop, who was killed during the attack. The fighting was heavy; the Turks had several machine guns in position. The New Zealanders lost around 100 men clearing the outposts. The attack was successful but the plan was now two hours behind schedule, making it doubtful the summit could be reached before dawn.

The three battalions on the north side of the spur were in position by 4:30 am, shortly before dawn. They advanced to a point called 'the Apex', 460m from the summit, where there were few defenders. The Canterbury battalion on the south side of the spur got lost and delayed. Colonel Johnston waited for the last battalion to arrive before attacking the summit, disobeying his orders not to halt for any reason.

The supporting attack planned at the Nek for 4:30 am to coincide with the New Zealanders' attack on the rear of the Turkish position on Battleship Hill was a crucial part of the plan. Despite the now-delayed New Zealand attack, the Battle of the Nek went ahead on time, but without the planned assault on their rear the Turks were able to concentrate all their fire on the Nek.

By daylight, after an exhausting climb and faced by increasing opposition, the prospects for a successful New Zealand assault against the peak looked bleak. Johnston made a request to wait for the cover of nightfall before pressing his assault on the summit, but General Godley ordered him to attack. Two hundred yards beyond the New Zealanders' position on the Apex was a knoll called 'the Pinnacle', from where it was a straight climb to the summit. Off to the side of the spur to the north was the small plateau known as 'the Farm'.

Johnston ordered the Auckland battalion to attack the Farm at 11 am. About 100 men made it onto 'the Pinnacle', where they desperately tried to dig in on the hard ground. The casualties rose to about 300 between the Farm and the Apex. Johnston ordered the Wellington Battalion to continue with the attack. The battalion's commander, Colonel William Malone, refused the order, not willing to make his men carry out a hopeless attack, saying his battalion would take Chunuk Bair that night.

Two disastrous charges had been made before the attack was called off by Godley. Hundreds of Anzacs were dead or lying wounded below the summit of the Apex.

Godley spent the rest of 7 August planning another attack. He sent up reinforcements including the British 13th Division, the 7th Battalion of the Gloucestershire Regiment and the pioneers of 8th Battalion, the Welch Regiment. The Auckland and Canterbury Infantry Battalions were relieved by the Otago and Wellington Infantry Battalions, which would lead the new attack. A forty-five-minute naval bombardment was planned for 3:30 am the next morning. Twelve machine guns would provide covering fire to the attacking forces.

Following the pre-dawn naval bombardment, the Wellingtons, followed by the Gloucesters, reached Chunuk Bair virtually unopposed. The naval barrage had driven most of the Turkish defenders off the top. But it was only possible to scrape shallow trenches in the rocky ground and the peak was exposed to a heavy crossfire from Turkish positions on Battleship Hill to the south and from Hill Q to the north. If the assault plan had succeeded, Hill Q would have been in Allied hands. Allanson's battalion of Gurkhas reached it the following day but were only lightly armed and could offer no relief to the New Zealanders still hanging on at Chunuk Bair.

At 5:00 am, the Turks counter-attacked the Wellingtons' position. The New Zealanders fought desperately to hold them off, firing their rifles and those of their fallen companions until they were too hot to touch. The Turks reached their trenches and·fighting continued with the bayonet. The battle continued all day as the trenches filled with the New Zealand dead. Around 5:00 pm, Malone was killed by a misdirected artillery shell. The Wellington Battalion had advanced to just below the summit; they could see the straits of the Dardanelles. For a day the Wellingtons withstood devastating Turkish counter-attacks, Bean described them when they were relieved:

Of the 760 of the Wellington Battalion who had captured the height that morning, there came out only 70 unwounded. Throughout that day not one had dreamed of leaving his post. Their uniforms were torn, their knees broken, they could only talk in whispers; their eyes were sunken; their knees trembled; some broke down and cried.

Charles Bean, *Story of Anzac*, Vol 2, 1924, p 279.

As darkness fell on 8 August, the Wellington Battalion was relieved. Malone had resisted sending his men on a suicidal attack on 7 August, but a day later the outcome was the same. The New Territorial Army battalions had also been sacrificed. There were 417 casualties of the Welch pioneers and 350 among the Gloucesters, including all the officers of the battalion. Some of the wounded crawled for three days down Rhododendron Spur back to the beach just a kilometre away.

The Farm

At his headquarters near the beach, Godley was basically uninformed of the state of the attack. The main force was the 38th Brigade, commanded by Brigadier General Baldwin, but the situation was so disordered that the force he led towards Hill Q contained only one of his battalions, the 6th East Lancashires. He had the 9th Worcestershires and 9th Warwicks from the 39th Brigade and the 5th Wiltshires from the 40th Brigade, two 10th Irish Division battalions, and, from the 29th Brigade, the 10th Hampshires and 6th Royal Irish Rifles.

This force was to climb Hill Q from the Farm. The New Zealanders on the right of Chunuk Bair and units of General Cox's Indian Brigade on the left would also attack the hill. The plan failed when Baldwin's battalions became lost in the dark trying to find the Farm and didn't reach it until after 6 am. The only force to reach Hill Q was Allanson's battalion of Gurkhas. They suffered the same fate as Colonel Malone, shelled by their own artillery, and unable to dig in on the stony ground.

Again the offensive had stalled; the New Zealanders on Chunuk Bair had to endure another day of Turkish harassment. As night fell, the last surviving New Zealanders moved back to the Apex to be replaced by the 6th Battalion of the Loyal North Lancashire Regiment and some of the 5th Battalion the Wiltshire Regiment from Baldwin's force.

At the north side of Rhododendron Spur, the Turks then attacked the small plateau of the Farm, overrunning Baldwin's brigade; the Warwicks were almost annihilated, the 6th Royal Irish Rifles lost half their number and Baldwin was killed. The Turkish infantry fell back to the main ridge and the Farm plateau became part of no man's land. Colonel Kemal's force had held the summit and it would remain in Turkish hands for the rest of the campaign.

Chunuk Bair is the site of two memorials, one for the New Zealand forces that died in the fateful attempt to capture the summit and outflank the Turkish defenders. The other is the Kemal Atatürk memorial, standing on the site where he had arrived just in time to turn around his retreating soldiers and issue his famous order: 'I don't order you to attack; I order you to die. In the time which passes until we die other troops and commanders can take our place.'

There is a small cemetery on the summit where I read the inscription on the headstone of Havildar (Sergeant) Punahang Limbu, 10th Gurkha Rifles, died 10 August 1915. I imagined his wife scraping by on a widow's pension in a small hillside village in faraway Nepal, perhaps little changed from when he had left to serve with the Gurkhas of the 29th Indian Brigade. For him and other Gurkhas, joining the British Indian Army was a prized occupation that he may have thought would support his family and elderly parents, and provide the money for his children to go to school.

Later I looked up Punahang Limbu's service record. He had served in a proud regiment. The 10th Princess Mary's Own Gurkha Rifles, a regiment of the British Indian Army, formed in 1890. It became the 10th Gurkha Rifles in 1901 after a reorganisation. Its assigned recruiting area was the Limbu and Rai tribal region I had recently trekked through. I wondered if I had ever been in his home village when I was in the Limbu region of eastern Nepal, from where he had taken his surname. The battalion was composed of Gurkha recruits from the 42nd, 43rd and 44th Gurkha Rifles, and equal numbers from the hill-tribes of Assam, including some Jhurwahs, and Dogras.

His regiment had once fought on the Afghanistan frontier during the nineteenth and early twentieth centuries, before taking part in WW1 and WW2. Following Indian independence in 1947, the regiment was transferred to the British army. In the 1960s it took part in the Malayan Emergency and the Indonesian Confrontation. On 1 July 1994 on the parade ground at Gallipoli Lines, Hong Kong, the regiment was rebadged as the 3rd Battalion – The Royal Gurkha Rifles. It had lost its number 10 designation after 223 years.

Punahang Limbu was awarded the 1914–15 Campaign Star; he was also entitled to receive the Allied Victory Medal and the British War Medal – awarded for death on active service. I wondered if his family had received his medals or ever learned the details of his fate, or if any of his relatives had seen his final resting place. He was one of the few killed in the assault on Chunuk Bair whose remains were identified by name; most were never identified: their names are commemorated on inscriptions at Chunuk Bair memorial.

It is hard now to understand the value of a soldier's life in 1915. The Ottoman infantry in the sultan's service were just as expendable as those fighting in the king's service at Gallipoli. Colonel Kemal's orders to stand and die were obediently followed; to do otherwise would have meant death anyway. Few Turkish soldiers were known by name to their officers and no records were kept, making estimates of Turkish losses difficult.

Today, Turkish farmers, factory workers, housewives and school children from every remote Anatolian village make pilgrimages to Chunuk Bair in their thousands to spend an hour or two at this sacred summit. School trips of children and their teachers arrive from every village, town and city. It is humbling to witness some in tears for their grandfathers and great-grandfathers killed here. Wars don't end with the silence of the guns.

Historians all agree Colonel Kemal's victorious actions and leadership had enormous consequences for modern Turkey. Here was an unknown colonel, with many enemies, among the 'Young Turks Movement' in political power in Istanbul. His victory at this place would make him the greatest leader of Turkey, 'Atatürk': Father of the Turks.

After visiting the New Zealand monument to the missing with its evocative inscription – 'In honour of the soldiers of the New Zealand Expeditionary Force 8th August 1915, From the Uttermost ends of the

Earth' – I made my way to the Farm Cemetery, with its 652 burials, 634 of them unidentified reading the headstones of the few identified, then set off back past the Nek to Walker's Ridge.

The offensive on Walker's Ridge between 7 and 10 August 1915 had resulted only in more mass slaughter on both sides. Wounded men were lying all over the heights and valleys. Those capable of walking or crawling made their way to aid posts at the end of the valleys. The scene was recorded by Sergeant Harold Jackson:

> From the trench down to the beach, about 4 miles [6.4km], is one long line of grey stiff bodies of men who have died trying to get down to the beach unassisted.
>
> **Sergeant Harold Jackson, 13th Battalion AIF, 1DRL/0592, Australian War Memorial.**

Private Ormond Burton, of the New Zealand Medical Corps, tried his best to care for them:

> Nobody appeared to be responsible for them and men lay out in the noon day sun with no food or water. Some, from where they lay dying, could see the white-painted hospital ships off shore.

Burton gave his water bottle to a Turkish officer with some of his men lying dying nearby:

> He gave every drop to his men and took not a mouthful himself. I saw nothing more dreadful during the whole war than the suffering of those men.
>
> **Burton quoted by Chris Pugsley, *Gallipoli: The New Zealand Story*, 1998, p 305.**

Before the New Zealand infantry could make their way up the valleys during the night of 6 August, some Turkish outposts had to be captured. This job went to the New Zealand Mounted Rifles and men of the Maori Contingent. The Maoris attacked in traditional style, yelling as they went, with bayonets fixed, 'Ka mate, ka mate! Ka ora, ka ora!' 'The lads hurled themselves at the foe like a band of destroying angels; with bayonet and rifle butt they cleared the trench; only the dead and dying remained. Some Maoris fell, but the victory was with them'

(James Cowen, *The Maoris in the Great War*, 1926, pp 40–41).

Before going into battle in the 'August Offensive', one young Maori wrote to his parents:

We Maoris are now off to strike — to finish what we came here for. The head officers of our party are here after greeting us, and are now instructing us in methods of warfare. Your letter of love has come to me. I am well; my only grief is I hear nothing but the English voice. It is so; therefore, I must not grieve. I now feel my spirit, my soul, my whole body are not mine. Never mind.

James Cowen, *The Maoris in the Great War: A History of The New Zealand Native Contingent and Pioneer Battalion*, 1926, p 25.

William Rusden, New Zealand Expeditionary Force, recalled the Turkish bullets that made the journey down from the heights so dangerous:

We were being fired at, but barring a graze on my hip I escaped scot-free, others, however, not being so lucky for I saw two stretcher bearers and their burden all fall to snipers in about 20 seconds.

Corporal William Rusden, letter, AWM 3DRL/2287 (AWM C02422).

Colonel Mustafa Kemal had ordered a massed bayonet attack to drive the British off Chunuk Bair. Kemal later wrote:

> The blanket of dawn had lifted. Now was the hour for the attack. I looked at my watch. It was nearly 4.30 am. I greeted the men and addressed them: 'Soldiers! There is no doubt that we can defeat the enemy opposing us. But don't you hurry, let me go in front first. When you see the wave of my whip all of you rush forward together'. Then I went to a point forward of the assault line, and, raising my whip, gave the signal for the assault.

There are no survivor accounts of this overwhelming bayonet charge; one historian doubts the defenders had time to get one shot off before the charge was upon them. No first-hand accounts exist because no one came through it to record what happened. In a matter of minutes the Turks were through; nearly 1,000 British troops were killed, many of them teenage territorial volunteers from the Lancashire mill towns, facing their first action inexperienced and poorly armed.

These teenage youths were not conscripted by parliamentary law but by a more powerful one, the law of social blackmail. Edward Villiers Stanley, the 17th Earl of Derby, was the aristocratic landowner of much of Lancashire and a Tory MP. Lord Derby owned the whole of Bury and much of Lancashire, including sixty tenanted farms around the town, 500 workers' houses and the land on which 2,000 mills and commercial businesses stood and paid rents to him, and rents from two collieries.

The family wealth went back centuries but their greatest luck came during the Wars of the Roses. Thomas, 2nd Lord Stanley, recruited 4,000 men from Lancashire and led them at the Battle of Bosworth field in 1485. A loyalist, he intended to fight for King Richard, but, being unsure of the outcome and a cunning cove, he held his men at a short distance from the battle. As the fight began to favour Henry Tudor, and King Richard's army were taking heavy losses and seemed unlikely to win, Stanley saw his chance, changed his allegiance and threw his army into the battle against King Richard. His well-timed strategic intervention quickly brought victory. King Richard was dead and Henry VII was proclaimed king of England. Lord Stanley was rewarded with the title Earl of Derby; it included much of Lancashire and all of Bury.

Edward Villiers Stanley, the 17th Earl, was considered a benevolent man and far from the worst of Britain's hereditary aristocrats; he was known for cancelling the rental debts of his tenant farmers when times were hard. Nevertheless, he became the government's recruiting sergeant for the North of England, where his influence was strongest. Though he owned estates in other parts of the country, Lancashire was his stronghold owing to his ancestor's timely change of mind. The local population knew that their jobs and the roofs over their heads depended on his generosity, which in turn depended on his standing in Parliament and success as the recruiting sergeant for Lancashire. The town of Bury did not let him down, sending their sons off to the war.

These inexperienced teenagers had been sent forward to take over the front-line trenches and relieve the exhausted New Zealanders, who had suffered terrible casualties and needed to withdraw. The New Zealanders were not impressed by the territorial reserves, noting their poor physiques and lack of fighting experience. Many of the Anzacs expressed concerns: some were sympathetic, knowing a counter-attack was imminent and doubtful these youths could repel it.

One New Zealand veteran who witnessed the counter-attack interviewed years later said that these teenagers should never have been left to defend the position with their lack of experience, poor weapons and poor training, saying that some of our officers and NCOs should have stayed on to show them the ropes. Of course they should: what was the point of risking a critical position after so many New Zealand soldiers had just given their lives taking it if it were going to be left to inexperienced, untrained teenagers to defend against a major counter-attack? The Turks brought up battle-hardened reinforcements for the big counter-attack on the exposed position. It was yet another hopelessly thought-out plan by the generals at the rear.

The Turkish force rushed down the slope overwhelming the

teenage defenders; many Turks and some defenders were killed by New Zealand machine gun positions from a nearby hill, unable to distinguish friend from foe as they fought hand to hand. The August Offensive became yet another siege. Although they held out another three and a half months, this was the last advance of the Gallipoli campaign; Chunuk Bair would never be taken.

It was getting hot as I walked down the track from Walker's Ridge till it faded into a goat path. Looking back, I was still in sight of the cross of sacrifice at Walkers cemetery. I took stock of the way down or what I could see of it; the steepest parts I couldn't see at all. What to do now? Continue down the path or turn back up and take the ridge road down, a longer walk? I thought of the soldiers risking their lives carrying heavy loads as they fought their way up to Walker's Ridge while being sniped at. I would only be descending without a burden to carry, and so down it was.

Straight ahead, the Aegean Sea sparkled in the sun. Here I was walking where the whistling bullets and shrapnel had once flew so thick that to have stayed still for a few seconds would have meant certain death from a sniper or a machine gun.

It was hard to imagine that so many had died all around where I stood as I looked down on the beaches of Anzac Cove, where they had come ashore. It lay less than a mile away. A large raptor was soaring on thermals over the cliff face they had named the Sphinx to my right, and I wondered what it was. Months later looking up bird books I thought it was most likely a white-tailed eagle; they are widespread in Turkey and the Mediterranean, preferring habitats of open water and high cliffs, just as it was here.

I started working down between chest-high bushes and stunted holly oaks; as bees droned past I imagined them as snipers bullets: a small sense of how it once was, uncaring, knowing a sting would be all I felt instead of a deadly bullet as they climbed these slopes not knowing what lay ahead. Not even knowing where they were in the general confusion; they weren't even supposed to be in this area on that first day.

The goat path petered out and I was in thick bush. Getting directionally lost wasn't possible; I only had to head towards the lowering sun to come out at Anzac Cove. The issue was how long it would take and could I get through the thick undergrowth at all? And I had only a small amount of water left. It wasn't too late to turn around, only a ten-minute climb back to Walker's Cemetery. I hesitated a moment, then I thought of all those who had fought their way up here; they weren't for turning back. I started pushing through the gaps between the bushes.

The remains of some of the missing would certainly be lying under the earth around me. Many who died on these slopes were never recovered by the burial parties, their bones scattered by animals and spates of water that sweep down the gullies after heavy rains. I was conscious that here I was on hallowed ground. I sensed the past as the gentle breeze rustled the bushes, and bees droned past as eagles soared above. It was a peaceful silent place for those whose bones still lie thereabouts.

On my right was the cliff known as the Sphinx, a landmark familiar to them as they climbed these hills. Its steep southern flank was only 200 metres away from me. A small ridge with patches of open ground lay between me and the Sphinx. I followed a narrow watercourse down through the thick undergrowth. It would lead to the beach eventually I thought it might be the quickest route down. I didn't want to be here when darkness fell; it was hard enough making headway in daylight.

A trickle of water was running down the brook but the vegetation was too thick along its banks to follow it. I came back up and turned north towards the Sphinx; this too was overgrown and I was forced to retrace to where I had a clearer view. The ground was overgrown with bushes and stunted trees: a hiker's nightmare. I was scratched and thirsty, taking small sips to conserve my water, just as the troops had to. It was no place to be lost in, and I was acutely aware of the dangers of an accident here: no one knew where I was or would come looking for me if I had a bad accident.

I tried another way; a small ridge running down between me and the Sphinx looked promising. If I could get on it and follow it down, perhaps it would be easier, it wasn't as densely overgrown, with some open patches from where I hoped to pick a way ahead. First I had to work down and across the gully in-between; it was steep, unstable ground. If I slipped I would fetch up thirty metres below, probably with a broken bone. It seemed a long time getting down, but was probably just a few minutes. From the bottom I scrambled up the far side and reached the crumbly ground of the ridge.

It was a scary prospect. The ridge fell away steeply to the bottom of the south flank of the Sphinx. A fall down there would result in serious injury or death. I stepped back from the edge so that if I lost balance I would fall back the way I had come: less steep and less distance to fall. I needed to rest. I drank the last of my water and estimated I was half way down from Walker's Ridge, in height but not in distance forward. However, this was no help as I had no idea of the best way down from here or how long it might take.

After some minutes I moved off along the ridge, still unable to see a way out of the difficult country. I toyed again with the idea of going back up. I could find my way back, I knew, but it would be dusk when I came out at the top and a long walk in the dark from there. I told myself to toughen up; the troops had come up through this country, carrying heavy packs of rations, ammunition and rifles, sniped at as they stumbled up these gullies and ridges or crawling down, wounded, to the beach.

Reaching a flat area of ridge, I rested, determined now to get down, it was too far and late to go back; the steep slope ahead would have to be my way out. I knew if I got down to the ravine below I had a good chance of getting down; from there it was less densely vegetated. The rough slope was of yellowish loose scree and I was forced to kick steps into it. I was wearing my hiking boots, which had been my comfortable support act for six weeks in the mountains of Nepal. I was more in need of them here than I had been in the Himalayas.

Taking it slowly, I worked across and down in zig-zag traverses to lessen the steepness of the descent, kicking a shelf and stamping it flat to make steps that sometimes gave way beneath my foot, forcing me to lie into the slope and grasp at the loose ground for a purchase. I was aware of the danger of causing a land slip; it was no place for clumsiness or rushing.

In places it was as steep as 60 degrees, with little vegetation to stabilise the soil. I knew these slopes were resting at their 'angle of repose' – the angle at which a soil type will rest without slipping under its own weight. But by adding surface weight through rain or my own weight it would be likely to slip. This is how avalanches start. One slip and I'd be slip-sliding away. I started humming the tune to keep myself focussed.

After some careful minutes I got down far enough to run the last metres across the slope to some small bushes, then another short rest to get my breathing back to normal. From here the slope lessened and the ground became more stable and I reached relative safety.

The big decision was made: there was no way I could get back onto the ridge; it was all down now. I couldn't see the best way so I just made for the sun, setting behind the next scrubby knoll, taking the easiest path through the bush. I felt comfortable now as the risk of a bad fall had lessened to the risk of a turned ankle. But I was tired and thirsty, with no idea of where I was, only that ahead lay the sea and the track along the shore. The bushes were becoming taller and thinning out at the lower elevation, then I came across pig tracks and a twelve-bore shotgun cartridge: this was boar hunting country.

I found a winding foot track with what I guessed to be boar prints in the damp earth where it crossed a rivulet. It was still hard going, bending under bushes and climbing over fallen branches, but I was happy to see the scrub holly oaks, pines and rhododendrons growing; it meant water. I knew the small wash-away would become a brook soon. There was more litter, a tin can and more shotgun cartridges, then I saw a cigarette packet and almost burst into song: it couldn't be far now.

A small brook appeared and I filled my water bottle. I was able to push down its bank, crossing over and back as the undergrowth demanded. I took a few minutes' rest, knowing I hadn't far to go. Then, with the light dimming under a canopy of taller trees and bushes, I pushed through the last 200 metres of scrub. Suddenly I was out of the trees and bushes: in front was Ari Burnu Cemetery. It seemed like an anti-climax to be in a familiar place after the rough country I had scrambled down.

In that tangled country it would be easily done to twist an ankle or break a leg. I thought about that a few times; my worst imagining was being unconscious after a fall. No one would miss me; no one knew I was there. I would not have been missed till my pensioni realised I had not returned. Eventually the alarm would be raised, the police would be called and a search started. I would have been pig and ant food well before anyone found me, if they ever did.

It wasn't a pleasant thought being converted to bacon; considering it, I wondered if any killed in action had suffered such a fate. The Turks, being Muslims, would have shot any wild pigs they saw, to prevent such a thing. And it's doubtful any animal bigger than a rat could have survived the shrapnel and shells that flew everywhere hereabouts. Perhaps there had been no wild boar here then; I have not read an account mentioning any in the books and diaries.

I had time for a short look at Ari Burnu Cemetery overlooking the seashore. A peaceful place, the more so now in late afternoon, still and quiet. I was certainly the last visitor for the day and perhaps the only one that day. I walked around the cemetery, wished them a peaceful night and set off along the track. If anywhere deserved to be left to its nightly stillness, it was this fateful shore and the tragic heights above it.

The men who landed on the beach here had climbed the ridges and gullies I had just come down fully laden under fire. They never knew what lay ahead or if they would live through the day. What were my problems? Sore feet, stiff legs, some cuts and scratches. I started walking along the shore known to them as Brighton Beach.

It was the pleasantest walking of the day, the sun setting into the

Aegean, pleasantly cooler than when I set off up Artillery Road to Chunuk Bair. I made a mental note not to return in a summer month. Late summer or early spring is ideal for walking here. I trudged along, feeling a bit tired, the setting sun reflecting orange, pink and purple as twilight began creeping across the sea.

It felt good walking the lonely coast, thinking over the day's sights and long-past events, reflecting on my small adventure at this battleground of history. This remote corner of Europe had hastened the end of the Ottoman Empire and the slow decline of the British Empire, and brought a coming of age to Australia and New Zealand, but, for all its heavy cost in lives, it had brought no result.

The sun soon dropped out of sight across the Aegean behind the ancient Greek island of Imbros – today's Gokceada – and the distant mountains of Olympus far beyond, where the gods of ancient Greece lay in their brooding mountain abodes. I imagined them getting ready for bed as night came on, cleaning their teeth with sulphur after a hard day hurling molten lava and bolts of lightning across the heavens. Travelling alone can cause you to think too much.

Dardanelles Straits

The Dardanelles Disaster, by the naval historian Van Der Vat, gives a good concise account of the Royal Navy's actions at Gallipoli, the Aegean and the Dardanelles. The failure of the Navy's warships to break through the narrows and reach Istanbul was its only major defeat of WW1. On 15 March Admiral Carden told his vice admiral, De Robeck, and his commodore, Roger Keyes, that he felt he could not continue in command. A naval doctor assessed Carden to be on the verge of a nervous breakdown. This was not the time to have one and he sailed for home.

The attack on the narrows was due to commence on 17 March. Churchill quickly promoted De Robeck to fleet admiral, with the sanction of Admiral Wemyss, in command of the naval base at Lemnos, who was the senior officer on the Mediterranean station but who had not been involved in the naval operations at Cape Helles, as De Robeck had.

Churchill had brought Sir John Fisher out of retirement at age seventy-four to take the post of First Sea Lord. Fisher is an interesting character, with a lifetime's naval career in the mould of Nelson when that great admiral's memory still influenced the Navy. Fisher's godmother, Lady Horton, was on neighbourly terms with Admiral Sir William Parker, who had been one of Nelson's fleet captains. Using her 'influence', she prevailed on Parker to put her godson up for naval selection. At his board of examination, he was required to write out the Lord's Prayer and jump naked over a chair. There were good reasons why the Royal Navy ruled the waves.

Having passed the academic and physical requirements of the selection committee with flying... – well, you get the gist – he entered the Navy aged thirteen in 1854 as a midshipman joining HMS *Calcutta*, an old wooden ship of the line with a crew of 700, where strict discipline was enforced by Captain Stopford. Fisher fainted when he witnessed eight men being flogged on his first day aboard. But he soon toughened up and became, in the Royal Navy's hierarchy of famous admirals, second only to Lord Nelson.

It was to become one of those odd associations. Fisher, the old seadog with sixty years' naval tradition, and Churchill the young politician and First Lord of the Admiralty: the partnership made for some lively discussions. But the failure of the Navy to force its way through the Dardanelles Strait would tarnish both their reputations and ultimately cost the lives of thousands of servicemen.

Some British and French ships that attempted to get through into the Sea of Marmara with the objective of taking Constantinople still lie on the seabed their crews within them. The dreadnoughts attacked Kum Kale and Sedulbahir forts, with little success. Though they inflicted some damage, they never silenced the guns of the forts, concealed behind earthworks; the Turkish gunners were adept at moving their guns quickly with teams of oxen and horse when the Navy's gunners found their range.

At dawn on 18 March De Robeck, in command of both French and British squadrons, ordered his captains to clear stations for action and the fleet steamed out of its anchorage at Tenedos. In line 'A' was the admiral on his flagship, *Queen Elizabeth*, followed by *Inflexible*, *Lord Nelson* and *Agamemnon*, the most powerful ships in the fleet. They were attended by the battleships *Prince George* and *Triumph* to each flank. A mile behind them, in line 'B', Admiral Guepratte led the French squadron of *Bouvet*, *Charlemagne*, *Gaulois* and *Suffren*, with the British battleships *Majestic* and *Swiftsure* flanking them.

As the battleships entered the straits at 10:30 am the Turkish forts opened fire with all they had at the valuable targets as they steamed towards their designated positions. At 11:30, line A opened its barrage, with *Queen Elizabeth* bombarding the two forts either side of Chanak (Cannakale) with her fifteen-inch guns, the biggest in the Navy. *Agamemnon, Inflexible* and *Lord Nelson* began firing on the forts at Kilid Bahr on the European side of the straits.

The defenders, too far out of range, conserved their ammunition and ceased firing. The fleet continued firing from their stations until 12 am. Though the forts were hit many times, damage was limited. De Robeck judged it was time to move in close to fire point blank at the forts. The French admiral Guepratte known as a fighting sailor was popular among both the French and British sailors. He had requested De Robeck allow him to take his squadron close in to attack at Chanak, as De Robeck had gone in close at the entrance forts. The French admiral wanted his turn and De Robeck called him to bring his squadron forward.

Guepratte took his ships through the British line well within the range of the enemy's guns, and fanned out to allow the British ships to fire through them. Then they began heavy shelling of the Chanak forts. We can imagine the scene: flames from the ships guns and explosions on the shore as the shells found their targets; the smoke and noise when a shell from the shore batteries found its target, causing the sailors to attend to fires; and the hectic action on the gun decks as the gun crews reloaded and found their range as the ships moved to new positions.

Gaulois was hit and holed below the waterline; *Inflexible* was holed in its side. *Agamemnon* was hit twelve times and had to come out of the action to a safer position. At 1:45 De Robeck called the French squadron to retire and brought in his own battleships. *Suffren* led the French squadron out of the action along Eren Keui Bay, close to the Asian shore. As they passed the British line a great explosion shook *Bouvet*. Witnesses described it: 'A column of smoke and flame shot through the decks to the sky and she heeled over still steaming fast and capsized.' An observer watching from a British ship said, 'It was over in two minutes she just slithered down as a saucer slithers down in a bath.' Her captain and 639 crew went down with her.

The Turkish gunners took heart, renewing their fire on the fleet still in range. De Robeck ordered the minesweepers to come up. The sweepers were just converted North Sea fishing trawlers, too underpowered for the strong currents. They destroyed three mines, but when they came under close fire the four trawlers retired back to safety.

Then at 4:11 pm *Inflexible* suddenly listed. It had hit a mine close to where *Bouvet* had sunk. *Phaeton* rushed in to take off the crew. The explosion flooded the torpedo deck killing twenty-seven sailors; the lights went out and fires and smoke began spreading. The ventilation fans failed and the heat below decks became extreme. Captain Phillimore decided to run for Tenedos to save his ship, calling the lower deck crews to come up on deck, in case he had to abandon. To a man they volunteered to stay below, working in darkness, smoke and rising water to close the watertight doors and fight the fires. As *Inflexible* steamed through the fleet, the men not needed below stood to attention on the deck as the other ships' crews cheered them past, and safely made it to Tenedos.

Five minutes after *Inflexible* left the line, *Irresistible* was seen to be flying a flag to indicate she was in trouble. She was the closest ship to the Asian shore, the Turkish gun crews, seeing her unable to manoeuvre, were shelling her heavily as she drifted. The destroyer *Wear* went to assist, taking off over 600 crew and several dead; the captain and ten men stayed to attach towing lines. By 5 pm two battleships were out of action and *Bouvet* had been sunk.

The bay where they had all been hit had been swept, and De Robeck thought the Turks were floating mines down the straits from further up. He sent Keyes on *Wear* to *Irresistible* with the battleships *Ocean* and *Swiftsure* in attendance to help. As *Irresistible* drifted close to shore, Turkish batteries were pouring salvos in on her. It looked hopeless; however, Keyes decided it was his duty to try and salvage her and ordered *Ocean* to come and take her in tow. *Ocean*'s captain replied he could not as the water was too shallow for his ship. Keyes then ordered the captain of *Wear* to get his torpedoes ready to sink *Irresistible* if it could not be salvaged.

Keyes took *Wear* in so close to the shore to take depth soundings that the crew could see the enemy gunners working their guns. *Ocean* and *Swiftsure* were steaming back and forth, shelling the shore, it seemed to Keyes with no real effect for the risks to themselves. Leaving *Irresistible* drifting, Keyes sped to *Queen Elizabeth* to suggest that De Robeck send the trawlers in with their shallower drafts after dark to take *Irresistible* in tow.

Meanwhile, *Ocean* had taken *Irresistible*'s remaining crew off; as *Wear* approached *Ocean* to tell its captain to withdraw there was a huge blast and *Ocean* began to list. Destroyers rushed in to take off the crew as the Turkish gunners increased their fire. When Keyes got back to *Queen Elizabeth*, De Robeck was in discussion with the captains of *Ocean* and *Irresistible*.

Keyes had plenty to say on the failure of *Ocean* to take *Irresistible* in tow and tensions were high in De Robeck's cabin. He convinced De Robeck to let him return to *Wear* to torpedo *Irresistible* and attempt to recover *Ocean*. Badly damaged, her crew and the survivors of *Irresistible* were taken off by destroyers and *Ocean* was left to sink in Morto Bay.It had been a bad day for the combined fleet, signalling the end of any hope for a quick naval victory.

Naval guns are not designed for use against fortifications. They fire shells on a flat trajectory designed to hit other ships at long range and high speed; they could not lob a shell to fall over the walls of fortifications.

Admiral Nelson was well known to have strong opinions on the dangers of naval operations against land fortifications. He was successful in 1801 after his barrage at Copenhagen but only just at short range, where the targets were visible. To neutralise the Dardanelles forts the fleet would have to stay out of range of the Turkish shore batteries and hope they would hit their targets. They thought they had silenced the fortress guns but it was just good tactics to conserve ammunition and create a false impression.

There were other red herrings. The Turkish garrison had built dummy gun emplacements using terracotta drainpipes mounted on timber carriages, viewed through telescopes they looked like cannons, luring the Navy's gunfire from the real guns hidden behind their defences. A signal would be given to the sewer pipe gunner at the moment a live shot was discharged from a hidden gun. A black powder charge would be ignited in the sewer pipe; a flame and puff of smoke would be seen by the observers on the ships and a round of shells would fly to it.

One of these terracotta pipes had over 500 rounds of shells expended on it, probably the most shelled sewer pipe in the history of warfare. It was a good ruse, especially as the Royal Navy was short of high-explosive shell. As soon as one was destroyed, another sewer pipe took its place. The naval gunners never suspected they were firing at clay pipes. It was only after the 1919 armistice that Royal Navy officers visited the forts and discovered how little damage they had caused.

Cannakale

At Chunuk (Cannakale) on the Asian side of the straits is a good museum with displays of cannons and howitzers from the campaign, and a history of their actions and makers – French, German and British. The museum's star attraction is a replica of the minelaying boat *Nusret*, whose achievements during the naval campaign were out of all proportion to its size. The tiny vessel effectively prevented two of the world's most powerful navies entering the Dardanelles and reaching Istanbul (Constantinople). Every Turkish child knows the story and many school trips come to visit the full-size replica. It is the Turkish equivalent of HMS *Victory*.

Nusret served as a minelayer during the Gallipoli campaign. She was built in 1911 at Kiel in Germany and commissioned into the Ottoman navy. Armed with two 47mm and two 57mm quick-firing guns, she had helped sink the French submarine *Sapphire* when it attempted to get through the Dardanelles into the Sea of Marmara in January.

The Turkish defenders were outgunned and low on ammunition; however, during the naval manoeuvres, Turkish and German observers had noted the British and French battleships after advancing and firing on the forts used Eren Keui Bay to turn around before retiring to the rear, to allow sea room for the next battleship to advance. Captain Hakki Bey, commander of the minelayer *Nusret*, was instructed to lay his last string of mines not across the strait, as the other strings had been, but parallel to the shore in Eren Keui Bay. Although Captain

Bey had earlier suffered a heart attack, he readily agreed to the risky assignment.

On 8 March, under darkness and without lights, *Nusret* slipped unnoticed into Allied-controlled waters, carrying twenty-six mines, all the Turks had left. British boats patrolled the area under searchlights, yet *Nusret* went unseen as it laid its twenty-six mines at hundred-yard intervals close to shore, away from the centre channel, where the Allied ships moved forward. When *Nusret* safely docked, Captain Hakki Bey suffered another heart attack and died, never to see the effect of his actions.

On 18 March, the Allied navies had entered the straits, minesweepers leading the way. Their flanks were not swept properly as the underpowered North Sea trawlers employed as sweepers could not make headway against the strong currents. The battleships began shelling the Turkish positions at 2 pm, and the Turkish fire dropped away. As the French battleship *Bouvet* steered out of the line to let those behind take up a firing position she turned into Eren Keui Bay and ran into one of *Nusret*'s mines. *Bouvet* capsized within two minutes, taking 640 of her crew to the bottom with her.

As the battleships HMS *Irresistible* and HMS *Ocean* finished their attacks and pulled out of the line, they too became victims of the minefield. Admiral De Robeck assumed the Turks were floating mines down the Dardanelles and ordered the fleet to withdraw. In the confusion of this manoeuvre, the battlecruiser HMS *Inflexible* hit another mine and was heavily damaged, as did the French battleship *Gaulois*. Beyond the Narrows there were no mines to stop the ships. They could easily have crossed the Sea of Marmara unopposed and taken Constantinople. If proper minesweepers had been employed instead of North Sea fishing trawlers, the advance might have succeeded.

This defeat was the catalyst for the Admiralty decision that the Dardanelles could not be taken by naval forces alone; the Admiralty then demanded a combined naval and land operation. The army was to capture the high ground around Achi Baba, from where it was thought artillery could be used to neutralise the forts and make the strait safe for the navy to advance to Constantinople.

As a result of the failed naval operation the invasion of the peninsula went ahead on 15 April 1915. The Turks used the time gained to prepare their beach defences. It was well known to the Turks that the Allies were assembling a fleet of troop ships, escorts and equipment in Egypt and at the Greek island of Lemnos, where the invasion fleet was collecting in Mudros Bay.

As the fleet was making its failed attack at the Dardanelles on 18 March, trains had been waiting to evacuate the sultan and his government from Constantinople to the interior. The battlecruiser *Goeben* and light cruiser *Breslau*, given by the Germans to Turkey, waited at Constantinople ready to make a dash for safety into the Black Sea, where they would have been followed by the Allied navies and certainly sunk. But it was never to be: Captain Hakki Bey had changed the course of naval history with his tiny ship *Nusret*, a forty-metre-long 250-ton minelayer.

It was to be a costly failure for the alliance, perhaps the costliest naval failure in lives ever. At the end of the nine-month campaign, when the Allies evacuated Gallipoli in late January 1916, British, Indian, Australian, New Zealand and French forces had suffered 220,000 casualties out of 570,000 troops. The Turks had 250,000 casualties, out of 315,000 troops. The Turkish numbers are estimates as few records or names were kept.

North of Ari Burnu

North of Ari Burnu is the small Canterbury Cemetery, made after the armistice. It contains the graves of twenty-seven men of the Canterbury Mounted Rifles. The cemetery sits at the bottom of Walker's Ridge. It is the only cemetery at Gallipoli where there are no inscriptions on any of the headstones. The Canterbury Mounted Rifles operated in this area for most of the campaign. On the beach just north of the cemetery is the wreck of a landing barge, visible at low tide. Looking south, the north face of the Sphinx is clearly seen. It is a peaceful, little-visited place.

No. 2 Outpost Cemetery is next along the road. Nos 1 and 2 Outposts were established by the Nelson Company of the Canterbury Infantry Battalion on 30 April. It is the final resting place of some of those killed when the 7th and 12th Australian Infantry Battalions landed nearby on 25 April. No.2 Post saw heavy fighting on 28, 29 and 30 May. It was one of the starting points for the Battle of Sari Bair. The best water available in the Anzac theatre was from a well dug there; 16th Casualty Clearing Station and a New Zealand dental clinic were located nearby. The cemetery was made during the occupation: 152 men are commemorated, sixty-six burials are unidentified and special memorials commemorate forty-eight casualties believed buried among them.

Across the road is Embarkation Pier Cemetery. Early in August 1915, this area was occupied by the headquarters of two divisions, and later by the 16th British Casualty Clearing Station. A pier was built to evacuate the wounded from the Battle of Sari Bair, but it came under continuous rifle and shell fire and had to be abandoned. Besides five original burials, the cemetery is made up of burials brought in after the armistice from the cemeteries of Chailak Dere Nos 1 and 2, Mulberry Tree, and Apex, and from isolated graves close by. There are 944 Commonwealth servicemen buried or commemorated here, and memorials to 262 unknown casualties believed buried among them; 662 burials are unidentified.

The Special Memorial to Captain Chaplain Andrew Gillison in Embarkation Pier Cemetery is a reminder of the dangers faced by clergymen attached to fighting units. Historian Michael McKernan wrote of these military clerics:

The padre was on the whole older and unused to rough conditions. He was a man of peace swept up into the horrifying insanity of war. At the nightly burial parties he was closer to death than most — he saw each night the cost of the campaign. The padre did not have the release of action, wildly firing off a rifle to avenge a mate. The padre could not rage against orders or the fates when things went awfully wrong; the padre was a man of peace and comfort.

Michael McKernan, *Padre: Australian Chaplains in Gallipoli and France*, 1986, pp 41–42.

Scottish Presbyterian minister Andrew Gillison enlisted in the AIF in October 1914. Involved in the 'armistice' of 24 May 1915 to bury the huge number of Turkish and Australian dead lying out in front of the Australian trenches, he described the scene:

Our dead were the result of the first days advance. I never beheld such a sickening sight in my life, and hope it may not be my lot again. The way that rifles and equipment left behind on the battlefield were wrecked with bullets, was a revelation of the extent of rifle and machinegun fire.

Andrew Gillison, diary, 3DRL/6277, AWM.

On the morning of 22 August, Gillison was preparing to read the burial service over the bodies of men who had been killed the previous day in heavy fighting at Hill 60 when he heard someone groaning in the scrub on the ridge. He called two men of the 13th Battalion, Corporal Robert Pittendrigh, a Methodist clergyman, and another Australian soldier, to assist him. The three crawled out and reached the wounded man, but both Gillison and Pittendrigh were severely wounded by a sniper before they could drag the wounded man to safety. Another padre, Walter Dexter, was with Gillison at the end:

> Several of the Padres were with him and while conscious he spoke to them. Just a servant gone to His Master, but Oh, his poor wife!

I paused here to rest a bit; the sun was high and I was getting a bit tired. I sat drinking my water and eating the boiled eggs and bread I had brought in the shade of the pine trees, a silent, leafy place where the bees drone and flycatchers chase them.

A kilometre on is 7th Field Ambulance Cemetery, named after the 7th Australian Field Ambulance, which landed in September 1915. It is situated further off the road, down a rough track. Over 350 burials were brought here from smaller burial grounds including Bedford Ridge, West Ham Gully, Waldron's Point, Essex, Aghyl Dere, Eastern Mounted Brigade, Suffolk, Hampshire Lane Nos 1 and 2, Australia Valley, 116th Essex, 1/8th Hants, Norfolk, Junction, and 1/4th Northants. The majority of those lying here are from the 54th (East Anglian) Division.

This was as far north as I could go if I was to get to Eceabat before dark. I had not seen a vehicle pass by all afternoon. I preferred the quietness and feeling of isolation seeing no one for hours. Today the main sites, especially Lone Pine, see many Australian visitors; at Chunuk Bair there is a daily queue of buses from all parts of Turkey bringing pilgrims and school outings, so many cars and buses that a large car park has been built over what was once a battleground.

I decided on an early night: tomorrow would be my last day and I wanted to visit the Hellespont sites I had not yet seen. I also wanted to see the Turkish memorial to their dead and missing, then go on past Skew Bridge for a last look at the beaches of the Hellespont and, if time, up the coast road to Pink Farm and Twelve Tree Copse cemeteries.

The first book I read ever about the Dardanelles campaign was *Gallipoli* by Alan Moorehead.

Moorehead dealt mainly with the Anzac landings and situation in that theatre. He largely overlooked the equally disastrous slaughter of British and French forces at Cape Helles. It can give an impression he was seeking written revenge for the wasted lives of so many young Australian and New Zealand soldiers. He was entitled to be angry about it, as are all who visit here, but a great many young men of India, Nepal, Britain, Newfoundland, France and Senegal were also killed.

His anger can be understood: the military incompetence of the generals, admirals and politicians, especially Churchill, Hamilton, Hunter-Weston, Carden and De Robeck and many other commanders at Gallipoli, would make a saint angry. Australia too had its share of incompetent commanders at Anzac, though you won't find much mention of them in Moorehead's book. Written history is meant to be unbiased, and there is not enough balance in Moorehead's account.

Churchill's writings seem designed to deflect attention from his overambitious misreading of the whole operation, not the least being his misinterpretation of the Turkish army's resolve to defend their land, the topographical complexity of the terrain, and perhaps most crucially the ineffective use of the world's most powerful navy to shape events.

The cost in lives on both sides is incalculable, as were the grief and poverty this caused. Little wonder Churchill suffered from the depressions he called the black dog for the rest of his life; no doubt so did many others. Over the years suicides were still happening, not just of those who had made bad judgements, causing the deaths of others, but ordinary soldiers who just couldn't keep on living, some because they felt guilty they survived when many of their friends had not. Many survivors brought their mental scars home and their families suffered: wars linger long after the treaties have been signed. If the cemeteries of Gallipoli don't make you think about life and luck, nothing can.

First Battle of Krithia

Over the peaceful farmland to Krithia had marched the men of the Wellington, Canterbury and Auckland Battalions from Helles over rough ground (there was no road then) on the morning of 8 May. They were to relieve the 88th Brigade on Fir Tree Spur and make yet another attempt to break through the Turkish lines. It was to fail with huge losses. The Wellington, Canterbury and Auckland Battalions advanced through Fir Tree Wood to a place they named the 'Daisy Patch', where they became pinned down and enfiladed from machine guns at Gully Ravine, they couldn't advance or withdraw without being killed. I was walking in their footsteps.

Twelve Tree Copse Cemetery lies a kilometre south of Krithia. The cemetery was constructed after the armistice from individual graves and smaller cemeteries around the battlefield. Bodies were brought here from Geoghan's Bluff Cemetery, which contained 925 graves from the Battle of Gully Ravine in June–July 1915, and from Fir Tree Wood Cemetery and Clunes Vennel Cemetery, which contained 522 graves.

It is one of four memorials on Gallipoli commemorating New Zealand soldiers whose graves are unknown; 179 names are of soldiers killed outside of the Anzac area. Special memorials carry the names of the 646 British soldiers, ten New Zealand and one Australian buried in the cemetery whose graves have not been identified.

In an unidentified grave lies Alfred Victor Smith (killed 23 December 1915). Smith was a twenty-four-year-old second lieutenant in the 1/5th Battalion, East Lancashire Regiment, who died in an action nearby for which he was awarded the VC. His citation reads:

> For most conspicuous bravery. He was in the act of throwing a grenade when it slipped from his hand and fell to the bottom of the trench close to several officers and men. He immediately shouted a warning and jumped clear to safety. He then saw that the officers and men were unable to find cover and knowing that the grenade was due to explode at any moment, he returned and flung himself upon it. He was instantly killed by the explosion. His magnificent act of self-sacrifice undoubtedly saved many lives.

In total, 3,360 men are buried or commemorated in the cemetery; 2,226 are unidentified. Memorials commemorate casualties known or believed to be buried among them, including 142 officers and men of the 1st Essex killed on 6 August, and forty-seven of the 1st/7th Scottish Rifles on 28 June.

Twelve Tree Copse was as far as the Allies reached. I picked up some pine cones from under the trees and slipped them in my pack. Then I set off, walking south over the ground they had advanced up. It was dreamlike: no road traffic, no one in sight, just the wind and pine trees gently creaking; in the distance a plume of white smoke from a farm kitchen blending into the hazy sky.

The 29th Division under Major General Aylmer Hunter-Weston came ashore on five beaches at Cape Helles on 25 April 1915. The main landing sites on V and W Beaches were well defended and heavy casualties resulted. The French Expéditionnaire d'Orient Division had made a diversionary landing at Kum Kale on the Asian side of the Dardanelles on 25 April. They later moved across the strait to positions on the right to reinforce the Allied line. By late afternoon of 27 April, the Allies had advanced two miles towards Krithia in readiness for an assault next day.

The strong Ottoman defences and coordinated disciplined Turkish rifle fire had led the British to believe they faced greater forces than were actually there. They assumed they were facing two divisions, whereas they outnumbered the Ottoman force by three to one: the Turks had only two understaffed regiments as they waited for reinforcements. Battle commenced at 8:00 on 28 April with a naval bombardment. The plan was for the French to hold a position on the right while the British line would pivot left from them, capturing Krithia attacking towards Achi Baba from the south and west.

The plan had been badly communicated to the 29th Division brigade and battalion commanders leading the advance. Hunter-Weston remained away from the front, unable to coordinate events as the attack advanced. Initially things went well, with only small pockets of Ottoman resistance. Some sectors of the line were held up, while others advanced, causing some units to become outflanked. The terrain worsened the further the troops advanced, and they ran into the four ravines running down from Achi Baba to the sea.

On the left of the advance was Gully Ravine. It was and still is a difficult obstacle. I walked its entire length, from beach to the Krithia Road. Two battalions of the 87th Brigade, 1st Border Regiment and 1st Royal Inniskilling Fusiliers tried advancing through the ravine but were halted by a machine gun position near Y Beach. Exhausted and leaderless, with many officers killed, the troops advanced as far as they could in the face of strong resistance. In places they were forced back to their starting positions. At 18:00 Hamilton called the attack off.

Fourteen thousand Allied troops took part in the First Battle of Krithia, with 3,000 casualties. This loss would be small compared to the later Krithia battles. Nonetheless, the first battle was significant in that it demonstrated that the assumption of a quick victory was wrong. Cape Helles was set to become a scene of grinding-down battles measured by small advances or the capture of a forward trench, then digging in to defend against the counter-attack.

Following the failure of the First Battle of Krithia, the exhausted British 29th Division dug in to consolidate, defending counter-attacks on 1 and 4 May. Counter-attacks against the Anzacs landing site on 2 May had been repulsed but not without casualties. The Anzacs were well dug in and able to hold their positions. General William Birdwood the commander of the Australian and New Zealand Army Corps was asked to send two of his brigades from Anzac to the Helles front for the next assault on Krithia. These were the Australian 2nd Infantry Brigade and New Zealand Infantry Brigades, about 5,000 men.

Other reinforcements included brigades from the Royal Naval Division and the 125th Brigade from the 42nd East Lancashire Division. The 87th and 88th Brigades of the 29th Division would be at the forefront of the attack. General Vaughn Cox's 29th Indian Brigade and the Anzac brigades would be in reserve. General Hunter-Weston's artillery lacked high-explosive shells – the Navy were reserving these for the assault on Constantinople – but they were never to get near it. The shrapnel shells they did use were mostly ineffective against the Turkish positions.

Cape Helles was a more open country than the harsher, broken country above Anzac Cove, though divided by four large deres, or gullies, that run down from the slopes of Achi Baba to Morto Bay. Gully Ravine, on the west, empties into the Aegean and is separated from the sea by Gully Spur. East of this is Fir Tree Spur, and Krithia Valley (Kirte Dere), then Krithia Spur. Krithia Spur was exposed, with no cover for attacking forces. Gully Spur and Fir Tree Spur had the best cover, so the main advances were made along these spurs in the shelter of the gullies.

Like the first battle, Hunter-Weston's plan for the Second Battle of Krithia called for a general advance along a line across the peninsula, as the first battle had: originality and alternative strategies were not his strong points. It was more of the same, resulting in more of the same. The attack was divided into three stages. First a general advance north across the whole front; this would take the French, on the right, to Kereves Spur, where they were to dig in and hold. The second stage was for the British, in the centre, to turn in from the French flank, then advance up Fir Tree Spur and Gully Spur and take Krithia village. The third phase would be an advance to capture Achi Baba.

After three days of fighting the Allies were forced to call a halt without completing even the first stage. The greatest advance was 550m. There was no clear idea where the enemy trenches even lay, aerial reconnaissance had failed to locate them. Artillery and naval bombardments before the advance were ineffectual. Again, Hunter-Weston had ordered the infantry to attack in full daylight, believing an attack in darkness would result in units getting lost. This was always his plan: the same thing even when it hadn't worked earlier; he was unable to think of or try anything new: the cannon fodder approach.

The advance began late, at 11:00 on 6 May, and was soon up against strong resistance. The 88th Brigade advanced on Fir Tree Spur and captured Fir Tree Wood. The 6th (Hood) Battalion of the Royal Naval Division advanced along Kanli Dere but never got further than 400m. The Turkish defences were not reached. The attack resumed again the next day, Hunter-Weston adopting the same strategy: full daylight advances across a broad front on entrenched unknown gun positions, with the same disastrous results.

On the morning of 8 May, the 88th Brigade on Fir Tree Spur was relieved by the New Zealanders, who made yet another attempt to reach the Turkish lines, with huge losses. The Wellington, Canterbury and Auckland Battalions gained 400m through Fir Tree Wood to a place they called 'Daisy Patch'; here they became trapped. Enfiladed on the left from machine guns on Gully Ravine, they couldn't advance or withdraw and had to scrape shallow pits to survive the firing.

Despite their hopeless position, Hunter-Weston ordered them to resume the attack at 17:30. The brigade commander, Colonel Francis Johnston, protested but Hunter-Weston insisted the attack be carried out. The brigade made another attempt to cross the Daisy Patch, and some men got within sight of the enemy trenches, but the attack was once again beaten off.

On the right, the French advanced at 18:00; making good progress, they reached the Turkish trenches on Kereves Dere, and managed to capture the Bouchet Redoubt but were forced back everywhere else, with high casualties.

General Sir Ian Hamilton then ordered a general advance at 17:30.

Brigadier General M'Cay's Australian 2nd Infantry Brigade was given thirty-five minutes' notice to prepare for the attack. They were to advance along Fir Tree Spur, on the right flank of the New Zealand Brigade, and had to march 800m from their position at the rear to reach the start line at Tommy's Trench. The brigade fought their way a further 500m past the start line, taking 50 per cent casualties.

The outcome of the Second Battle for Krithia was also disastrous, a third of the Allied soldiers becoming casualties. General Hamilton knew he could not sustain such losses; it was becoming difficult to hold even the little ground they had taken, let alone capture more. Once again, they dug in. The battle had been poorly planned and badly supported, with insufficient artillery and knowledge of the defences. It wasn't the only poorly thought-out strategy: medical provisions and evacuation plans for the wounded were almost an afterthought.

Insufficient stretcher bearers were available for the number of casualties; the few available had to carry the wounded all the way back to the beach. No forward dressing station or collecting base had been established where horse or mule ambulances could take the wounded back. The hospital ships, too, were inadequate for the task. Once the wounded were taken off the beach they would often be left in open boats for hours, unable to find a ship with space to take them owing to the high numbers of wounded. Each night those who couldn't be saved were buried at sea.

No advance succeeded in taking Gully Ravine till the night of 12–13 May, when the men of the 1/6th Gurkha Rifles overran the covering machine gun positions by climbing the 100m steep cliff the Royal Marine Light Infantry and Royal Dublin Fusiliers had earlier been unable to climb. The cliff is now named 'Gurkha Bluff'.

After the failure of the Second Battle of Krithia, Hamilton asked the British secretary of state for war, Lord Kitchener, for another four divisions. He should have had them to begin with, but Kitchener had kept them in reserve for setbacks on the Western Front. The third attempt to capture Krithia was not made till early June.

Four kilometres from Alçitepe is Pink Farm Cemetery (Sotiri

Farm), a little south of Gully Beach. Gully Ravine runs roughly parallel to the new road on the west of Fir Tree Spur. There are still some fir trees standing there, though most have been cleared for farmland.

Pink Farm was named for the pinkish-red soil in the area. There were originally three cemeteries around the farm, the first made after the First Battle of Krithia. After the armistice, Pink Farm Nos 1 and 2 Cemeteries were relocated to the site of No. 3 Cemetery. Graves from smaller cemeteries were later moved there from 29th Divisional, 52nd Divisional, Aerodrome, Oak Tree, Gully Beach and Gully Farm. A total of 602 servicemen are buried or commemorated in the cemetery. Of these, 250 burials are unidentified; memorials commemorate 219 casualties known or believed to be buried among them.

Pink Farm is a peaceful cemetery, shaded by fir trees of the kind on Fir Tree Spur in 1915; they surround the site, isolating it from surrounding farmland. I wouldn't want to say which of the Gallipoli cemeteries is best; they are equally poignant and special, yet each is different. Lone Pine has beautiful views of the Aegean, as do others. Pink Farm is serene and sylvan, isolated in a flat landscape, priceless, like an old master in a hushed gallery.

Third Battle of Krithia

Only very small gains of territory had been made during the Second Battle of Krithia. Commander-in-Chief Sir Ian Hamilton told Hunter-Weston to continue with a 'ceaseless initiative' against the Turkish trenches that ran for 7km across the peninsula. Hamilton was still determined to seize the prominent hill of Achi Baba, 2km behind Krithia village. Since the landings the advances had been held back by entrenched artillery positions on Achi Baba.

Hunter-Weston still thought Krithia and Achi Baba could be taken with further reinforcements. Neither he nor General Hamilton had yet got a grasp on the realities of what was needed to take Achi Baba. Hunter-Weston's obstinate confidence overrode the little strategic planning abilities he had. Hamilton was in overall command and could have overridden him, but felt he must trust to the officers he had given the responsibility for planning the battles and so never countermanded Hunter-Weston's plans. Krithia was Hunter-Weston's show, though he had no new ideas, only blind faith, blinded by the goal of Achi Baba at any cost.

In early June a series of night advances on 18, 23, 24 and 27 May resulted in the Allied line gaining three-quarters of a kilometre with as few as fifty casualties. By comparison, the one-kilometre advance during the Second Battle of Krithia had been at a cost of 6,000 casualties. This success gave Hunter-Weston confidence he could take the objective this time. It was to be a false dawn. At this time the Turkish cause was also given a confidence boost. The sinking of the battleships *Triumph* on 25 May and *Majestic* three days later in the Aegean with torpedoes from a German submarine greatly affected naval ability to support land operations by shelling Turkish positions from offshore.

On 24 May the British divisions at Helles were regrouped as VIII Corps, with Hunter-Weston in command. Hamilton was becoming wary and issued instructions limiting his aims to his own given objectives. He abandoned hope of taking Achi Baba in a single day, in preference to taking and then holding the Turkish forward trenches as a springboard for a future attack. Battle commenced at midday on 4 June, as a joint initiative of Hunter-Weston and the new French commander, Henri Gouraud. Gouraud's relationship with the British was stronger than General d'Amade, whom he had replaced. During his service at Gallipoli the luckless Gouraud had both legs broken and lost an arm.

The advance was preceded by ineffective shrapnel bombardments from eighteen-pound artillery. Early gains were made by the 42nd East Lancashire Division on the right. The French, on the extreme right, found the terrain harder and were held up. The attack was planned in two waves: the first wave was to capture the Turkish front-line trenches and hold them; the second wave to advance through them. An hour after commencement, the only progress made was in the centre, by the 42nd East Lancashire Division. To each side of them the flank attacks had been fended off. At this stage Hunter-Weston and Gouraud decided to commit their reserve battalions to the flanks.

This is now thought to have been a crucial moment and a critical mistake. A strong thrust to support the 42nd East Lancashire Division's central advance – they were within a kilometre of Krithia village – would have seen them take the objective and put them in a position to outflank the Turks. But it was not to be and the chance was lost. The attackers had been held back by determined Turkish soldiers under the command of General Liman von Sanders. Gains were minimal but the casualties weren't: 6,500 in total – 4,500 British, including Anzac numbers, and 2,000 French were added to the cost. Turkish losses were estimated between 9,000 and 10,000 men.

On 5 and 6 June, the Turks counter-attacked, hoping to push the Allied force back to the beaches and into the sea. Hunter-Weston's reserve battalions had already suffered high casualties supporting the failed 4 June attack. The Allied forces just managed to hold off the Turkish counter-attack, Hunter-Weston saying that the way his territorial force held their lines was even more impressive than their capture of them on 4 June. But it was yet more casualties for no territory gained.

In London, Lord Kitchener was dismayed at the news from Gallipoli and the casualties during the latest futile battle. Only now did he give Hamilton more reinforcements; had there been enough reserves earlier in support of the 42nd East Lancashire Division's advance, it could have been so different. Following the failure of the Third Battle of Krithia, Hamilton decided to dig in below Krithia, rather than sacrifice more men on Achi Baba, and to turn his attention towards Anzac Cove.

From Pink Farm the road sweeps round a bend by Gurkha Bluff alongside Gully Spur. On 25 April X Beach was a smaller landing north of W and V Beaches. The troops who landed at X Beach were reserve units with no defined objectives; their task was to secure the beach, then wait for orders. It was to be another lost opportunity.

Two companies of the 2nd Battalion Royal Fusiliers came ashore on X at 6:30 am from the battleship HMS *Implacable* without casualties. Turkish opposition was weak, though wire obstacles and a difficult cliff had to be overcome. X Beach was also known as the 'Implacable Landing', the battleship's fifteen-inch guns provided devastating covering fire as the landing pinnaces came in.

Once the beach was secure, the 1st Border Regiment and 1st Royal Inniskilling Fusiliers began to land. At this point, artillery fire from the direction of Krithia caused some casualties. Advance parties signalled back to *Implacable* and the Turkish gun was silenced by its fifteen-inchers. The 2nd Royal Fusiliers then moved inland to help capture Hill 114, linking with the 1st Lancashire Fusiliers coming up from W Beach.

A counter-attack was repulsed later in the day. The three battalions at X Beach dug in, awaiting the advance of the main force from V and W Beaches. Poor planning and lack of clear orders meant the easier landings on X were not exploited and didn't get further inland while it was possible to. Had reinforcements been sent to X Beach in time, they could have quickly outflanked Turkish positions. X was used to bring in men and supplies during the months ahead. A series of dugouts called 'Officer's Walk' were constructed there, but I could find no trace of it.

There have been ideas about how to keep the memory of what happened at Cape Helles alive in the future, including talk of excavating some old trench lines and dugouts back to what they were. I hope not: though many positions can be identified, they can never be the same. And, because many men's remains still lie at the bottom of old trenches, they should be left undisturbed. Where they buried their friends, played, prayed, hoped and died can never be recreated. It is best left as it is, to the goats, foxes and sheep, and the birds soaring overhead.

Whatever may happen to these old battlefields I hope we never see any re-enactments like those of the Napoleonic Wars, with cocked-hat generals on white horses and middle-aged pot bellies charging each other with wooden lances, before retiring to the pub to lick their wounds. Trivialising this moving place and its quiet fields and cemeteries by turning it into a theme park would be mockery.

Skew Bridge Cemetery was named after the skewed wooden bridge on the track from Cape Helles to Krithia. It contains the remains of 607 Allied troops, including the youngest British soldier, fifteen-year-old Joseph Aloysius Townsend, D Company, 1/4th Battalion East Lancashire Regiment, killed on 18 May 1915, the son of Charles Henry and Mary Jane Townsend, of Accrington near Bury.

The cemetery was started during the fighting of 6–8 May and used until the evacuation in January 1916. It originally had fifty-three graves but was enlarged following the armistice with reinterments from Backhouse Post, Orchard Gully, RND and Romano's Well Cemeteries.

Joseph was not the youngest soldier to lose his life at Gallipoli.

Australian James Martin, aged fourteen years, nine months, died of typhoid on a hospital ship and was buried at sea. Hasanoglu Ahmet was also fifteen years old when he was killed; he is buried in the Turkish cemetery at Morto Bay, all teenagers too young to vote but old enough to carry a gun and be sent to die.

Redoubt Cemetery takes its name from the redoubt line the Allies dug across the southern end of the peninsula; this is as far as they were to get in the battles for Krithia, the line on which the advance faltered in May. Today 2,027 servicemen are buried or commemorated in the cemetery; 1,393 are unidentified and special memorials commemorate the 349 casualties known or believed to be buried among them.

Redoubt Cemetery also contains a memorial tree to Second Lieutenant Eric Duckworth that his parents planted in 1922. He was killed on 7 August 1915 and his body was never found. The memorial oak tree is unique as the only private memorial within a CWGC cemetery at Gallipoli.

Redoubt Cemetery was begun by the 2nd Australian Infantry Brigade in May 1915 after the Second Battle of Krithia and used until the evacuation. It was increased after the armistice when the battlefields were cleared and graves brought in from the smaller cemeteries of Krithia Nullah Nos 1 and 2, West Krithia Nullah, Brown House, White House and Clapham Junction.

Redoubt Cemetery is two kilometres south of Alçitepe (Krithia), down a track lined by pine trees, at the heart of the Australian battlefield. In early May the 2nd Victorian Brigade AIF (5th–8th Battalions) and the New Zealand Infantry Brigade were brought from Anzac as part of the British advance during the Second Battle of Krithia; it was yet another disastrous action.

The Australians went forward across what was described as a 'wide, dry, level, grassland'. There were no trees then as there are today. The Australians ran forward into Turkish artillery and small arms fire. 'The heavily loaded brigade,' wrote Charles Bean, 'hurried straight on, heads down, as if into fierce rain, holding their shovels before their faces like umbrellas in a thunderstorm.'

The Australians advanced about 900 m, but Krithia was still far off and the Turkish line was not reached. More than 1,000 Anzacs were killed or wounded in the attack, some of them now lie among the unidentified graves in Redoubt Cemetery.

Lieutenant Colonel Robert Gartside, aged fifty-two, lies just inside the gate to the right. He was commanding the 7th Battalion (Victoria) AIF. Gartside was the first man buried in the cemetery of 2,027 graves, less than 20 per cent of them identified. He was killed during the Australian advance, shot in the stomach by a machine gun as he led his last charge. 'Come on, boys; I know it's deadly but we must go on' were his last words.

Near Skew Bridge is the French cemetery and memorial at Morto Bay, with 3,236 graves and four ossuaries containing the bones of 12,000 unidentifiable soldiers of France and its colonies. French sailors from warships such as *Bouvet* are remembered here on memorial plaques. The French force was called Corps Expéditionnaire d'Orient, comprising French and colonial African troops. The Corps fought on the Allied line at Kereves Dere, the gully north of the Turkish Martyrs Memorial.

At Kereves Dere the French made a number of attempts to advance against Turkish positions. So heavy were the French losses there that they named it 'Ravin de la Mort', Ravine of Death, where men of France, Algeria and Senegal fought and died on these little-visited battlefields. Dr Subin, a French medical officer, wrote in his diary, 'Wounded everywhere! The killed lay in confused heaps which increased as you advanced, the bodies had swollen and their uniforms were tight and narrow. It was awful.'

During the campaign, Morto Bay was exposed to shelling from Kum Kale fort across the straits. Dr Subin had a dressing station under the cliffs, not far from where the Turkish memorial is today. On 8 May 1915, the day of the Australian attack at the Second Battle of Krithia, the French tried to advance. Dr Subin described the scene: 'We laid the poor fellows in rows groans were piteous to hear, bandages soaked in blood, clothes torn to ribbons, ever more wounded arriving.'

The Turkish memorial at Morto Bay is the largest monument on the peninsula. It is triumphal architecture: four massive corner columns support a squat concrete capital. It commemorates the Gallipoli service of about 253,000 Ottoman soldiers and the memory of the missing dead. It was started in 1954 and opened on 21 August 1960. It can be seen from most of the peninsula at night, when it is floodlit. A long memorial wall with the names of those known to have died, and a series of panels depicting the stages of the campaign are commemorated, including one dedicated to Colonel Kemal Atatürk.

The huge structure is a visible landmark to shipping passing through the Dardanelles. An inscription with verses from the Turkish national anthem, reminds visitors:

> Do not ignore the ground on which you have walked,
> It is not ordinary soil.
> Reflect on the thousands of people, who lie beneath
> Without a shroud.
> You are the son of a martyr –
> Do not hurt your ancestor,
> Do not give away this beautiful motherland,
> Even if you have the whole world.

A monument commemorating the soldiers and officers of the 57th Regiment of the 19th Division, who were all killed in action, was added later in 1992. It is a three-storey tower with a relief inscription of Lieutenant Colonel Kemal's famous command on the morning of 25 April 1915 to his soldiers, who had run out of ammunition and had nothing left but bayonets to meet the Anzacs on the slopes of Chunuk Bair (Conkbayırı):

> As a sign of respect, there is no 57th Regiment in the modern
> Turkish army.

The road continues around the shore of Morto Bay to Seddülbahir and its ruined castle. At the east of Morto Bay is the site of S Beach, where three companies of the 2nd South Wales Borderers came ashore. Their task was to seize and hold a disused gun position called De Tott's Battery, then dig in and wait orders. It turned out to be a much easier landing than V or W Beaches, with only one platoon of Turks defending it. Turkish resistance was soon overcome and the Borderers dug in. Had they advanced, climbed the hills and marched to the flank of V Beach, they could have taken the pressure off the struggling attackers there. Hundreds of lives might have been saved and the beach secured, but their orders were to wait.

I walked through the village of Seddülbahir and on to V Beach Cemetery, which stands only metres from the sea in which many buried there had been killed trying to get ashore, sniped at from concealed positions. V Beach is about 10m wide and 400m long, backed by a low earth scarp a metre high.

V Beach Landing

V Beach was defended by a company from the 3rd Battalion 26th Regiment Turkish infantry with four machine guns. Fort Etrugrul was on the left of the attackers and Sedd el Bahr castle on their right. Ahead was Hill 141, one of the first objectives of the landing.

The *River Clyde* held 2,000 men from the 1st Battalion of the Royal Munster Fusiliers, two companies of the 2nd Battalion the Royal Hampshire Regiment and one company of the Royal Dublin Fusiliers. The ship was deliberately run aground on shore so the men could disembark as quickly and close to shore as possible.

To form a bridge from the grounded *River Clyde* to the beach, the steam hopper *Argyll* was to beach itself ahead of *River Clyde*. However, *Argyll* lost steerage and ended up broadside to the beach, unable to tie up to *River Clyde*. The captain of *River Clyde*, Commander Edward Unwin, led a crew to manhandle three lighters into position to form a bridge of boats. Two companies of the Munsters rushed out from the sally ports and along the boat decks to the beach but they were shot down, taking 70 per cent casualties. Around 9:00 another company attempted to land and also failed, with many casualties.

Captain Unwin won the VC for his actions that day. His citation reads:

While in River Clyde observing the lighters that were to form a bridge to the shore had broken adrift, Commander Unwin left the ship and under murderous fire attempted, to get the lighters into position. He worked on until, suffering from the effects of cold and immersion, he was obliged to return to the ship, where he was wrapped up in blankets. Having to some degree recovered, he returned to his work against the doctor's orders and completed it. He was later again attended by the doctor for three abrasions caused by bullets, after he once more left the ship, this time in a life-boat, to save some wounded men who were lying in the shallow water near the beach. He continued his heroic labour under continuous fire, until forced to stop through pure physical exhaustion.

An officer who witnessed the landing reported the carnage as follows:

The tows containing the Dubliners came in at 6:00. All appeared lifeless following the bombardment. As the boats were about to land, the Ottoman defenders opened up, laying down a withering fire. The guns in the fort and castle enfiladed the beach, slaughtering the men in the boats. As they came down the gangways they continued to be mown down. A few made it ashore and sought shelter under a sand bank at the edge of the beach where they remained, pinned down. Out of the seven hundred men who went in, only three hundred survived, many of whom were wounded.

Hunter-Weston was unaware of the slaughter taking place at V Beach. At 9:30 he ordered the covering force at V to link up with W Beach. A third attempt to get ashore by a company of the Hampshires also led to nearly all being killed. Brigadier General Napier, the commander of the landing, was also killed in attempting to lead his men ashore. Finally, Hamilton, watching the landing from HMS *Queen Elizabeth*, ordered Hunter-Weston to abandon V and land the main force at W Beach. One thousand men waited aboard *River Clyde* until darkness before making it ashore. It should never have been attempted in daylight, but such was the thinking.

Six Victoria Crosses were awarded at V Beach, including sailors from the Royal Naval Division who held the bridge of boats together and recovered the wounded from the blood-stained sea: Captain Unwin, Seaman George McKenzie Samson, and two midshipmen, George Leslie Drewry and Wilfred St Aubyn Malleson. William Cosgrove of the 1st Royal Munster Fusiliers also won a VC.

Gully Ravine

During the Second and Third Battles of Krithia, the Ottoman army suffered huge casualties in Gully Ravine. An estimated 16,000 were killed during the Third Battle of Krithia.

Ellis Ashmead-Bartlett, the official war correspondent for the *London Telegraph*, walked over the ground shortly after the battle and reported:

> The trenches are packed with debris, like the Gully. The same awful stench pervades everything, and the flies swarm in millions. In one corner seven Turks, with their rifles across their knees, are sitting together. One man has his arm round the neck of his friend and a smile on his face, as if they had been cracking a joke when death overwhelmed them. All now have the appearance of being merely asleep, for of the seven I only see one who shows any outward injury.

Ellis, *The Uncensored Dardanelles*, 1928, p 143.

The use of the word 'uncensored' in Ashmead-Bartlett's book title was deliberately intended to make the British public aware they had not been told the whole story of the failures at Gallipoli by the heavily censored official government releases.

Turkish historian Prof Dr Abdülkadir Noyanis is quoted from a witness account of the aftermath at the battle for Krithia:

The views of the first trenches were very distressing and painful. Our martyrs, intermingled with the fallen enemy soldiers were laying so dense that it resembled the courtyard of a mosque during the Friday praying hour. In the mouths and noses of the dead, flies had been laying eggs and the maggots who had feasted on these corpses had appeared. There was an unbearable stench everywhere. These heroic Turkish soldiers who had repulsed the enemy attacks day and night had done so with courage, faith and determination.

Abdülkadir Noyan, Son Harplerde Salgin Hastaliklarla Savaslarim, pp 45–46.

Robert Rhodes James quotes this account of the same sights as late as the 1960s.

The loss of five lines of trenches on Gully Spur stung them (Turkish) into a series of desperate counter-attacks in the Gully Ravine area, and between June 28th and July 5th they suffered the staggering number of over 16.000 casualties. Hamilton refused a Turkish request for an armistice to bury their dead, as the local commanders considered that the Turks were more worried by the effect on the morale of their troops attacking over the bodies of their comrades than by any humanitarian considerations. Over 10.000 Turks had been killed in the area, and nothing at Anzac compared with the dreadful scenes on either side of Gully Ravine. In the 1960's the piles of grinning skulls are everywhere to be found on the Spur and in the Ravine; in the scrub one only has to kick the ground to send a cloud of bones scuffling through the dust. 'the mangled bodies of the dead, unburied, half-buried, or partially dug up by shells, under the fierce heat, with loathsome clouds of flies, could only be dealt with by fire', a chaplain attached to the 52nd division has written. 'The valley with its heaps of rotting refuse, its burning pyres and sickening stench, was a veritable Gehenna.'

Robert Rhodes James, *Gallipoli*, pp 230–231.

Many of the fallen of both Turkish and Allied at Gallipoli were the result of snipers.

It is an ideal place for snipers, as the Australians and New Zealanders soon found to their cost. On the other hand, the Colonials proved themselves adept at this kind of warfare.

In the early part of the day heavy casualties were suffered in the boats conveying the troops from the torpedo-boats, destroyers, tugs, and transports. The enemy's sharpshooters, who were hidden everywhere, concentrated their fire on the boats.

When close in, at least three boats broke away from their tow, and drifted down the coast without control, and were sniped at the whole way, and were steadily losing men.

The work of disembarking proceeded mechanically under point blank fire, but the moment the boats touched the beach the troops jumped ashore and doubled for cover. From hundreds of points this went on during the landing of troops, ammunition, and stores.

In fact, I have never seen anything like these wounded Colonials in war before. Though many were shot to bits, and without hope of recovery, their cheers resounded throughout the night and you could see in the midst of a mass of suffering humanity arms waving in greeting to the crews of the warships. They were happy because they knew they had been tried for the first time, and had not been found wanting.

Ashmead-Bartlett, 'Snipers at Work'.

Australia's best-known sniper at Gallipoli was Private William Edward Sing DCM, 31st Battalion. Sing was born on 2 March 1886 in Clermont, Queensland, Australia.

As a boy, Sing was known for his shooting skill, but was the subject of prejudice owing to his Chinese ancestry. Sing became well known for his marksmanship, both as a kangaroo shooter and as a competition shooter. He won many prizes for his shooting and was also a keen cricketer.

On 24 October 1914, two months after the outbreak of war, Sing enlisted in the 5th Light Horse Regiment of the Australian Imperial Force. He was accepted into the army only after a recruitment officer disregarded Sing being part Chinese; at the time, only those of European ancestry were generally accepted for Australian military service.

Sing was known by the nickname 'the Assassin' for his skill as a sniper. Each morning before dawn he sought out a place to hide and watch the Turkish trenches, waiting patiently with a spotter. When an enemy soldier revealed himself, Sing would strike. The snipers stayed in their position all day till darkness fell to avoid giving their location away. Sing's fame spread as his tally mounted his skills being reported in Australian, British and American newspapers. He was credited with 201 official kills, and up to 300 unofficially as every kill had to be independently witnessed.

In an effort to stop him taking more of their soldiers' lives the Turks brought in their best sniper, named Abdul but known to the Australians as 'Abdul the Terrible'. Abdul came very close to killing Sing. In August 1915, he fired a single bullet at Sing and Sheehan's position that passed through Sheehan's telescope, injuring both his hands, and through his cheek, continuing on to hit Sing in the shoulder, but he was back in action after a week's recuperation.

Eventually it was Sing who killed Abdul as the two were sighting each other through their scopes, but Sing got the decisive first shot off. Minutes later, Turkish artillery fired on Sing's position, destroying it. But Billy and his spotter had left just in time when they realised they were being targeted.

Sing was mentioned in dispatches by General Sir Ian Hamilton, and awarded the British Distinguished Conduct Medal in 1916 for:

Conspicuous gallantry from May to September 1915 at Anzac as a sniper. His courage and skill were most marked and he was responsible for a very large number of casualties among the enemy, no risk being too great for him to take.

Another Australian, Alexander Aitken, described his introduction to sniping and how it affected him.

I slid the rifle-sight to '450', aimed and fired. The Turk plunged into the trench in a swirl of dust. This, of course, was what I was there for, but it seemed no light matter, and kept me awake for some time. I would come to no conclusion except that individual guilt in an act of this kind is not absolved by collective duty nor lessened when pooled in collective responsibility. I further found that I bore the Turk no trace of enmity — nor for that matter did any of us; he was to us 'Johnny Turk' or 'Joe Burke', almost a fellow sufferer. We were not indoctrinated against him, as we had been against the Germans by propaganda, the cartoons of Louis Raemakers, and tales of atrocity. But I saw, still further, that this Turk, at the moment of shooting, had not even been a person; he might have been big game. It was a single step to the thought that certain 'colonial' campaigns, not infrequent in our annals, might have been conducted in almost this game-hunting spirit. Here I balked; to become analytical might lead to doubt of the cause for which we were fighting; for this had been called, in those early years, the 'war to end war'. I was far from such doubt then, and would have repudiated pacifism.

Alexander Aitken, *Gallipoli to the Somme*, pp 33–34.

Ashmead-Bartlett

Ellis Ashmead-Bartlett was the English *Daily Telegraph* correspondent at Gallipoli, where he was instrumental in the birth of the Anzac legend. By his outspoken criticism of the conduct of the campaign, he helped bring about the dismissal of commander-in-chief, Sir Ian Hamilton. He had gone ashore at Anzac Cove at 9:30 pm on the evening of the first day's landing wearing a non-regulation green hat; he was arrested as a spy and only released when the boatswain who brought him ashore testified for him, saving him from being shot on the spot.

His report of the landing was published in Australia on 8 May, ahead of the reports of the Australian correspondent, C.E.W. Bean. His colourful writing style, though less accurate and detailed than Bean's dispatches, was well received by the Australian and New Zealand public.

'There has been no finer feat in this war than this sudden landing in the dark and storming the heights, and, above all, holding on while the reinforcements were landing. These raw colonial troops, in these desperate hours, proved worthy to fight side by side with the heroes of Mons, the Aisne, Ypres and Neuve Chapelle,' he wrote in his first dispatches.

On 27 May 1915, Ashmead-Bartlett was on-board the battleship HMS *Majestic* off W Beach when it was torpedoed by the German U-boat *U-21*. Two days earlier he had witnessed HMS *Triumph* torpedoed off Anzac, the first victim of *U-21*, aware *Majestic* might suffer the same fate. On the night of 26 May he helped drink the last of the ship's champagne, and had his mattress brought on deck so that he would not be trapped below in the event. As he lay there a rating ran by and told him a torpedo was approaching. He and most of the crew jumped overboard and survived but he lost all his kit. He sailed for Malta to acquire a new wardrobe: the naval hand-me-downs were not quite to his taste; correspondents of the *Telegraph* could do these things.

Instead of returning to the Dardanelles from Malta, he went on to London, to report in person on the conduct of the campaign. He met most of the senior political figures, including Winston Churchill. He met Arthur Balfour, Churchill's replacement as First Lord of the Admiralty, and Herbert Asquith, the prime minister. He was also interviewed by the secretary of state for war, Lord Kitchener.

Things now began to change in the war rooms and cabinet meetings in London. Hamilton's and Hunter-Weston's disastrous full-frontal daylight assaults on strong defensive positions were being questioned and reported on by Ellis Ashmead-Bartlett. The repeated incompetence and bad strategies the junior officers and men had known about for months were finally being heard in London.

Back at Gallipoli, Ashmead-Bartlett had become battleship-shy and made his HQ on the island of Imbros, the site of Hamilton's headquarters, complaining he had to live in a flapping tent on the hot sand. Hamilton, who didn't trust him, could keep a close eye on him there. But he lived in great comfort compared to the men at the front: no bully beef and biscuits for him. He had brought his own larder and supplies from London and his own chef from Paris.

In the August Offensive he witnessed the landings at Suvla the final desperate attempt to break the deadlock, reporting – 'Confusion reigned supreme. No-one seemed to know where the headquarters of the different brigades and divisions were to be found. The troops were hunting for water, the staffs were hunting for their troops, and the Turkish snipers were hunting for their prey.'

On 21 August he had been watching from Chocolate Hill as the

British IX Corps launched the final attack of the campaign, the Battle of Scimitar Hill. While filming with a camera brought from London, the only live footage taken during the land campaign, he was buried in earth when an artillery shell burst near him and had to be dug free.

The Australian journalist Keith Murdoch arrived on Gallipoli in September, and Ashmead-Bartlett found a willing listener for his opinion of the way the campaign was being run. Murdoch took a letter from Ashmead-Bartlett back to London. Whether Murdoch knew the contents damning the campaign isn't proved but thought likely. The letter described the offensive as being 'The most ghastly and costly fiasco in our history since the battle of Bannockburn'. The letter, intended for Asquith, was intercepted in Marseilles by the censors and Ashmead-Bartlett was ordered to leave Gallipoli.

Evacuation

Following the failures of the August Offensive, the Gallipoli campaign stalled. The criticism of Hamilton's performance by Keith Murdoch, Ellis Ashmead-Bartlett, Stopford and others contributed to the decision to withdraw. Hamilton resisted, fearing a withdrawal would badly damage British prestige in the region, but was replaced by General Sir Charles Monro. Following a rapid assessment Monro was of the opinion the force could not survive a winter campaign. Winter brought relief from the heat but also gales, snowstorms and flooding.

Monro recommended evacuation to Kitchener, who had visited Gallipoli in early November and was dismayed by what he had seen of it. After consulting with the commanders of VIII Corps at Helles, IX Corps at Suvla and Anzac, Kitchener agreed and made a recommendation to the British Cabinet to evacuate. Owing to the winter weather and the narrowness of the beaches, high casualties were anticipated during the withdrawal.

The unsustainable Allied position was made apparent by a storm at Suvla on 26 November. The downpour lasted three days. Rain flooded trenches, drowned soldiers and washed corpses into the lines; a snowstorm followed and more men died from exposure. Suvla and Anzac were evacuated on 20 December.

Decoys, such as William Scurry's self-firing rifle, rigged to fire by water dripped into a can attached to the trigger, were used to make the Turks believe the trenches were still occupied. At Anzac Cove, the troops kept a strict ceasefire and silence, when the Turks ventured out to inspect the trenches they assumed to have been deserted the Anzacs opened fire. Thinking further silences to be a tactical ruse, they kept to their own trenches as the Anzacs silently crept down the valleys to the waiting boats. The force was embarked without casualties but large quantities of equipment were abandoned.

Cape Helles was still retained but a decision to evacuate it was made on 28 December. Unlike at Anzac Cove, Turkish forces were now alert to signs of evacuation. In the meantime, the Turks had brought reinforcements up and mounted an attack at Gully Spur on 7 January 1916 with infantry and artillery but it was a costly failure to them.

Lying offshore in the shallows at Gully Beach are the rusting remains of the lighter that went aground in the dark on the night of evacuation 8 January. Two lighters had been sent to take off a party of men of 13th Division from Gully Beach, but one of them ran aground. The 150 men who could not fit aboard the other lighter had to make their way in darkness along the shore to W Beach to be evacuated. They set off at 2:00 am under General Maude. Barbed-wire defences had been placed to delay any Turks following; they had to cut the wire and then re-lay it as they went.

In the confusion, General Maude had left behind his briefcase, containing his papers and personal effects. With time running out, he returned to collect it. As the minutes ticked by with no sign of the general and with dawn not far off, Brigadier James O'Dowda, in charge of the evacuation on W Beach, sent Lieutenant Steele to look for him, while the two last lighters waited at the pier.

One can imagine the thoughts of the men nervously waiting in the lighters to evacuate: they had survived it all when so many of their friends had not and they had been minutes away from going home to safety; now they were in danger of being caught in open boats if the Turks attacked, as they surely would if they were still there at dawn. There was another problem: charges had been laid, set to explode the abandoned munition magazines at 4:00. As the minutes ticked by, the tension started to mount.

While they waited and Lieutenant Steele was searching for General Maude, Brigadier O'Dowda found time to write a limerick. The first verse was: 'Come into the lighter, Maude, For the fuse has long been lit, Come into the lighter, Maude, And never mind your kit.'

Steele eventually found Maude and got him back to the pier at 3:55; as they climbed aboard the first charges went off, showering the boats with debris. One man had his arm broken; we aren't told what he thought of Maude: perhaps he was just happy to still be alive. As the two lighters pulled away, the second magazine went off, this time without casualties. The withdrawal of those who had survived eight months on the peninsula at least was a success.

Despite predictions of heavy casualties, 35,268 troops, 3,689 horses and mules, 127 guns, 328 vehicles and 1,600 tons of equipment were taken off; 508 mules had to be killed and 1,590 cart vehicles were left with smashed wheels. As at Anzac, some horses were slaughtered to deny them to the enemy.

On my last visit to W Beach I picked up some fragments of broken pottery that had once been an S.R.D. rum jar. Thousands of these were sent to Gallipoli during the campaign, containing rum and lime juice. The initials 'S.R.D.', for 'Supply Reserve Depot', were redesignated by the troops to 'Seldom Reaches Destination'.

After WW1 the borders of Turkey were redrawn and many Greeks in Turkey left for Athens. Some went to Australia and America; some ethnic Turks in Greece resettled in Turkey. Turks fleeing Bulgaria and Romania were also resettled, some going to the war-devastated landscape of Gallipoli, to become farmers in the areas I had visited and walked through around Krithia and Seddülbahir.

Thrace

In 1980, Gallipoli was undeveloped, much of it still as it was in 1915; the roads to many cemeteries and monuments were just dirt tracks and the remoter sites were difficult to access, I'd only seen the more accessible ones. It was still a wild peninsula of famous history and much of it still is, with its myths of Jason and Leander, Xerxes and Alexander, ancient Greek legends and tragic battle sites.

Today it is still a little-visited place of brooding ranges, tangled hills and narrow ravines, where the storm floods rush down the gullies in winter still unearthing the bones of the dead after a century, to whiten in the sun when summer comes.

Tomorrow I would leave; there was much I hadn't seen but it would have to wait till another time. On my final evening I ate at one of the small cafes on the waterfront by the ferry terminal at Eceabat, enjoying what would be my last Turkish dinner: corba soup, stuffed capsicums and baklava washed down with an Efes lager.

Afterwards I walked along the waterfront watching the ferries busily crossing the strait, dodging between the big ships coming and going to Istanbul and the Black Sea ports beyond. Then I went early to bed, thinking of the days walking the CWGC cemeteries and monuments, and the gullies and beaches I had trudged along in the heat of each day, wondering, coming down through the tangled bush from Walker's Ridge, whether I too would become a casualty.

I left my pensioni after a last Turkish breakfast of bread, cheese, olives, boiled eggs and tomatoes: a breakfast I never tired of. I refuelled and rode back up the peninsula without stopping to Kesan, where I had a last lunch of corba, another meal I never tired of. An hour later I reached the border at Ipsala. Some cursory checks and I was through the formalities and out of Turkey on '8 V 80', as the exit stamp in my passport shows it.

Many of the small villages I passed through from the border to Alexandroupoli are still populated by ethnic Turks, as the mosques and minarets testify, surviving from the time that Thracia was under Ottoman rule for five centuries, and where the Turkish language is still the only one spoken by many of the elderly.

I took the smaller coast road along the shore of the Thracian sea to avoid the faster traffic; the sun was warm in mid-afternoon and the narrow road uncrowded winding along the sparkling Aegean Sea. After so many potholed roads in the past weeks it was enjoyable, relaxed riding, the sun warming my back and anticipating a cold beer at day's end. I stopped for petrol and to stretch my legs in Alexandropoulos.

There was something I needed to buy: finding a pharmacist sign I went in and hesitantly spoke the word diarrhoea. Though the word originates from the Greek *diarrhea* (coined by Hippocrates), literally 'a flowing through', I was greeted with a vacant stare – where I was brought up this would be called a 'gawp'; I believe 'gobsmacked' is the newer term for it. Hoping I wouldn't need to mime its meaning, I said it again in a half whisper; other customers were now gawping. Luckily someone spoke English and translated it to 'diarrhoea' in the local accent, then we all linked arms and did the Zorba.

The small city seemed crowded and hectic after the villages, lonely roads and farmlands of Gallipoli. After refuelling I rode on to Makri and found a small campsite by the beach. There were no holidaymakers in early May and it looked to be closed, I went to the nearby cottage to ask, and an elderly woman in black widows' clothes answered the door. Happy to see a customer early in the season, she showed me to a small wooden chalet, with a shaded veranda overlooking the sea.

It felt idyllic later sitting on the veranda watching my washing flap in the warm breeze, while relaxing with beer from the village shop, looking out across the Aegean. Fifty kilometres away lay the island of Samothrace and another fifty beyond that the fateful hills and ravines of Gallipoli, and its silent, isolated cemeteries and monuments to the fallen. It all seemed surreal – had I really been there that morning?

On my peaceful veranda watching the sun reflecting off the waves, I thought on the similarities of Gallipoli's twentieth-century battles and that of Alexander's 'Battle of the Carts' in 335 BC in ancient Thrace, how the mule- and horse-drawn wooden artillery carts used at Gallipoli to haul munitions and supplies up Artillery Road, where I had walked, yet 2,250 years later, were hardly any different to the horse carts of Alexander's time for much the same purpose. It seemed odd that two thousand years later some technology hadn't changed and would have been familiar to the soldiers of both eras.

To safeguard his northern borders, in the spring of 335 BC Alexander advanced into Thrace to deal with a revolt by the Illyrians. The Macedonians marched on Mount Haemus to do battle with the Thracian garrison on the heights. The Thracians had constructed a palisade of carts, with the intention of rolling them down the hillside to crush the Macedonians as they climbed. Alexander arranged his infantry in loose formation, ordering them to open their ranks and lie flat on the ground under their shields when the carts were loosed at them. The Thracians held a good position, but they were drawn out of it by Alexander's light infantry. The carts proved ineffective and Alexander's tactics succeeded; when the Macedonian infantry reached the top of the mountain the Thracians were routed, leaving 3,000 dead on the battleground.

More than 2,000 years later, the British and Ottoman empires would also engage in battles that left thousands of dead on the battlefields of Cape Helles, Lone Pine, Chunuk Bair and Krithia, not far away across the sparkling Aegean.

The widow brought me a plate of cheese, olives and bread, to go with the sardines and beer I had bought in the village: all I needed to round off the day's travel. I had supper on my veranda in the cool of twilight, thinking of the difficult days riding Baluchistan's desert roads and the energy-sapping heat in my weakened state, and the daily stresses racing through Iran, all of it now just a memory. Had it really happened? As I relaxed with a last beer overlooking the sea reflecting on it, I saw the AA badge glinting in the late sun on the Enfield's handlebars an arm's length away – it really had.

I knew I had been lucky to have only come off the bike twice in all those miles since Delhi. I raised my glass and toasted my Indian Enfield 3.5-horsepower gunmetal-grey hero, and those who built it all those miles away in the Madras factory, to withstand the potholed desert roads and hot, dusty days of the Baluchi desert.

In the morning after a Greek breakfast identical to the Turkish breakfasts of the Gallipoli villages, I considered staying for another night. It was peaceful and the beach perfect for a bit of sun and swimming, but after checking my funds I decided to go on to Salonika, where I wanted to spend a second day. I checked the Enfield's oil level and adjusted the chain tension: it was still stretching after all this distance. The tyre pressures were still right, but the tappets needed setting, a task I was now proficient at. This done, I packed my damp laundry in the panniers, said my *efcharisto*s to my host and saddled up.

I stopped at the port of Kavala for a lunch of sardines, watching the ferries and ships docking, and the bustle of the small waterfront, it was another world after the desert days, the smell of the sea and shore such a welcome one. I found a campsite on the edge of Thessaloniki and set up camp for the night and in the morning I walked into the centre.

Thessaloniki

At the tourist information office, no one could tell me where the CWGC cemetery was. Whatever tourists visit Salonika for, it's not cemeteries, but I am not a bona fide tourist. I was the only customer and the young assistant was happy to help; he dug into the cabinets to find out, and when this showed no result he made a phone call to the British consulate – now that's service. Then he marked the Lembet Road Cemetery on a map and gave me the bus number. I said, 'It's ok, I'll walk' he said, 'You can't, it's three kilometres from here.' I said, 'Ten kilometres uphill is fine.' He wasn't to know I had recently spent six weeks trekking up to 30km a day in Nepal. It was a fine day, and there is no better way to see something of a city than on foot.

He hadn't known there was an Allied WW1 cemetery tucked away off a main road in his own city. I explained a little Balkan history of how those buried there had come to be there, and to my pleasure he said he would make a visit to improve his knowledge of Thessaloniki's history. I hope he did: everybody who lives near a CWGC site should know why it is there.

At the invitation of the Greek prime minister, M. Venizelos, Salonika (now Thessaloniki) was occupied by three French divisions and the 10th Irish Division sent from Gallipoli in October 1915. Other French and Commonwealth forces landed later in the summer of 1916. In August 1916, a revolution broke out at Salonika, causing the Greek national army to come into the war on the Allied side.

The soldiers were sent to support the Serbians, who were under attack by German, Austro-Hungarian and Bulgarian armies. The Allied intervention came too late to save Serbia and, after a winter campaign in severe weather on the Serbian frontier, the Anglo-French forces pulled back to Salonika. After preparing Salonika's defences, especially of the port, the armies returned and dug in.

Contingents of Serbian, Italian and Russian troops arrived and offensive operations culminated in the fall of Monastir to Franco-Serb forces in November 1916. A second offensive in the spring saw the British take part in the First Battle of Doiran (April and May 1917), but made little impact on the Bulgarian defences. The front line remained static until September 1918, when another offensive was launched. The British attacked at Doiran for a second time in September 1918. A breakthrough by Serbian forces west of the river Vardar forced the Bulgarian army into retreat. The campaign ended with the surrender of Bulgaria on 30 September 1918.

The British Salonika Force was commanded by Lieutenant General George Milne. At its height – late 1916 to early 1917 – it comprised six infantry divisions, grouped into two corps. The British Salonika Force suffered 10,000 casualties in its three-year existence. The earliest Commonwealth burials were in local Protestant and Catholic cemeteries. Salonika Military Cemetery was begun in November 1915, with British, French, Serbian, Italian and Russian sections, and remained in use until October 1918.

Most burials were of soldiers who died in local hospitals. In February and March 1917 Salonika was subjected to air raids; many of the graves north of the cross of sacrifice belong to those killed in the bombing. The cemetery contains 1,650 British burials, fifteen from the Malta Labour Corps, and three Canadian nurses who worked in the hospitals during the campaign. After the armistice, some were brought in from cemeteries in Macedonia and Albania, and from Scala Cemetery, on the island of Thasos.

The headstones at the Lembet Road Cemetery are different from those on Gallipoli: not the ground-level stone plinth with its bronze plaque; they are the more common upright Portland stone seen in parish churchyards all across Britain. With the crest of the casualty's regiment above his name and rank, below this is the epithet his family may have requested, or, in the case of those who could not be identified, the epithet 'Known unto God'.

Unidentified burials always carry the words 'Known unto God', penned by Rudyard Kipling, who was chosen by the CWGC to author its inscriptions at the end of WW1, when the huge task of establishing cemeteries and reinterring the dead from hastily made graves into properly constructed cemeteries was begun. There are over 23,000 CWGC locations, in more than 150 countries, remembering the 1.7 million dead honoured in them.

The most notable grave at Lembet Road is that of Mrs Katharine Mary Harley, Croix de Guerre, who died 7 March 1917. She was the sister of Field Marshal Sir John French, C-in-C of the British Expeditionary Force in France and Flanders during 1914–1915. Mrs Harley led a group of British nurses serving with the Serbian Army and was killed in an air raid. Her grave has a private memorial as well as a CWGC headstone. The private memorial was erected in 1917 by officers of the Serbian Army and inscribed in English capital letters:

THE GENEROUS ENGLISH LADY AND GREAT BENEFACTRESS OF THE SERBIAN PEOPLE MADAME HARLEY A GREAT LADY ON YOUR TOMB INSTEAD OF FLOWERS THE GRATITUDE OF THE SERBS SHALL BLOSSOM THERE. FOR YOUR WONDERFUL ACTS YOUR NAME SHALL BE KNOWN FROM GENERATION TO GENERATION – From the officers of the Serbian command – Mikkra.

Somehow Lembet Road Cemetery seemed a sadder place than the Gallipoli cemeteries; though peaceful and meticulously kept, there were no open vistas here, no views over the blue Aegean to where you could direct thoughts, or scenery reminiscent of the homelands they came from. Here were manicured lawns, pencil pines in straight, orderly rows and borders of clipped shrubs, formal like a country park but close to a main road and surrounded by buildings in the suburbs of a city. Gallipoli's cemeteries are wilder and more natural, within a harsher landscape of national park, much as it had always been, and I preferred that.

Istanbul is at heart a Middle Eastern city with European influences. In Thessaloniki I was everywhere reminded I was now in Continental Europe. If Thessaloniki was economically poor, it was also lively and without the level of poverty I had become used to in Asia. I went sightseeing, walking down the promenade, where many elderly men were fishing to supplement their pensions. I watched one man wearing a suit and tie, casting his line into the oily sea, pulling out small fish and putting them in a bucket. Only in Europe, I thought, would you see a man fishing in a suit and tie: perhaps his only set of clothes but I like to think he had high standards and wasn't going to lower them for a fish.

Early next morning I set out on rural roads for the 200-mile ride to Igoumenitsa, over the Pindus mountains of Ioannina, across the Katara Pass at 1,705m, one of the highest roads in Greece. It was a ride I was looking forward to after the long, flat hauls of Iran. A shorter day over wild mountains much as they'd always been, with a long descent to the coast, was a pleasant prospect, although I underestimated how cold it still was in the mountains. Not since the high plateau of Anatolia's snow-swept roads had I needed to put on all my clothes against the morning's chill.

It was a rare enjoyable day of riding: cold and clear-skied, a day of silent mountain roads and mountain views, the first since the Himalayas. There was no time pressure now and I stopped whenever there was a view to admire, taking ten minutes for a smoke and to warm my hands on the exhaust pipe, as I had often done crossing the Anatolian plateau. The road was roughly paved but with mercifully few potholes, nothing an Indian Enfield with its heavy frame and forks designed for the rough roads of India couldn't handle. It was me that was the weak link, but at least the diarrhoea that had been such a longstanding part of the journey was easing, and I was riding without the bung.

The switchbacks and sharp bends with their dangerous drops to rock-strewn valleys below reminded me of northern India and its equally spectacular scenery all those weeks ago. As the sun crept higher I warmed up happy at the prospect of reaching Italy in a few days.

That night I camped on wasteland near the ferry terminal at Igoumenitsa, to be ready for the morning ferry to Corfu, where the following night I made my camp under an ancient gnarled olive tree in a grove that might have been cultivated for a thousand years, such is Greece's timeless history. After a day sightseeing I rode up the ramp of the ferry to Brindisi, lashed the Enfield securely to the rails of the car deck, and slept between rows of plastic chairs in the deserted cattle-class lounge.

There were no formalities in Italy and I was quickly out of the Brindisi terminal and onto the Bari road among the speeding freight trucks from the ferry. I pulled into a layby to let the racing mob pass while I had a smoke and tried to work out the best route north. Somewhere near Molfetta I found a desolate tourist site of holiday chalets; it was out of season and closed. It was dark and I rode quietly onto the site, looking for a place to camp. I noticed some chalets under construction and found an unlocked one and wheeled the Enfield behind it out of sight, and spent a fitful night sleeping on the floor. During the night I saw lights flash as a watchman patrolled the site but he never checked the door of my chalet. I was gone at first light before any of the builders turned up.

I made a stop at Naples at a backstreet pension in a rundown street. I left the bike in the courtyard, padlocked to an iron fence under the guard of a friendly dog. Later I walked warily around the locality and ate at a cheap pizzeria, still the best pizza I ever had. Fires of garbage were burning on street corners where prostitutes gathered, gesticulating at me to come and warm my hands, but it wasn't really all that cold. Next day I rode cautiously up the peninsula. I hadn't been in traffic this fast before and found it a bit scary after the uncrowded roads I was used to.

I bypassed Rome. I had no money for sightseeing in such an

expensive city, and no desire to tangle with its traffic. I camped on a littered beach south of Livorno and dined on tinned sardines and bread. Again I left at dawn – I always woke at daybreak – and set off riding past Genoa to Turin, where I stayed on an expensive campsite, but at least it had hot showers. Again, I left as the sun came up, wanting only to make the crossing through the Alps to France. Once again I needed to wear every item of clothing I had, and still the alpine climate penetrated through to my bones. I was shivering with cold when I reached Mont Cenis.

I went through Mont Cenis Tunnel to Modane on the train separated from my Enfield, in warm comfort in a heated carriage, while the Enfield was unceremoniously roped on a flat wagon for the ride through the chilly tunnel. It was the first time we had been separated since setting out, and I felt a bit guilty. At the station as I unroped the Enfield from the flat wagon a couple of lads came over to see the unusual bike, and we chatted about my journey. I tried kickstarting it and for the first time it wouldn't start; perhaps it wasn't happy at being left on a flat wagon in the cold tunnel while I was seated in warm comfort. Eventually it came around, pulsing into life to the delight of the small crowd that had assembled to watch the strangely dressed unshaven freak and the show.

On wet roads we arrived in Lyon. I treated myself to a night in an overpriced, dreary pension and too late I found it had no hot water, and a bed so hard and lumpy it reminded me of a Baluchistan road. I felt cheated and forty years later I still do. After a breakfast of croissant and coffee, which at least was hot, I was happy to be gone from Lyon's grey, damp, dreary streets.

Somewhere riding through forest north of Auxerre, I rounded a sharp bend and met with a Citroen corrugated job stationary on double white lines. There was never a chance of pulling up in time: the brakes on an Indian Enfield take longer to stop than a bout of diarrhoea, and I still had some of that. I hit its offside rear wheel arch, and came off. A bit shocked, I quickly picked up the Enfield before anything else came round the bend and wheeled it to the roadside and onto its stand. The driver made a fuss, offering to take me to a hospital. But, apart from a small cut on my leg and some grazing, I was ok, and having no insurance or any other documents that entitled me to be in charge of a motorbike on the roads of Europe I declined; I didn't want the police involved, and after the bed I'd paid good money for in Lyon I didn't want to test any in a local police cell.

The Enfield had come out of it with a dented exhaust pipe and scratched mudguard; the 'cissy bars' (leg protectors) I'd had fitted in Delhi had saved us both from any serious harm. By comparison the Citroen had a dented wheel arch and some missing chrome off the dented rear bumper. I thought it a fair swap and congratulated the Indian engineers who had built the bike to withstand a bombing raid and not felt it was necessary to lower the iron content of the frame and mudguards; it might not be a lithe and lively steed but its solid iron frame and fittings were made of the right stuff. After a smoke and a tidy-up and with no hard feelings, just grateful to still be in one piece, we said adieu and I carried on, albeit sedately.

I made it to Paris after dark and decided not to stop, I didn't want to pay for another bad pension, preferring the free hard ground to another pricey hard bed. At a fuel station I asked a driver for directions to the Calais road. His English was poor and my French was worse but he gesticulated to follow him, and took me 10km through the Paris suburbs to the Calais road. Merci, mon ami: you are a gentleman and a scholar, and there's not many of us left.

About 11 pm I came across a crumbling air-raid shelter by a field of wheat near the roadside and stopped. I was tired and hungry and had come far; it would have to do. I was too weary to go on to the ferry terminal at Calais. I pushed the bike out of sight behind the graphited WW2 masonry and made my bed alongside it on the weed-grown hard ground, the very last time I used the blue plastic groundsheet bought in the Old Delhi bazaar. I ate my last tin of sardines with half a stick of French bread. In my little corner of a foreign field I fell asleep gazing at the stars happily, knowing I would be on the ferry to Dover next morning.

I was up, packed and away in the chilly dawn after a breakfast of the last of my French stick. Soon after I was treating myself to café au lait et un croissant at the ferry terminal café. I hadn't long to wait; riding up the ramp into the ferry's warm diesel-scented bowels among the revving trucks and cars, I felt a rush of relief, but also regrets. I was almost home after a lot of dangerous miles. The adventure was ending, and after all that had happened that was no bad thing. But due to – as they say – 'circumstances beyond my control' I had missed a lot of the sights and whatever fun may have been.

On 18 May 1980 I rode off the ferry ramp and through immigration without a glance from the customs officers. I rode out of the terminal and into Dover. On the road three lads on their motorcycles saw me and followed to see what this strange road-grimed, dishevelled combination was. I stopped to chat with them and ask directions to the centre and as the four of us were talking a police car pulled up; off they shot like the hounds of hell, leaving me to explain myself. The cops had stopped because we looked likely to be causing the good citizens of Dover a nasty shock on their way to church that Sunday morning.

They noticed the Enfield's registration plates were foreign, and once again I showed my Indian documents and pointed to the AA Upper India badge still shining on the bars. They didn't want to know any more; I was in the too-hard basket: I could go. For the third time I had been stopped by police on the journey, once at gunpoint while having a smoke at a fuel station, once while sleeping under a flyover bridge and now on the road into Dover. Each time I had been told to move on; none of them wanted us on their patch; we were in the too-much-paperwork category. I was used to daily difficulties by now, I felt like I could have dealt with anything. But what I wanted most was a couple of pints of the local bitter, fish and chips for supper, a hot bath and an early warm bed, so off I went looking for it.

The tourist office was closed but there was a notice in the window for local B&Bs. I found one in the backstreets, with, of all things unexpected, a double bed in a heated room, and a bathroom with a bath in it, and a proper breakfast to look forward to in the morning. All of this for half the price of the damp, mouldy walls, cold water and stale croissant of the grim dungeon in Lyon. I had a hot bath, washed some grimy clothes, changed into my not-quite-clean best daks and least stained army surplus jacket, and went looking for a pub.

I sat with a pint, reading the Sunday paper, the first news I'd read for two months. When the fish and chip shops opened that evening, I was the first through the door. I ate them on the seafront with the cool wind of the Channel in my face, happier and cleaner than I'd been in months. Then a last pint and early night in a big bed; after all the camp beds on hard ground and cold dewy nights, I felt like I was staying in a five-star hotel.

After a welcome lie-in I had my first English breakfast since leaving Australia five months earlier. I must have looked in need of it; the landlady asked if I wanted more toast, and yes I did. I hadn't had toast with butter and marmalade for months; it's funny the big things you forget and the small things you don't. I rode to Hastings and the village of Battle to spend an hour at this iconic site where the Battle of Hastings had taken place; every schoolboy of my generation was taught the significance of this site. From there I rode to Croydon to visit Don.

It was good catching up with Don again. We had once worked in the west Australian town of Dampier in the dusty red Pilbara, in what now seemed like a previous life. We went immediately to Don's local for a few Guinnesses and after closing time back to Don's flat, where we finished the bottle of Grant's I had bought on the ferry.

Next morning I set off on the final leg up the M1 and M6 to Lancashire: not the most enjoyable or interesting route but the quickest. For the first time on the entire trip I ran out of petrol on the M6, twenty miles short of my destination of Leyland. Of all coincidences, an AA van stopped to see if I needed help and I bought half a gallon of petrol from him.

That night I told my parents of the journey from India. I hadn't wanted to worry them by telling them before; I had sent occasional postcards but they thought I was travelling by bus and train. Next day I did a tidy-up of my things and looked through all the old documents, emptying everything onto the bed, throwing away stuff no longer needed, like the Indian school atlas's tattered pages of the route across Asia.

As I rummaged through the pockets of my money belt, a square of folded paper fell out, sealed with gum. At first I wondered what it was and then remembered. I unfolded the page torn from an Indian school exercise book, remembering the young Sikh and his cart outside the pilgrim hostel in Amritsar, all those weeks ago. I looked at what he had written. It wasn't much, just a date: 'May 18 a good day for you.' How could he have known I would arrive in England on the morning of 18 May 1980?

The disabled teenager vendor of combs and cigarettes, who had wrongly guessed the name of the flower I had chosen, had prophesied the date I crossed the Channel to England at the journey's end. In safety, like he said, as long as I didn't open the folded paper till I reached my destination, as he insisted. His prophesy was fulfilled: I was home and safe without incident. Unless you counted falling off the Enfield three times, being tear-gassed among rioting students, taken into custody at gunpoint, a nasty customs officer I had escaped from, a collection of grazes and gravel rash, and far too many forced toilet stops – nothing any old India hand would have thought worth mentioning.

That night as I lay on my bed thinking of the day's past and considering my changed circumstances – no rattling air conditioner struggling to cool a hot caravan here, my bedroom window wide open, the sleeping temperature perfect – I fell asleep thinking of the sweating Pilbara days, roofing in the 40°C temperatures and wondered if Ted had had his man killed or was still losing his wages in the Sunday two-up game at the rubbish dump.

Postscript

I have likely made many more mistakes in my life than the average man of my age; riding an Indian Enfield 350cc bullet from Delhi to Leyland Lancashire wasn't one of them. It was just bad timing.

I sadly lost contact with the Enfield, it spent some years in my parent's garden shed, and I couldn't justify the cost of shipping it to Australia when I returned there in late 1980. In 1989 I returned to live in England when my mother became ill and my father who had less than 20% sight couldn't manage to take care of her. I sold the Enfield to a man from a nearby village for a lot less than its value, but as no one else wanted a bike with Indian registration plates and jobs were scarce I accepted the offer.

Following my parents deaths some years later I contacted the new owner only to learn he had sold it on to someone else, and didn't know where it was.

If by some million to one chance someone reading this book has an Indian Enfield – Engine number 204334. Chassis number B/204334/ DBX – original Indian registration – DEX 2723 – I would be truly grateful to know what happened to it and whether it is still bupping along the roads.

MW

22   23

VISAS   VISAS

ESS AAR MOTORS

Authorised Main Dealers :-
ENFIELD MOTOR CYCLES, SCOOTERS & SPARES
1E/13, Jhandewala Extn, **NEW DELHI** - 110055

Dated 17/3/80

No. 232

MR. MICHAEL R WHITTLE S/O JAMES
TOUREST CAMP, OPP. IRWIN HOSPITAL
DELHI

Quantity	PARTICULARS	Part No.	Rate	Amount Rs.	P.
One	Enfield Motor Cycle Bullet			9972	50
	Model Bearing				
	Engine No 204384				
	Chasess No B/204384/0BX				
	as per Standard				
	Specification				
				Total 9972	50
	M R Whittle	@10		S. Tax . 997	25
	Customer's Signature.			A. L. 10969	75
				G. Total	

All vehicles are stored at owner's risk.

Signature.
